GET

"In this compelling guide to approaching conflict in our most intimate relationships, Jayson Gaddis offers a science-informed, practical toolbox for resolving the inevitable tensions that arise in our personal and professional lives. Filled with useful concepts and readily applicable steps to sensing and solving interpersonal challenges, repairing ruptures when they occur, this book is *not* about trying to achieve a life without difficulties in our relationships, but is about moving toward a receptive state of calm and clarity—a state our author names as "zero"—in which we can engage our inner life and our connections with others with kindness and presence that research suggests are at the core of mutually rewarding, generative ways of living with compassion, connection, and well-being."

—DANIEL J. SIEGEL, MD, executive director,
Mindsight Institute; *New York Times* bestselling author
of *IntraConnected, Mind, Mindsight,* and *Aware*

"Jayson Gaddis has written, in our view, one of the most clear and helpful books on this endemic feature of our humanity: conflict. If you want to know what conflict is and how to resolve it, *Getting to Zero* will give you to that destination. We recommend this book to everyone who has ever felt that twitch which plunges us into darkness. While it is replete with accessible theory about what is happening in your mind and brain, it is even more generous with practical guidance from that will lead you from conflict to connection."

—HARVILLE HENDRIX, PhD, and Helen LaKelly Hunt, PhD,
authors of *Getting the Love You Want: A Guide for Couples*

"Jayson Gaddis's excellent new book, *Getting to Zero,* is a fabulous couple guide to conflict solutions interspersed with inspirational self-disclosures of Jayson's own life and relationship experiences.

He provides valuable conceptual framing and techniques for managing conflict. His detailed insights will be of great value to readers interested in effective loving relationships."

—STAN TATKIN, PsyD, MFT, developer of the
Psychobiological Approach to Couples Therapy (PACT)
and author of *We Do* and *Wired for Love*

"Jayson Gaddis has dedicated his life to understanding the dizzyingly complex, emotionally charged territory of relationships. The knowledge he has accumulated is a gold mine for anyone looking to create deep, fulfilling connections with others. This book is a lifeline for anyone who has wondered how to thrive in relationships."

—CORY MUSCARA, host of Mindfulness.com
and author of *Stop Missing Your Life*

"Jayson Gaddis has done it! He has written a brilliant, practical book that leaves no stone unturned in its quest for healthier relationships. Far too many relationships fall apart because humans have never been taught how to convert conflict into transformation. This book stops the bleeding, and provides the tools and techniques that every relationship needs to get to the other side."

—JEFF BROWN, author of *An Uncommon
Bond* and *Grounded Spirituality*

"As a couples' therapist, professor, and relationship educator, I am excited to recommend *Getting to Zero* to my clients and students. Jayson Gaddis is a magnificent teacher—thoughtful, warm, nerdy, practical, and wise. The approach he offers on these pages is one that serves our bodies, our minds, our hearts, and our souls. Dive in! You are going to be so glad you did . . . and the people you love will be so glad too!"

—ALEXANDRA H. SOLOMON, PhD, faculty, School of
Education and Social Policy, Northwestern University;
author of *Loving Bravely* and *Taking Sexy Back*

"Finally, a book that gets right to the heart of how to work with relational conflict! Jayson Gaddis brilliantly helps the reader understand what conflict is, why it arises, and offers a roadmap through these challenging times. His ability to weave together psychology, human behavior, and interpersonal dynamics leaves no stone unturned. Thank you, Jayson, for your tremendous contribution to this part of the human experience that many find themselves lost in. This book is a must-read for everyone."

—LISA DION, LPC, RPT-S, president of the
Synergetic Play Therapy Institute and
creator of Synergetic Play Therapy

"*Getting to Zero* is the ultimate loving relationships guide for anyone who would love to transform disconnection to connection, conflict into communication, victim mentality into victory mentality, survival into thrival, and inauthenticity into authenticity."

—DR. JOHN DEMARTINI, international
bestselling author of *The Values Factor*

"*Getting to Zero* holds the keys to deepening your relationships and exponentially up-leveling your joy in life! Jayson Gaddis has written the step-by-step guide on resolving conflict from the inside out. As founder of The Relationship School and relational expert, Jayson seamlessly untangles the complexity of resolving conflict to makes the process accessible to all of us if you want to be seen, heard, and understood in your relationships."

—TERRI COLE, psychotherapist,
relationship expert, and author of *Boundary Boss*

"*Getting to Zero* is an excellent guidebook for anyone looking to improve their conflict management skills. Jayson's storytelling is impactful, his insights are wise, and his message is clear and heartfelt."

—"COACH MIKE" BAYER, *New York Times*
best-selling author of *Best Self* and *One Decision*

GETTING TO ZERO

GETTING TO ZERO

*How to Work Through Conflict in
Your High-Stakes Relationships*

Jayson Gaddis

hachette
BOOKS

NEW YORK

Copyright © 2021 by Jayson Gaddis

Cover design by Terri Sirma
Cover copyright © 2021 by Hachette Book Group, Inc.

Hachette Go, an imprint of Hachette Books
Hachette Book Group
1290 Avenue of the Americas
New York, NY 10104
HachetteGo.com
Facebook.com/HachetteGo
Instagram.com/HachetteGo

First Trade Paperback Edition: October 2022
Hachette Books is a division of Hachette Book Group, Inc.

The Hachette Go and Hachette Books name and logos are trademarks of Hachette Book Group, Inc.

Image credits: Martin Tabanag.

Print book interior design by Linda Mark.

Library of Congress Cataloging-in-Publication Data
Names: Gaddis, Jayson, author.
Title: Getting to zero : how to work through conflict in your high-stakes
   relationships / Jayson Gaddis.
Description: First edition. | New York : Go Hachette Books, 2021. | Includes
   bibliographical references.
Identifiers: LCCN 2021019564 | ISBN 9780306924811 (hardcover) |
   ISBN 9780306924828 (ebook)
Subjects: LCSH: Conflict management. | Interpersonal relations. |
   Self-actualization (Psychology)
Classification: LCC HM1126 .G33 2021 | DDC 303.6/9–dc23
LC record available at https://lccn.loc.gov/2021019564.

ISBNs: 9780306924804 (trade paperback); 9780306924811 (hardcover);
   9780306924828 (ebook)

Printed in the United States of America

LSC-C

Printing 1, 2022

First and foremost, this book is for me. May I take all my own advice and continue to get better at conflict in my own life.

To the parents who are willing to learn how to navigate conflict. We can't expect our children to get this unless we model it every day. Thanks for being one of those people.

To all the schoolteachers out there. We expect way too much of you. This book's for you, too, so you and your students have a map on how to get back to a good place again. I want this book in every high school in the United States.

To all the growth-oriented people in the world who are willing to learn how to navigate conflict in a way that improves your relationships and the world around you.

Contents

PART 3

DO'S & DON'TS OF CONFLICT—HOW TO STAY AT ZERO

PART 1 | BEFORE CONFLICT— WHAT IS CONFLICT AND WHAT IS ZERO?

My Life of Conflict

Being able to resolve conflicts peacefully is one of the greatest
strengths we can give our children.

—MISTER ROGERS

CAME IN FROM RECESS, SAT DOWN IN MY SEAT DIRECTLY BEHIND
Casey Henderson, and accidentally kicked the back of his chair.
He turned around and asked if I wanted to fight after school. Fear
washed over me. My mind went blank. Despite my tough exterior, I
was actually a sensitive, emotional, and empathic sixth grader. The
last thing I wanted to do was fight this kid. If I said yes, I'd risk getting
my ass kicked. Or I could be true to myself and say no, yet risk the
humiliation of being called a wimp or a loser. Two bad choices.

So, what did I do? I went against everything in me and agreed to a
fight. Almost every boy in the sixth grade showed up to watch. Casey
and I were on the far side of the playground surrounded by a circle
of boys yelling, "Fight! Fight! Fight!" There was no escape. I remem-
bered, suddenly, the words my dad had said to me a few times: "If you
ever get in a fight, throw the first punch." I didn't know how to throw
a punch, so I slapped him. There was a roar from the circle around

us. Suddenly, Casey and I were on the ground. Casey was a wrestler and nearly had me. Then the animal in me took over; the adrenaline I summoned helped me throw him off.

As we got to our feet, I remember time stopping, just for a second, while Casey's fist came flying through the air and hit me right above my left eye. In the same moment, one of the boys yelled, "Mr. Tonnison is coming!" The principal was running full speed toward us, his tie flying in the wind over his shoulder. Everyone fled in all directions, and I ran home as fast as I could, crying in shame and fear the whole way.

At home, my mom was aghast that I'd gotten into a fight but quickly helped me with my swollen eye. When my dad got home from work, I couldn't look at him. Smiling, his first question was, "Well, did you throw the first punch?" He offered zero sympathy. After I spent a night filled with confusion and humiliation at home, I went back to school the next morning, my head hanging low. Our teacher, Ms. Jameson, pulled both Casey and me out into the hallway and shut the door behind her. "I heard you two got in a fight yesterday," she said. We nodded. "Well, say you're sorry."

"I'm sorry," I said. Casey said the same. She dismissed us back to the classroom and that was the end of our conflict.

Or was it?

WHAT I LEARNED ABOUT CONFLICT

Even though my father taught me to throw the first punch, I also got the message from him and my mother that conflict—fighting and arguments—was bad. After all, they *never* fought. At school, I thought that bad kids got into conflicts and good kids didn't. Casey was a "bad" kid, and now so was I. A few months later, I entered middle school with no friends.

That fight was the first of many to come. It was an initiation into conflict, the kind that leaves its mark. This pattern would last for years: fighting, not speaking, leaving, more fighting, avoiding, and so on.

One contradictory lesson I took away from this experience was that when you get in a conflict with someone, you can simply say, "I'm sorry," and everything is made better. But nothing about my experience and relationship with Casey was ever "better." I eventually realized that apologies were like Band-Aids, simply covering up the wound: they got people off my case for a while and allowed me to move on, to a certain degree. But even though I kept apologizing, the conflicts never felt resolved. The wound still festered.

Like you, I have witnessed and experienced countless relationship situations go awry and never get resolved. I saw this at home, at school, during sports, and eventually at every job I had. Not to mention my own relationship failures that kept me stuck and depressed for years. As a kid, I continually felt disappointed in grown-ups, because they didn't seem to know how to work things out. And these were grown-ups who supposedly cared about each other.

After feeling rejected, bullied, and lonely in middle school, I realized, in a much more profound way, how important relationships were. Fitting in, and being liked, became the only thing I really cared about. Belonging is a central need in the human experience. Relationships are everything.

The Harvard Study of Adult Development confirmed that good relationships are the cornerstone of a well-lived life.[1] The tapestry of our lives is woven by everyone we come into contact with, with the most important relationships taking up the most space, color, and meaning. Think about the most meaningful experiences in your life, both good and bad; they were likely shaped by other people, friends, family members, lovers, partners, and even coworkers. Other people provide us with the most joy and the most pain in our lives. Good human relationships are crucial for longevity and good health, and yet, more often than we realize, our unresolved conflicts gnaw at us, leading to ailments that keep us exhausted, stressed, and sick.[2] Without good people near us, loving us, and cheering us on, we feel alone. And it's said that loneliness is more lethal than obesity or smoking fifteen cigarettes per day.[3]

WHY CONFLICT IS IMPORTANT

If good relationships are so important, why do we struggle when things get hard in those relationships? Conflict in our closest relationships is scary because so much is at stake. If the disagreement or conflict doesn't go well, not only do we feel judged, hurt, and criticized, we could lose our marriage, our family, or our job, all of which are connected to our security and our survival. And we'll do just about anything to not lose those relationships, including avoiding conflict, betraying ourselves, and being dishonest. Ironically, these adaptations create even more conflict. This deep-seated fear of rejection and abandonment runs our lives, and it won't change unless we learn how to embrace conflict and work through it.

I've had years of study and training as a psychotherapist and direct hands-on experience with thousands of people as a relationship coach over the past two decades, and I see over and over again that the crux of good, strong, long-lasting relationships is not the absence of conflict but the ability and willingness to work through it. No good relationship can bypass learning about conflict. Conflict is the key to any relationship progressing from bad to good and good to great. And, of course, conflict can also be that thing that tears relationships apart.

If you don't work through adversity with other people, your relationships will never reach their potential, and you'll never know the magic of what a strong friendship or partnership is like. You'll stay stuck in superficial or failed relationships, where you don't feel emotionally safe or seen. You'll rob yourself of fulfillment and personal empowerment. And you might just blame all of that on others for the rest of your life.

---

*The crux of good, strong, long-lasting relationships is the
ability and willingness to work through conflict.*

It's a fantasy that a "good" relationship is free from conflict. This cannot be further from the truth. As you will soon learn, great relationships are built over time through the ability and willingness to work through what I call the *Conflict Repair Cycle*. Changing your mindset about conflict is the key to having satisfying relationships.

MY JOURNEY

When I finally found a group of friends that accepted me in high school, I felt like I had a home, yet every girl that I liked didn't like me back. For years I faced rejection after rejection. After my awkward high school years and freshman year of college, I finally figured out a way to get girls to like me (thanks to a lame strategy taught by my best friend).* Then I had no trouble attracting women, yet I kept them all at arm's length and avoided anything that resembled conflict. When things became remotely conflictual, I'd "fire" whoever I was dating and move on to the next woman. Rinse and repeat for ten years.

Had I been paying attention I would have seen that each of my intimate relationships held an invitation for deeper intimacy and self-understanding. I would have seen that the external conflicts I was avoiding could have guided me to resolve my growing inner

---

* My friend was good with girls and I felt very insecure. So, I asked him how to get girls to like me. He said, "It's easy. Act like you don't care." I tried it and it worked. Isn't that interesting that women were drawn to me when I was dismissive of them. That should be very concerning. . . .

conflict (more on this soon). But I continued to miss all of the sign-posts because I wasn't in enough pain yet. I was trapped in the valley of victimhood and looking for answers outside of myself. After all, my strategies were working—er, sort of. I had great friends and had no problem with dating. So nothing was wrong, right?

When things got hard in my intimate relationships, I'd drink, go skiing or climbing, or go to work. I did my best to find jobs where I could work outside and take my mind off my problems. I bussed tables, worked winters as a ski coach for young kids, and spent my summers with troubled teenage boys in a variety of wilderness therapy settings. Al-though I loved the work and was praised for helping these boys, I some-times felt inadequate, like I didn't have the skills necessary to truly help them. Some of these kids were dealing with major internal and external conflicts, from depression and feeling suicidal to drug addiction. All had enormous family conflicts and problems. I needed more training.

THE BREAKUP THAT WOKE ME UP

About this time, I had chalked up six failed relationships over the course of nine years, and my frustration and pain were at an all-time high. By the time I turned twenty-nine, Andrea and I had been dating for almost a year, one of the longest relationships I'd had. She was amazing, and all my friends and family adored her. She wanted to get married and have kids. I wanted nothing of the sort. So, anytime she brought up this conversation, I'd find a way to dodge the question and change the subject. To me, it registered as "drama." And drama felt like conflict. And conflict was off-limits for me. For example, anytime she wanted to discuss her feelings, I'd get super uncomfortable, try to "fix" it by offering solutions to her issues, and then tell her I had plans or wasn't feeling great, or I'd change the subject. Anytime she wanted to talk about my feelings, I turned the attention back to her and her problems as a way to avoid mine.

Somehow, I bought into the notion that when you find "the one," or meet the "right" person, it should always feel good and the two of you should never fight. Of course, this is absurd, but you'd be surprised how many people believe this. I concluded that the drama had to be because of her. She was making me feel this way. I had to end it. Best to just walk away, like I had so many times before.

But this would take me months to do. Breakups meant conflict, which might mean crying, anger, tears, and a bunch of other stuff I didn't want (or know how) to deal with. I didn't want to hurt her feelings like I had with so many other women. I kept hoping she would break up with me so I wouldn't have to be the bad guy.

I was torn between two shitty choices. If I broke up with her, I'd be alone again and face-to-face with that empty feeling that I tried to fill with women (and drugs and extreme sports). And I'd be repeating this pattern yet again. Nothing really would be different. If I stayed with her, I'd be lying to her—and myself—implying that I wanted to continue the relationship, and that would feel like I was betraying myself each and every day the relationship continued.

The breakup talk eventually happened in Andrea's car in the Whole Foods parking lot. We had agreed not to meet at my house or hers since the relationship was hanging on only by a thread, so we drove to the store separately. We needed neutral ground. Even though I'd had this kind of painful conversation many times before, I was still freaking out inside. But I was determined to be an adult and muster the courage to tell her face-to-face. I owed it to her.

As I sat in the passenger seat of her car, in my mind I kept rehearsing the speech I had come up with. "I need to be honest," I said, breaking the awkward silence. (Looking back, I now know that I was experiencing a lot of compounding shame for all the previous failed relationship moments like this one.) Then I stumbled over the words: "I want to break up." I was squirming. I wanted to run from the car.

Even though she knew it was coming, or so she'd later tell me, her first question was, "Why?"

My first thought was, *Because of you.* I genuinely felt like my relationships all ended because of the woman I was with, not because of anything I did or didn't do. And yet in the next moment, I thought of that old cliché, *It's not you; it's me.* In the past I had used this line as a cop-out, a dodge to make it look like I was self-aware and had a part. But this time, it felt true. Something clicked. It rocked me to my core. *Wait, it really is me!* For ten years straight, I'd rejected every good woman I dated. Ten fucking years of me not being able to figure out how to have an intimate relationship. That was my issue, *my* problem. I was the common denominator in all of these failed relationships. In that moment, the issue switched from being about her to being about me. The light started to seep in. I saw that if I was really the problem, then I also had the power to change it. I felt energy rush into me.

Excited, I looked at her and shared my insight. She wasn't exactly as fired up as I was, but she suggested, with both grace and tears in her eyes, that I get some counseling. I agreed even though I didn't know what counseling was. I wasn't even defensive. Breaking up was the right choice. It was time to go deal with my issues—alone. We hugged and wished each other the best. We'd managed to respectfully get through the breakup—the first conflict I'd ever experienced that came to a semi-successful completion.

I got back into the driver's seat of my own car, and as I drove away, I made a commitment to myself that I was going to learn everything I could about love, conflict, and relationships. I was determined to figure this out. I felt liberated, not because I'd weaseled out of another painful and uncomfortable conversation but because, for the first time in my relationship life, I was taking responsibility.

The combination of hitting a ceiling in my ability to help troubled boys and feeling like a failure in my intimate relationships led me back to school. I was finally ready to learn. I searched high and low for a program that would force me into a petri dish to examine my own issues. One graduate program in psychology would train me to become a psychotherapist and require that I do thirty hours of psychotherapy as a client. Perfect! It was time to stop running away from my problems and start facing myself.

In grad school, I studied humanistic, transpersonal, and Gestalt psychology. (The fundamental principle in Gestalt is asking the client to take personal responsibility on a moment-to-moment basis, the opposite of what I'd been doing for decades.) I devoured everything I could that would get to the roots of my problems. I quickly signed on as a crisis worker for the local mental health center, then as a family therapist. I learned solution-focused therapy, motivational interviewing, strengths-based planning, and how to diagnose someone with a major mental illness. I even co-led groups for perpetrators of domestic violence. At the same time, I got extra training in a three-year Gestalt therapy program. And because I was determined to get to the bottom of my own relationship problems, I enrolled in very intense, regular therapy that lasted for years.

I also started meditating and joined a Buddhist community. Through the Buddhist teachings of meditation and mindfulness, I learned that when we resist our inner emotions and feelings, seeking pleasure but avoiding pain, we create more suffering for ourselves. Duh, why hadn't I learned this sooner! Meditation was helping me deal with my fears, feelings, and anxiety. Soon I became a meditation instructor.

After I received my master's degree, I became a family therapist at a local wilderness program and then eventually started my own counseling practice. I saw how terrified people were at working through conflict. Yet it appeared to be the root of people's problems. So I began to study trauma and how to resolve the conflicts between people.

In my second year of graduate school, I started dating the woman who is now my wife. Early in our relationship, I put on my training wheels around conflict. Instead of leaving the relationship, I stayed, even though every part of me wanted to run (I actually did run twice, but I came back both times). You can imagine two budding therapists trying to get to the bottom of an argument. It went something like this: "You're projecting!" "No, you're projecting!" Round and round we'd go. Practicing my new therapy tools, I'd try to process a fight or argument for hours, analyzing her reactions and telling her all the ways in which *she* was making it worse. I learned that approach was emotionally exhausting and took way too long. Needless to say, I was pretty slow and sloppy with conflict for the first three years we were together. However, over time, we got more efficient and learned how to dissolve arguments quickly.

Then, because I kept seeing similar issues with my clients, I'd take what I was learning at home and try it on them. My clients started having success working through conflict in their high-stakes relationships. I kept reading, attending workshops, and studying with the best teachers and mentors. I was always surprised that no one had a system for working through conflict successfully. So, I created one. And since then, I've discovered some incredible tools, made modifications, and developed the Getting to Zero method that I now teach to people all over the world.

I truly believe that I've come up with one of the most effective ways to work through conflict with fellow humans. I've put that program into this book for you to learn and practice in your own life. Because if we don't start learning how to work through conflict, we'll repeat what we've always done, and our high-stakes relationships will never reach their full potential.

WHY I WROTE THIS BOOK

Like me, you may have left a wake of relationship carnage behind you. You've probably blamed, run away, or shut down—actions that never help the relationships you care about get any better. Married people get rid of their "difficult" partner all the time because, instead of learning how to work through conflict, they "fire" the person and feel better. They conclude the problem was the other person. But what happens when the next partner comes along?

Through my work as a therapist, coach, and founder of The Relationship School, I've met and worked with some of the most courageous people in the world. Mothers, midwives, monks, veterans, CEOs, professional athletes, and rock climbers. People who stare death in the face almost daily. People who seem to be fearless. Yet all of them, without exception, become deeply afraid when it comes to conflict with other people. They, like I was, are afraid that if they are really honest, the other person will leave. This is one of the most fundamental fears human beings have. And because of this fear, we end up trading our true self-expression in exchange for connection. As you will soon see, this tradeoff is at the root of our inner conflict as social mammals. Why do we do this? It all stems from an unwillingness and inability to engage in conflict and a lack of experience with the fact that conflict done well makes us and our relationships better. You can learn to work through fear and overcome just about any difficult or uncomfortable issue with another person.

Take Jared, for example. Jared is a talented extreme athlete, respected by almost everyone. His stories of climbing the world's highest peaks are insane. The guy is a fearless beast when it comes to staring death in the face in big wilderness. But his interpersonal relationships were a mess. When things got hard with his girlfriend, he'd just shut down, shut her out, and go climbing. Eventually, Jared had to wake up to the fact that if he didn't want to lose her, he'd have to become a student of conflict. I taught him the basics of the Getting to Zero method, and soon Jared's girlfriend became his wife. Their conflicts shrank over time, and they got more efficient at moving through their disagreements. Now, Jared and his wife have become a strong resource for many people, and the results they see in their own life are incredible.

Diane hadn't spoken to her sister in over eleven years. After learning the Getting to Zero tools outlined in this book, she reached out to her sister, took ownership of her part of the conflict that happened many years ago, and the door cracked open between them. Within two months, they were having dinner together and celebrating their newfound relationship.

Every day, I see people open their hearts to each other after hours, days, or years spent feeling hurt, resentful, and disconnected. Imagine what could be possible for you if you just apply yourself here in these pages and learn.

To see conflict as the incredible opportunity that it is, we have to remodel our beliefs about it and truly embrace the idea that conflict makes us better, stronger, and more relationally adept human beings. That's what we'll do here, chapter by chapter. By the end of this book, I guarantee you'll be armed to handle just about any hard conversation, especially with the person you care most about. You'll increase your self-worth and boost your self-confidence and in doing so improve and deepen your relationships. These are permanent and long-lasting changes because the Getting to Zero approach deals with how you are fundamentally wired.

HOW TO USE THIS BOOK

PLEASE NOTE

ALTHOUGH MANY PEOPLE REPORT THE TOOLS I EXPLAIN IN THIS BOOK help them work through conflicts that have been stuck for decades, this book is not meant to resolve trauma or get rid of pain. This book does not cover rape, murder, war, or other massive conflicts. In those tragic events, any of us would be a victim of a horrible act against us and many more resources outside the scope of this book would be needed. If you have significant trauma, please continue to work through it with your own highly trained trauma specialist.

This book is also not meant to guide you through conflict in abusive relationships. Although some of the tools may help, the Getting to Zero method is not a recipe for the level of challenge someone faces living in fear and abuse every day. If you are in an abusive relationship, get out and find resources that will help support that move.

In a few cases, no matter how perfectly you do what's outlined in this book, nothing will work. I get that. There is one type of person for whom this method of working through conflict is barely effective because they can't and won't take personal responsibility for their part. I'll say more about this person later, but it's important to know you can't help people who don't want your help and you can't work through conflict with someone who won't even come to the table.

You'll hear me use the term *intimate relationships* in this book frequently. Intimate relationships are your closest relationships (family, deep friendships, and a partnership). These might also be your "high-stakes" relationships. It's important to make the distinction between "intimate" and "everyday" relationships, because more is at stake with intimate relationships than any other type of relationship and conflict tends to be more challenging with these people as a result.

This book takes you through the steps I've used countless times when I help two people move through a painful conflict and into a place of greater understanding and connection. You'll soon understand great relationships are earned, not given. And all great relationships have one common attribute: the willingness and ability to work through conflict. If you don't learn how to handle yourself and your reactivity, who will?

In the pages that follow, I will help you "get to zero." *Getting to zero* is a term that I use to help people measure their level of resolution and connection after a conflict. If we use a 0 to 10 scale, zero means that you have closure and you feel connected. Getting to Zero is the name of the process whereby you and another person in conflict move from disconnection to connection, acceptance, and understanding. Zero is that happy place where you feel good and content. This consilient approach blends spirituality, interpersonal neurobiology, attachment science, several branches of psychology, and my own experiences.

To go along with this book, I suggest you dedicate a journal to take notes and draw graphs and charts in. In addition, an accountability partner can help you integrate the material and see more tangible results. Whereas learning in isolation is fine, learning together is better. Think of an accountability partner as someone you can practice the skills with and someone who will hold you accountable to speaking up, setting a boundary, or finishing the book. Find someone you can share openly and honestly with about what you're learning, someone who will practice the listening and speaking exercises with you.

This is a personal growth book. *Personal growth* in this context means that you are investing time, money, and energy into learning how to work through conflict with the people you care most about. Because personal growth work is a privilege, it's important to mention that if you're in survival mode, it's much harder to face your inner life and apply what I'm about to teach you. To grow and develop in an optimal way, a certain level of physical and emotional safety is required. I'm grateful you are in a resourced enough place to take in what I'm about to share.

I can assure you, if you have avoided conflict your entire life or you've never seen it go well, it's not because of some personal defect in you. You are not broken and nothing is wrong with you. Working through conflict is a skill that anyone can develop.

The following chapters are laid out as a progression: before, during, and after conflict. Part 1 (before) sets the context for why conflict is so hard to face and what we are all up against. I dive into what I call your *relational blueprint*. You'll learn how your earliest relationships laid the template for how you do conflict later in life. I cover the inner conflict, which will help you see where you might be stuck within yourself and with other people. Part 2 (during) gives you practice tools to calm yourself and the other person when in conflict, how to listen better, and how to speak better, and Part 3 (after) highlights the most common fights, the roadblocks to reconnecting, and how to establish agreements. The book concludes with some tips for you if you get stuck and what to do if people won't meet you halfway. And, at the very back of the book, you'll see a resource guide if you want to dig a little deeper, download some free meditations, or hire a coach.

If you're eager to use something tangible immediately, I recommend skipping to whichever chapter most applies to what you're wanting. You can always come back later and fill in the context. But no matter what order you approach the text, you must read "How to Listen During and After Conflict" because the tools in that chapter alone will change how you do conflict immediately.

Finally, you'll see that a few action steps are listed at the end of each chapter. These challenge you to reflect, practice, and integrate what you're learning. Here is an example of action steps to come. I suggest you pause, do these now in your journal, then proceed to the next chapter.

I'm grateful you are here with me and I look forward to being your guide.

ACTION STEPS

1. Write your "conflict story" in one paragraph. Here are a few sentence stems to get you started.
   A. My current relationship to conflict is . . .
   B. Growing up, conflict was . . .

C. When conflict shows up in my relationships now, I typically . . .

D. The person I have the most conflict with is . . .

2. Share this with someone close to you or your accountability partner. Read it out loud and ask the other person not to judge you or laugh at you. Tell them to just be supportive for now.

3. Write down your accountability or practice partner's name here: _____.

What Is Conflict?

Many things make for a happy life, but few things have as
much influence and impact as our relationships do. Learning
how to not stumble through them like a drunken asshole and
how to exercise some conscious control of how you express
your emotions and intimacy is possibly the most life-changing
skill set I've ever come across.

—MARK MANSON

WHAT ASSUMPTIONS AND IMAGES COME UP FOR YOU WHEN
you see or hear the word *conflict?* Most people think conflict
equates to violence or a battle of some kind. The conflict I'm talking
about is not war, international political strife, or violent crimes, even
though those are obviously conflicts at an extreme.

Instead, I want to get personal—focus on your closest relationships. Most everyday conflicts with other people are much more subtle and nuanced, which is why so many of us seem to get by without
ever dealing with them.

Conflict is that hard conversation you're unwilling to have. It's
the breakup that probably needs to happen so you can both get on
with your lives and meet someone more suitable. Conflict is firing

that one employee who needs to go. It's that thing preventing you from reconciling with your brother after seven years of silence, and what you feel as you block your ex on your phone or Facebook (that's scary, right?).

And conflict is what you will have to go through to save your marriage.

Although conflict is, clearly, a lot of things, let's use this as our working definition: A *rupture, disconnection, or unresolved issue between two people (outer conflict) or inside of you (inner conflict)*. Resolving that disconnection is the process of getting to zero, which is the purpose of this book.

Getting to Zero is defined as follows: *The process of moving from disconnection to connection through a process of reconnection inside ourselves and with others*. This is the Conflict Repair Cycle. See Diagram 2.1.

When we get to zero, we've reconnected, repaired, and resolved the conflicts inside and out. The bulk of this book teaches you how to get back to a place of connection, or to zero, after any disconnection. This diagram represents the Getting to Zero process. I want to encourage you to take a snapshot with your phone

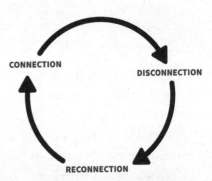

Diagram 2.1 Getting to Zero

and save it, or just draw this and put it on your fridge until you're done with this book, because the Conflict Repair *Cycle* means it will repeat throughout your life. It's not a one-time thing. Unfortunately, you can't live in a permanent state of zero—because no one is perfect and life throws us curveballs—so please don't create unrealistic expectations of yourself or your close relationships. But as you learn to handle inner and outer conflicts, you'll be able to get back to zero more quickly.

When I lead relationship events, I ask everyone in the room this question: "Who here has a disconnection or unresolved issue with at least one person in their life?" Every hand goes up. So, I'm going to ask you the same question: "Who do you have an unresolved issue with?" It doesn't matter what the issue is or who started it, as long as it exists and it currently bothers you. Think about that person you talk shit about, or the person who rejected you ten years ago. Think about the unspoken honest conversation you haven't had with that annoying roommate or family member. Sometimes conflict is the thing you are not saying, the truth you have not spoken.

Now let's get in there and deal with this person. Diagram 2.2 shows a conflict box. Draw this box on a piece of paper. You will use this box throughout the book and add rows to it later.

Write your person's name in the top row of the box. In the next row, write down what they did or didn't do in one to five words. In the third row, write down what *feeling* you get when you think of this person. Here are a few examples: *pissed off, hurt, sad, annoyed, guilty, disgusted, anxious, scared.* Don't write something like, "They suck." Although that might be what you're thinking, it's essential to identify what you're feeling because that's the clue to your disconnection.

In the fourth row, you're going to assign a number from 0 to 10 to

Person I'm in conflict with:
What they did:
The feeling I have when I think of this person:
0-10 scale:
Timeframe:

Diagram 2.2 The Conflict Box

that feeling you have. Ten is the worst; zero is the best. What goes into this ranking are answers to questions like: How complicated is the situation? How angry or hurt are you? How much or how little does this unresolved conflict impact your life? Think of that number as the amount of discomfort you feel in your body, how much it hurts right now, how much you ruminate about it, and how emotional you are about this person. Basically, your number is how much stress you're carrying about this particular relationship.

Keep in mind that the goal is to eventually get to zero, a phrase you'll hear me use a lot. Zero is baseline. Zero means that the conflict between you and the other person is finished and you both feel resolved. Zero is your sweet spot, where you feel emotionally safe, secure, and connected to your person. In the last row of the conflict box, below the number, write down how long the issue with this person has been going on. One day? Two months? Ten years? If it comes and goes, average it.

Now you should have something that looks like the conflict box shown in Diagram 2.3.

I'm always surprised by the time frames and how much stress people are carrying because of unresolved conflicts. Many people have learned to live with conflicts for months, years, or even decades. That low-grade stress isn't good for your health and well-being.

| Person I'm in conflict with: *Bill* |
| What they did: *Lied to me* |
| The feeling I have when I think of this person: *Angry* |
| 0-10 scale: *6* |
| Timeframe: *4 years* |

Diagram 2.3 Conflict Box Example

So ask yourself the honest question: Do you want to address this? Do you want to get to zero? If you died of a virus tonight, can you honestly say that you gave your all to get to a point of resolution? If the other person died in a car accident tomorrow, can you legitimately say you took the higher road and tried to have one last conversation with them? I know it's hard, uncomfortable, and scary to work through conflict, especially if you don't know how and it hasn't gone well in the past.

It's okay if you're feeling unsure, scared, or even defensive. If the prospect of confronting this person seems too daunting, you may need to pick a different person to make this first conflict repair more doable. I would encourage you to pick a relationship for which you feel intrinsically motivated to resolve the issue between the two of you because, to do this, you'll be investing your time and energy. Let's face it: some people are a lost cause. This process is about prioritizing the people you care about the most. Pick someone with whom you have a chance to get to zero. Either way, hang on to this conflict box because we'll come back to it. Right now, its purpose is to act like a scorecard to highlight where you're at in one of your high-stakes relationships.

Have you noticed that you become a different person during conflict? For most of us, this is when our mature adult goes out the window. You might throw a tantrum or go silent for days. Perhaps you get mean or intimidating. Or maybe you turn into a zombie, a ghost, or a stone wall.

I once ghosted a close group of friends when I lived in Maine. I told my closest friends I'd be staying for the winter. But then I changed my mind. I didn't want to disappoint them or create a conflict, so I said nothing about how I didn't want to be there. Instead of saying goodbye, I got up one morning while everyone was sleeping, packed up my SUV without leaving a note, and drove all the way to Utah. I disappeared. I never even returned their emails. As you can imagine, it created a conflict with my friends that I never properly dealt with.

I'm not saying this kind of behavior is okay. But for some people, this "ghosting" behavior—where you just disappear—can be the normal fallback position when they're stressed.

THE SCARED ANIMAL

Why do we behave this way? Why do we avoid conflict so often? And when we do actually get into conflict, why do we act like a wounded dog and lash out?

Your biology is geared toward both connection and protection. Protection usually trumps connection. In fact, to protect yourself, your brain often slants toward thinking of the negative, always on the lookout for both potential and real threats. I call this the *scared animal*, and the job of your scared animal's brain is to protect you from danger. If you've ever picked up a rescue dog at the animal shelter, you know that dog usually comes with some fear. A rescue dog might be happy to get a new loving owner, but it is also scared because of whatever it's been through prior to meeting you. Any dog owner understands that you must behave in a kind and safe way so as not to set off alarm bells in the dog. Because most of us have been hurt at some point in life, we sometimes act like scared rescue dogs.

For example, when you feel judged, criticized, or even blamed in one of your high-stakes relationships, the part of you I'm calling your scared animal will react. Your scared animal will perceive threats if a person or situation even slightly resembles a previous unsafe scenario. For better or worse, you cannot turn it off or get rid of this fearful part of you, no matter how hard you try. That reactive fear is there to protect you, but it can also lead to a disconnection between you and the people you care most about.

When you get really upset with someone you care about, a darker version of yourself comes out. You raise your voice, you shut down, you freeze, or you run away. Each of us has a pretty intense alter ego that shows up when another person challenges us. This is why it's so essential to learn to hit the pause button during a conflict (more on how to do that soon).

Wouldn't it be interesting if you could show this part of yourself on your dating profile? My bio might read: "Hey, I'm Jayson, and when I get triggered, I'll blame you and then shut down for days. Wanna get coffee?" My guess is we'd all be single.

WHAT CAUSES CONFLICT?

If conflict is a rupture, disconnection, or unresolved issue within ourselves or between us and another person, what causes those ruptures?

What causes us to disconnect in the first place and makes the scared animal freak out? Quite simply, conflicts are, at their core, triggered by feeling *threatened*—whether it's your sense of emotional or physical health or safety, your identity, your values, your morals, your property, or your loved ones. None of us likes to feel threatened, especially with things we value or care about. When we feel threatened, our scared animal reacts. Our guard dog comes out and either wants to run or fight.

But what causes the feeling of threat in the first place? To keep things simple, most relationship threats are created in two main ways:

* Too much closeness
* Too much distance

We hate and fear both of these situations because we are social mammals and therefore sensitive to both threats of attack (too close) and threats of abandonment (too distant). Let's unpack each one so that you can understand how they arise.

Too Much Closeness

Too much closeness can be defined as someone moving toward you in a confrontational way, raising their voice, getting bigger physically with their body language, talking too much, talking too loudly, furrowing their brow, pointing their finger, screaming, yelling, physically making threatening body gestures, and much more. All of these can be upsetting, and your scared animal might interpret any body language that feels like someone is coming too close as an act of aggression. If the person isn't backing down, moving away, or giving up, if they stare us down or continue to raise their voice at us, conflict is guaranteed. Even an angry or "dirty" look can send most of us into a defensive position where we scan, evaluate, and get ready to defend ourselves. A spouse raising their voice from the basement can feel aggressive and elicit a fear response in many of us.

Here's a mild example of too much closeness or intrusion: You come home from a super stressful day at work, eager to relax on the couch and scroll on your phone. But your partner wants to connect with you and share about their day. Even though you love this person, you're now irritable and edgy and your tone of voice shows it. You want space. They want connection. If you don't do a great job speaking up about your need for space, they'll assume you want to listen to them and connect. Because you're wanting space, their friendly gesture for connection feels threatening. This may lead to a fight or disconnection. You're reacting because you feel threatened with too much closeness.

Too Much Distance

Too much distance, on the other hand, can also feel threatening because we think that the other person doesn't care or, worst-case scenario, is leaving us. The other person's actions, such as the following, might signify too much distance to our scared animal:

- Silence
- Leaving the room
- Turning away
- Looking away
- Slamming doors
- Cutting someone off during a discussion
- Not returning a text, phone call, or email
- Avoiding a difficult conversation
- Never speaking to someone again
- Leaving a relationship

Out of all of those experiences, we dislike silence the most because we don't like not knowing. Let's say you come home from work wanting to connect, but your partner isn't home. They're always home at this time of day and you wonder where they are. You text them and get no immediate response. If you still don't hear from them within a few hours, you'll start to feel pretty threatened. If you've ever been on the receiving end of someone who doesn't return your texts or who just won't talk to you, their behavior can feel rude, heart-wrenching, and agonizing. If we feel threatened, we might think the person is giving us "the silent treatment." Some of us hate silence so much that we're willing to betray who we are to reconnect with a person who has hurt us deeply, even if things never got dealt with.

Not surprisingly, many long-term intimate partnerships end up with the dynamic where one partner wants more closeness and the other person wants more distance. This creates regular friction and frustration and will be what's lurking underneath most, if not all, of their fights—which will, in turn, trigger the scared animal, regardless of what the fight is about on the surface.

Getting triggered by too much closeness or too much distance, then, is normal. Staying triggered, though, is terrible for your mind, body, and health.

THE FOUR DISCONNECTORS

When stressed, your scared animal takes over, and often in its attempts to make things better, it makes things worse. The problem, however, isn't the scared animal; it's how you handle it. If too much closeness or too much distance feels threatening, typically you leave your center and disconnect using one of four coping strategies that I call the *Four Disconnectors* (see Diagram 2.4).

In the diagram, the center circle represents zero, where you're most connected to yourself and the people you care about. It's that warm, fuzzy place where you feel connected to your heart (that's our goal with this book!). The outer circle of the diagram represents a ten, where you feel most upset and disconnected. The best relationship moments happen when you are relating to people from zero, your center, because you are connected to your heart, your love, and your

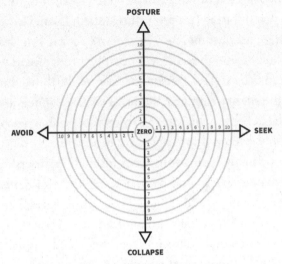

Diagram 2.4 The Four Disconnectors

self-care. As you get triggered, you move out of the center, your center, and begin to disconnect.

The Four Disconnectors are as follows:

1. Posture (puffing up)
2. Collapse (getting small)
3. Seek (invasion)
4. Avoid (distance)

By getting to know which disconnector or disconnectors you do,
you'll be able to recognize disconnection more quickly, which then
helps you reconnect faster. You can also let the people closest to you
know what your typical disconnector pattern is so they are better pre-
pared to deal with you during conflict and you can be more of a team.

Posture

Think of yourself in this behavior like a startled porcupine: your
quills stand up and point outward, attacking or blaming the other

person and protecting yourself. When we posture, we go straight to defending ourselves: "I didn't do that." "It was you, not me." When we posture, we react as a way to protect ourselves from further harm. If you dig a little deeper, you might find that right before you reacted, you were feeling shame about whatever just happened, perhaps over something you did or didn't do. But instead of slowing down to recognize or own our shame (which might feel too vulnerable), we posture and blame. We may try to get physically bigger, act like we are fine, and prove that we did nothing wrong. You might look and act big and strong, but chances are you're posturing to hide your vulnerability, defend yourself, and avoid ownership over your part in the conflict.

Collapse

Collapsing is the opposite of posturing. Like a hermit crab, you go inside to protect yourself. As with posturing, shame can be a big driver of a collapse. Instead of an explosion, we might implode, shut down, and go deeper into shame: "I'm such an idiot." "It's all my fault." In these moments, we might blame ourselves and think that it's all our fault, forgetting that there's always two sides to a disconnection. We might even feel depressed and hopeless in our collapse. People who collapse can stay shut down for days, and sometimes years!

Seek

Sometimes during a fight or when we feel another person pulling away, we might feel anxiety, fear, rejection, or abandonment, all of which compound the conflict. Because we feel so insecure and anxious in these moments, we'll likely move toward the other person in hopes of getting back the connection. We seek them out. Depending on *how* we do our seeking or pursuing, it can backfire and drive the other person farther away. Think of a golden retriever nuzzling into your leg and wagging its tail, saying, "Are we okay? Are we okay? We're okay, right?" It's okay to seek. We just need to learn how to do it more skillfully and with less desperation, while managing the emotions that drive it. Otherwise, the other person might feel threatened by the intrusion upon their space.

Avoid

When we perceive someone as "in our space"—too close to us, talking too much, or wanting things from us—we might feel trapped, engulfed, or invaded. Thus, like a feral cat, we might not want to come anywhere near the other person, so we avoid them and create distance between us. We leave the room, ignore their texts, or space out into the comfort of our thoughts and fantasies. Depending on how we take that space or ask for it, the other person might escalate and get even more anxious, creating more of what we're trying to get away from. Avoiding is just another way your scared animal protects itself.

As you can see, the Four Disconnectors pull us away from zero and away from feeling connected. Thus, conflict not only creates a disconnection between you and the other person but also creates a disconnect with yourself because, when you're scared, you move out of your normal way of being and into a stress response.

FACE YOUR FEARS

John reached out to me because he was in what he called "constant pain and anxiety" about his current relationship with his girlfriend. John was divorced and had two young kids from a previous marriage. Anytime he'd try to fix his relationship, his girlfriend experienced his attempts to connect as invasive (too much closeness). She would retreat (avoid), then John would feel anxiety because it felt like too much distance, so he would reach out to her in every way he knew how (seek). John wanted to get the connection back. His girlfriend wanted more space.

As we dug into John's situation, we found out that not only did his girlfriend go silent after their conflicts but also, when she finally came around, she made sarcastic comments (posturing) about his sensitivity. John was staying in the relationship because, quite frankly, he was afraid of being single and alone at this stage of his life. So, his scared animal was in control, trying to avoid abandonment by doing whatever she told him to do, which created inner turmoil. The relationship was taking a toll on his job, his kids, and his health. Finally, John realized that to break his patterns, he was going to have to start voicing his need for reconnection in a whole new way, which to him felt like creating more conflict.

I assured him that doing this would help him break his disconnection pattern and—more importantly—get what he wanted. He finally gathered the courage to use his voice, set some boundaries, and take a stand. John said to his girlfriend, "I'm unwilling to be in this relationship without a plan to reconnect. I want to be with a partner who will reconnect after any conflict." He realized that despite his fear of losing the relationship, it was too painful to stay in one where he wasn't getting a say or respect. The only way for him to have a different relationship outcome was to go into the fire of conflict.

Sometimes when one person advocates for themselves and for the relationship, like John did, the other person wakes up and is motivated to work on themselves and the relationship, too. Unfortunately, that did not happen this time. John's partner dug in her heels, blaming him for being too sensitive, which clarified John's commitment to being true to himself and getting respect. John got very clear on what he wanted in a partnership: when the inevitable conflicts happened, there was a plan and mutual buy-in to reconnect. John continued to advocate for his need for reconnection, and it created some intense conflicts with his partner. Three months into our work together, he left his girlfriend. This was a painful break, but two years later he found an awesome partner, and as their relationship became more serious, they set up some basic agreements about how they would deal with conflict. (We'll talk about agreements in Chapter 15.)

John's success hinged upon one thing: learning to face his inner conflicts and work through his outer conflicts. He became a student of conflict and changed his mind about it. Once he learned a few tools, his other high-stakes relationships started to improve, too.

Maybe you are like John. You've spent your life apologizing, avoiding, or collapsing. If so, it might be time to face your fears, work with the scared animal inside, and approach those difficult conversations. Or maybe you're more like John's ex, who avoids and postures. Interesting how John does the opposite: he seeks and collapses. Although it's very common to find yourself in a relational dynamic where the Four Disconnectors are opposing, it's not always the case. For example, in some high-stakes relationships both people can avoid and posture (blame). You've got some work to do also. No one likes being on the receiving end of your judgments, criticisms, or attacks.

At its core, conflict is a disconnection in the relationship. No matter how bad it is or how your scared animal reacts, there's a strong likelihood that you can fix it and get back to zero. Not everyone in your life will be onboard with using the Getting to Zero method, but for you and the people closest to you, it is worth the effort for an upgrade.

ACTION STEPS

1. What are your historical and current beliefs about conflict with others?
2. What is most threatening or triggering for you? Too much closeness or too much distance? List three examples of things that really trigger you (silence, too much talking, etc.) and place them in either the distance or closeness category. Ideally, think of the person you named in the conflict box when you complete this step.

3. Identify your main disconnector type—seek or avoid, posture or collapse.

4. What is your commitment to learning? Write it down like this:

My commitment around conflict is _____.

5. Send this statement in an email or a text to at least one person in your life, letting them know what you're committing to.

6. Share any or all of this with someone in your life.

How Most People Do Conflict

> If someone comes along and shoots an arrow into your heart,
> it's fruitless to stand there and yell at the person. It would be
> much better to turn your attention to the fact that there's an
> arrow in your heart.
>
> —PEMA CHÖDRÖN

CONFLICT DOES NOT ALWAYS INVOLVE A BIG FIGHT. IT'S OFTEN the day-to-day withholding and indirect communication that create conflict. Whenever you put off an uncomfortable conversation in the name of avoiding upsetting people, you're actually creating more conflict. Sure, short term, you are in fact avoiding feeling bad or making the other person feel bad. I get it—I've done this many times. But your upstream problem not only doesn't go anywhere but also becomes larger, heavier, and remains unprocessed. This is conflict avoidance.

Monika wanted help with her marriage, which she felt was lacking an emotional connection and physical intimacy. She observed other relationships where couples held hands, finished each other's sentences, and went on regular date nights, even after years of marriage. In her twelve-year relationship, the spark had left. Her husband had slowly pulled away after they had their first child; Monika poured all her energy into her kids and he focused on work.

When things got hard between them, her husband would posture, then avoid, and she would pursue, then collapse. They both were avoiding conflicts, which added more stress and distance between them. But as their kids grew older, she took even more notice of the distance and lack of sex with her husband. Her resentment grew. She finally tried to say something. But within minutes of her bringing up their relationship issues, he got defensive and shut down.

This confirmed Monika's worst fear: if she said something, it would make things worse. She wanted to feel closer to her husband, but now, many years later, she was still too scared to speak up. When I pressed her for why, she let me know that if she brought it up, she feared he might shut down, withdraw, and not communicate for days, like he had before. Even nonverbal overtures to sex were shut down with silence and negative body language.

"So, let me get this straight," I said, "you want more closeness with your husband, but you don't want to bring up this intimate conversation because he might retreat even more. Is that right?"

"Yes," she said. "That's exactly right."

"So then, what are you choosing to do now?"

"To not say anything."

"Right," I said, "and what kind of intimate connection does that get you?"

"Hmmm. I guess not much, but at least I have a relationship," she said with an awkward smile.

This is a classic relationship conflict: different desires for closeness and distance, and conflict avoidance at its finest. Monika's situation isn't that unusual. Most people rationalize themselves out of having an uncomfortable conversation in just this way because they have valid reasons to keep quiet. But here's the question you must ask yourself in this type of situation, and it's the one that I asked Monika: "What is the worst thing that will happen if you speak up?"*

"Well, he will shut down like last time," Monika said.

"Okay. If he shuts down, what's so bad about that?" I asked. "Let's play it out. He shuts down and then what happens?"

"Well, we definitely won't be having sex, and now he's mad at me."

"And if he's shut down and mad at you, then what? What's so bad about that?"

"Well, I guess we'd just be roommates, coasting by, and not really connecting with each other."

"Isn't that what's already going on? So, you're afraid of more of the same?"

"Well, yes."

"And if this lasted for many more years, what's so bad about that?"

Monika grew pale. "I can't live like that. I guess our relationship would end. He'd leave or I'd leave."

"Then what might you have to face?"

"Being alone, I guess."

"Bingo. So, you're afraid of being alone? Is that what's driving your fear of saying something to your husband?"

"Why, yes." She nodded. "I never thought of it that way."

"Okay, now we can get somewhere. It seems like you've got it boiled down to two bad choices. Speak up and end up alone, or don't speak up and keep whatever lame relationship you currently have. Sound right?"

I could see Monika had a lump in her throat. She sighed. "Yes."

"Okay, can you see why you're stuck? Those are two shitty choices."

Monika got it. Then we explored other possibilities that she couldn't previously see. The main one being that if she did speak up, her worst-case scenario might *not* happen and, instead, her hus-

---

* I learned this from one of my mentors, Bruce Tift, many years ago.

band might actually choose to connect with her emotionally or physically. Once she realized that her choice to not say anything left her powerless, she was motivated to try a different approach. To have a breakthrough here, Monika needed to step toward her fear, toward what was uncomfortable—a possible conflict. Monika wouldn't get a better relationship unless she took action.

She'd been making a lot of assumptions about her husband and had not even given him a chance. If we got to know her husband, we might learn that he has a long history of avoiding conflict in intimate relationships. We might learn his scared animal is more like a feral cat and that behind his feral cat is a hurt little kitten. Yes, her husband might shut down; it might turn into a big fight where he runs away even more. But by speaking up at least Monika would know firsthand what happens instead of making it all up in her head. And even if they do get into a fight and he retreats, is that a good enough reason to keep withholding her true feelings and desires?

VICTIMHOOD

We all have a tendency to blame others. Monika was blaming her husband's distancing for their lack of physical intimacy. Although it's understandable that Monika would blame her husband, the problem with blame—and it may be hard to accept—is that it turns us into victims. We believe that someone is doing something *to* us. Someone else is at fault. Or we blame ourselves for making a mess of a situation and get stuck as a victim of our own poor choices.

Anytime we feel hurt in a close relationship, we naturally move into the victim seat, which is unavoidable. Sometimes it's for a brief moment; other times, it's for years. Just think of the person in your conflict box right now, and consider how you're in the victim seat in relation to them. Not convinced? Consider a time when you were hurt by another person. I bet you see it as someone's fault, usually theirs, but sometimes yours. If so, you have fallen into the victim position.

If we remain a victim, for whatever reason, we are choosing to stay in a place where we blame. This is where a lot of us get stuck. If I'm in the bottom of this V, like a valley, my options are limited. (See Diagram 3.1.) I can't see the forest for the trees. I call the victim seat the *valley of victimhood.*

Down in the dumps in the valley of victimhood, we struggle to "see" more from a higher perspective. In fact, we have literally lost perspective and choice. If I blame you for our problems, I'm off the hook to do anything. It all rests in your hands. If I blame myself, you don't have a part and it's all me. So how do we recognize when we are playing this role?

Let's come back to Monika. She kept hoping her husband would change. Then she came to The Relationship School because of their unresolved conflict. Anytime she tried to broach the subject (seeking) with her husband by talking about this conflict of theirs, her guy would withdraw for days (avoiding). The very act of not fighting in itself is conflictual, especially when seekers are the recipients of this avoidance. Not dealing with the relationship itself is very stressful in high-stakes relationships. The pattern was that Monika would get anxious and try to reconnect (more seeking). Her husband

Diagram 3.1 Valley of Victimhood

would then defend himself (posturing), label her as too sensitive and too emotional, minimize their fights as "not that big of a deal" (avoiding), and ultimately shut down. Monika had been to talk therapy and felt like it never helped because she would just vent about her husband and the therapist would listen. But nothing changed.

Monika was stuck and at her wits' end. She didn't know what to do. She judged herself as too broken and too needy to be in a relationship. She also thought all men were like this and wondered if this was simply how relationships went. Monika was in the valley of victimhood, blaming herself and blaming her husband, with what seemed like no way out.

Monika had been putting a lot of energy into trying to change him. She would ask him to read books and listen to podcasts about relationships. If he changed, she thought, their relationship would be better and she would magically be released from the victim seat. When we are in the valley of victimhood, we tend to employ an "outside-in" approach, where we want other people to change (outside) for us to feel better (inside). But I helped her see that doing the opposite, taking an "inside-out" approach, would be far more empowering. This meant changing herself first (inside), then perhaps the outside (him) would change. I reminded her that because her guy was a conflict avoider, the only person who could help her move out of the valley of victimhood was her. In our first class together, I challenged her to take a new approach: stop pursuing her guy and start pursuing herself.

By taking an inside-out approach, where she would first look at what she could change inside of herself (inside), maybe her husband would change (outside).

THE TRIANGLE OF BLAME

Monika was slowly getting it. But we had to address one more bad habit of hers—venting to friends. When her husband would withdraw and Monika felt alone, she would sometimes text her closest girlfriend, Imani: "My husband is doing that thing again where he just shuts down. He won't connect with me; he's being such a jerk. It's like he doesn't love me [blame]. What should I do?"

Instead of getting legitimate support from a skilled therapist or coach and facing the deeper issue on her side, she chose to confide in a friend, which, in this case, did nothing to help her. Imani replied with: "I know, my husband may as well be made out of a stone wall. Lol. That's just how men are. I just give my man another beer so he lightens up. Works every time."

Did Monika get anywhere with her venting? No. She was still stuck, and the support from her friend did nothing to address her conflict. It's understandable that you'd want to vent to a friend as a way to relieve your hurt feelings. But often this doesn't move you forward because most people are just as confused around conflict as you are. When we reach out to friends or family members concerning a personal conflict, it can be like the blind leading the blind.

In family systems theory, which is a theory of human behavior that views the family as an emotional unit and uses systems thinking to describe the complex interactions in that unit, any relationship involving two people is an unstable system and can handle only so much stress or conflict. This is why we seek relief by bringing in a third person. The third person stabilizes the relationship because tension can move between people within the system. That tension can move in a functional way (which I'll explain shortly) or in a dysfunctional way, which is what was happening with Monika. This is called triangulation; "triangles" are natural and normal in relationship dynamics.* However,

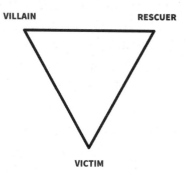

Diagram 3.2 Victim Triangle

that doesn't mean they'll help us work through conflict. As stated in Bowen theory, in a dysfunctional triangle, "spreading the tension can stabilize a system, but nothing gets resolved."[1] Case in point: Monika. She was stuck in the victim triangle, off-gassing (venting) about her husband the "villain" to her friend the "rescuer," as shown in Diagram 3.2.

Any dysfunctional relationship triangle involves three roles: the victim, the villain, and the rescuer. Reflect on the person in your conflict box from Chapter 2. Can you identify a triangle in that

---

* Murray Bowen is considered the first person to use the term *triangulation* in his work with families.

relationship? If you're the victim, and the other person is the villain, who's the third, the rescuer? If you look closely, you're probably still in a dysfunctional triangle with someone today. Perhaps the way you deal with your overbearing mother-in-law is to align with your spouse behind her back. Or maybe, like Monika, you vent to a friend and ask for advice, and she takes your side and derides your partner.

A dysfunctional triangle creates a sense of stability and allows people to stay stuck in their conflicts and remain powerless for years. As a victim, if I blame the other person (villain) and keep my attention on them and how they wronged me, I'm using the outside-in approach (mentioned earlier) and will remain powerless to find a solution. A victim thinks, *My hurt will get better if the villain does* _____ (fill in the blank with any solution). In other words, we relinquish any control or power over our own reactions to another person's behavior, usually giving our power to the person we perceive as the villain. The rescuer in the triangle continues to feed our victim the same old narrative that the villain is wrong and the victim is right. For example, Imani could rescue Monika, but they both stay stuck in the triangle and no one gets empowered because they are both blaming Monika's husband. If no one wants to change the triangle, it remains stable, like an embedded thorn in your side.

So how do you move out of the valley of victimhood and change a dysfunctional relationship triangle into a functional one? You must face the uncomfortable conflicts in your life. In doing so, you begin the transition out of victimhood and into a place of being the author of your life.

AUTHORSHIP

In your childhood, you may have been a victim of tremendous pain and trauma at the hands of other people. You didn't have choices back then and were powerless to do anything about it. As an adult, however, you have power and choices now, and at the very least, you can begin to put the pieces together differently and change how you see situations. As you take responsibility and look back to reflect on any past pain, you can become the "author" of a new narrative about it.

The path to authorship does not deny the pain and struggle you've been through. Nor does it make the victimized part of you "wrong." On the contrary, it reinforces the power you can gain by engaging in conflict and overcoming the pain. When attempting to overcome a conflict, think of yourself as a victim on the move, on your way to being the author who works through the conflict.

The trick is to make it an ongoing *movement*. The movement from victim to author must become a habit, not a one-time thing. As you can see in Diagram 3.3, the author has a much better view. It's like you're on a mountaintop. You now can see the forest for the trees. Your perspective is bigger, wider. You can see more options, more directions, more choices. Your confidence grows because you put one foot in front of the other and climbed your way out of the valley of victimhood. No one did it for you. You can even reflect on where you used to be and make meaning out of it.*

Diagram 3.3 Author on the Mountaintop

Once Monika grasped this concept, she hit the ground running. Now it was time for her to climb out of the valley of victimhood from the inside out. Monika wanted a deep relationship with her husband and finally understood that causing a conflict with him—the thing she'd been avoiding for years—was the path forward. And through practice role-play conversations with me, then direct practice at home with her husband, where she spoke up

---

* Making meaning out of our experiences, especially our difficult ones, is what builds self-trust and the self-confidence to keep going, and it is a hallmark of having healed through a trauma or difficult experience. We develop the ability to put any tragic situation in a bigger context that can empower us.

without blame and spoke honestly about her needs, she started getting stronger. I encouraged her to give him a chance to come forward and meet her halfway since she had been withholding for so long. But, alas, after a few months of her effort and him giving lip service to learning how to work through conflict, she finally accepted that her husband wasn't going to change. Now her fight was about her own dignity, self-respect, and self-worth. She sat him down and, with an open heart, let him know she would be leaving by the end of the month.

Her husband had heard versions of this before, but this time something was different about how Monika was saying it. For the first time, she had her own back, and he got it. This ignited a latent fear that he previously didn't have access to; he realized he didn't want to lose his relationship. That same week, on his own he called a relationship coach, joined a men's group, and started actively working to save his marriage.

JOURNEY TO AUTHORSHIP

How did Monika move from victim to author? She started where she was with what she had. She admitted she was ready for a major change. She took personal responsibility. She began to grow and develop. She embraced conflict and started to fight for herself. In her innocent attempt to not lose her husband by rocking the boat, she had lost herself over a period of years. But now? No way. She was super clear that she wouldn't lose herself anymore. She turned toward, not away from, the conflict inside. She never gave up on herself.

If we want to get empowered, we must engage in conflict whenever it arises, because it's the fast track to authorship. Brené Brown reminds us in her book *Dare to Lead* of a great quote by Marcus Aurelius, the last of the Five Good Emperors of Rome: "What stands in the way becomes the way." Monika finally took action and changed when the pain of trying to change her husband and blaming him for her problems was too much to bear. When you stop running from conflict and finally face it, you make a giant leap in your own development.

ACTION STEPS

1. What relationship triangles are you currently in? Draw the diagram and label your position in it. (Hint: Think of the family you grew up in.)
2. Victim or author? In relationship to the person in your conflict box, are you more in the valley of victimhood or in the author seat? How do you feel about that, and more importantly, what are you going to do about it?
3. Share any or all of this with someone in your life.

CHAPTER

4

How to Become a Relational Leader

You can be right, or you can be in a relationship.
—Stan Tatkin

WHEN YOU MOVE FROM BEING A VICTIM TO BEING AN AU-thor, you become a relational leader. A relational leader has a few characteristics that separate them from the herd. Relational leaders have a growth mindset. They learn and grow from experience in order to achieve a skill, overcome an obstacle, solve a problem, or master an ability. A relational leader asks for help and seeks out teachers, mentors, and guides. Leaders are always learning.

To become a relational leader, you need to do these four things:

1. Admit you're stuck and need help.
2. Take personal responsibility for the outcome you want.
3. Learn, grow, and develop.
4. Embrace and engage in conflict.

Let's go through these one at a time.

1. ADMIT YOU'RE STUCK AND NEED HELP

That day in the Whole Foods parking lot with my ex-girlfriend, I finally held up the white flag. I'd hit bottom and had no clue how to move forward. If you can't take this first step of admitting that you have something more to learn in life about yourself, you'll never get to the powerful next step of personal responsibility, and you definitely won't get any better at working through conflict. Sometimes it's not until we lose or completely fail at something that we're willing to make a change. Try on these statements: "I don't know how." "I'm stuck." "I need help." Just see how it feels to humbly admit you're in the weeds.

Sometimes just acknowledging that you are not great at something brings up fear and shame because we think we should already know how. We might feel afraid that people in our circle will "find out" that we are a beginner at conflict and we might feel shame because we think we "should know better."

Check yourself if you are unwilling to admit that you don't know how to work through conflict. Notice whether you have an inflated ego (posture), like I do at times. I ran on a bad knee for a couple of years before the pain was so great that I finally went in and found a physical therapist to help me. I hadn't been ready to admit that I had a problem and, therefore, something to learn. I kept minimizing it as "not that big of a deal." Because of my stubbornness, I now have permanent knee damage.

2. TAKE PERSONAL RESPONSIBILITY
FOR THE OUTCOME YOU WANT

My entire life changed the day I took responsibility for my relationship problems and said, "I'm the problem." I moved from being a victim and blaming all the women I dated for not satisfying me and my needs to finally seeing that I was the problem. Did they play a part? Sure, but I couldn't, and can't, do anything about that. In my marriage, my wife plays a part, but I can't address what's happening between us if I am unwilling to look in the mirror and take personal responsibility for my part.

Monika was no different. She was blaming her husband for her marital problems. But when she saw her part and that she could do something about it, everything changed. During conflict, the victim in us says, "Take my side, I'm right," whereas the author in us says, "Help me see my side; I'm open to being wrong."

When you finally take responsibility for your conflicts, something incredible happens. Instead of beating yourself up (self-blame) or blaming others for what happened (which is normal, initially), you use the conflict as fuel to help you learn, grow, and get stronger. You realize you are the author, and no one can take the pen from you. You stop trying to get the outside to change and you change only what you have control over—your thoughts, beliefs, perceptions, and actions.

As you take more and more responsibility and are willing to change and grow beyond the current dynamic, like Monika, you do a one-eighty and flip the victim position to the author position, creating a new triangle that looks like the one in Diagram 4.1.

As you can see, a big shift in the roles occurs. The rescuer is now seen as a supporter, and the villain is now seen as a challenger. The author welcomes both challengers and supporters

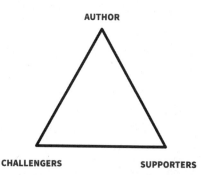

Diagram 4.1 The Author's Triangle

with the understanding that both types of people are a natural part of life and essential to our growth. The author understands that in order to grow, you have to be challenged regularly and supported regularly. I'm not talking about challenging people who trigger us or push our buttons. That's a given. Those people are everywhere. I am talking about close friends and allies that challenge us supportively, with our growth and best interests in mind.

Notice here that moving from victim to author is to become a relational leader.

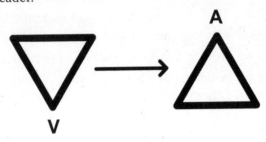

Diagram 4.2 The Path of the Relational Leader

For example, as a relationship coach, I support and challenge my clients. Without me challenging them, they wouldn't grow. Too much support leads to atrophy. Think of a great personal trainer. The personal trainer always challenges the client to push a little harder so the client can get stronger, lose weight, or stay in shape. Without this challenge, the client wouldn't get the same results. In fact, most of us are able to push our comfort zones a little more effectively when someone is in our corner challenging us in a supportive way.

My wife and I follow the "challenge and support" way of living in our home. For example, our kids don't get an allowance. If they want money, they work for it. We do buy them stuff, but if they really want something, they either help pay for it or pay for it themselves. This teaches them to take personal responsibility for getting the thing they want.

We also challenge our kids to go to bed on time, help out around the house by doing chores, and work through conflict. We don't let unresolved conflicts happen in our house. We challenge both of them to own their part and stay in the conversation until everyone is back to zero. We help them see that in life, people will challenge you and support you. We remind them that there is no magical world that is all support and no challenge. As much as I want to see my kids never get hurt and to protect them whenever possible, I know that's not the world we live in, and I want them growing up in reality.

3. LEARN, GROW, AND DEVELOP

Becoming a relational leader is a process, a practice, a movement from victim to author. Part of that movement is putting your student hat on and being willing to learn what you don't know or understand. You grow and develop yourself because you know it's the only way to turn that V into an A. By reading this book, you are learning about conflict. You are growing in the areas where you are limited. You are developing stronger conflict muscles to help you navigate the storms ahead. Growth is a mindset that embraces challenge and discomfort in the process of learning something new. As you acquire new skills and practice, you're lifting weights, combining all three in the context of conflict, and you grow into a stronger, more self-aware person.

Your brain changes and grows, too. Research shows that the brain can be rewired. In fact, how you think, what you think, and how you behave can change the structure of your brain. This characteristic is called neuroplasticity.[1] Thus, working through conflict is a learnable skill that can alter your brain for the better. And because our brains grow in the context of human relationships, it is through relationship that our brains can be reshaped the most.[2] In fact, your earliest relationships shape how genes express themselves in the brain. Relationships that did not go well can have detrimental impacts later in life not only on your brain development but also on your physical and mental health.[3] Because we are not taught this incredible life skill in school, all you need is the willingness to learn.

Growing and learning new things involves struggle, pain, and discomfort. Learning sometimes sucks. I get it. In one of my early jobs as the head ski coach of a developmental ski team (kids ages five to ten) at a major ski resort, I helped start a new kids' snowboard team.

But I was a skier, not a snowboarder, and because we were short a head coach, I arrogantly volunteered for the job! I quickly found out at least three of the kids were better at snowboarding than I, and they were half my age. I ate a shit sandwich almost every day on the mountain with these kids—I fell down countless times in front of them. Sometimes they would have to wait for me to catch up. I felt like such a victim. I wanted to give up and hand the job over to someone more competent. But I stuck that year out, and it turned out to be an incredible learning opportunity for me. I didn't realize it at the time, but every day I got back up and tried again, I showed the kids how to do the same in their own lives. And, yes, I did improve.

You will fall down, again and again. Just like a toddler learning to walk. Contrary to what a lot of self-help and personal development books might say, you won't just stay in the author's seat or "get over" your victimhood after a cool spiritual retreat, a deep coaching, or one therapy session. Growth-development-oriented people move in and out of author and victim roles as long as they are in relationships, as long as they are learning, and as long as they are alive. Ideally, your growth is like the line slanting up and to the right in Diagram 4.3. I call this upward trend *empowerment*. Empower-

Diagram 4.3 Empowerment and Evolution

ment means becoming a more confident relational leader, over time, through the ups and downs of learning.

Getting good at conflict has taken me years; I still get scared, I still blame, I still react, and I still fall down. I will be learning about human beings, conflict, and relationships forever. But because I continue to learn, my line is slanting up and to the right.

4. EMBRACE AND ENGAGE IN CONFLICT

Continue to watch your preconceived notions and judgments about conflict. Remember, conflict isn't the problem. Your way of doing conflict is the problem. The irony is that by learning how to do conflict, you'll move closer to what you want sooner. In other words, effective fighting is the path from victim to author that makes you a relational leader. You can't ever become a relational leader by avoiding conflict or hoping it never happens.

Whenever I fall down in life, I remember my heroes, like former South African prisoner turned president Nelson Mandela.[4] In 1964, he was sentenced to life in prison, where he would stay for twenty-seven years. He spent decades cut off from the world in an extremely inhumane environment, stripped of almost every right he had. For example, inside prison it took him fifteen years of fighting to ensure that African, colored, and Indian prisoners' meals were as fair as the other prisoners'.[5] While he was in prison, his mother died, and his eldest son died in a car accident. He was not allowed to attend either funeral. Black children were not allowed to visit prisoners until they were sixteen, so he finally saw one of his own daughters after thirteen years.[6] He hadn't seen her since she was three years old! He had to fight over and over to receive visits from his wife, and she fought the system to see him. At one point, he didn't see her for two years. He couldn't even touch her hand for twenty-one years.

Mandela became an author and global (relational) leader because he fought every single day, not because he avoided fighting.

With each passing year, he learned how to fight an apartheid government more effectively. He had countless setbacks and "failures." His commitment to fighting for freedom was relentless, and he was able to help dismantle the apartheid government and become president of South Africa. Through all his conflicts, he became smarter, stronger, and more resilient. He stepped into greater and greater levels of authorship and leadership. Mandela remains an inspiration to me. Find yours. Who inspires you to get back up when you fall down?

These four powerful steps—admit you're stuck and need help, take responsibility for the outcome, learn to grow and develop yourself, and embrace and engage in conflict—turn dysfunctional relationship triangles upside down. They move you from being a victim in conflict to being an author who works through conflict.

THE QUICKEST WAY OUT OF ANY FIGHT

Trudy was distraught because her adult son hardly ever called her and it upset her. But when she would speak to him about it, she would say, "You never call me—you don't care about me," which, of course, made him feel attacked. She had a tendency to start every sentence with *You* and would often follow that up with the word *always* or *never*, which sounds accusatory. Trudy had a huge breakthrough when she finally was able to lead her conversation with her son by focusing not on his behavior but on her own reaction. The next time she spoke to him, she said, "I'm hurt that you don't call me." Though this might not seem like much of a change, instead of defending himself, her son came forward in a new way. He realized he didn't want to behave in a way that hurt his mom. He was finally able to hear her in a way that he was not able to previously because this time she led with responsibility rather than blame. Trudy also acknowledged her part and was able to own another layer: "I'm anxious and feel unloved by you, and as a result, I judge you and attack you, which doesn't help me get what I want."

The quickest way out of any fight is to own your part and acknowledge where "I" went awry. As a way to start practicing, here's your first warm-up: Try taking responsibility for something you did or didn't do in the past few days. For example, "I raised my voice." Or "I was dismissive by not returning your text." Or "I pushed you away because I was hurt and angry." Beware that it is tempting to sneak in some finger-pointing under the guise of looking responsible. Trudy would say things like "You're being mean to me." Instead, I taught her to say, "I feel criticized."

Another easy way to practice taking responsibility is to simply lead with these three words: "My part is . . ." Look at your conflict box from Chapter 2. Let's add one more row so it now has six rows. In row 6, write: "My part in our unresolved conflict is [*insert your behavior, action, inaction*]." This is ownership. For example, your box now looks something like the one in Diagram 4.4.

When we keep our statements about ourselves, we can get to what needs attention and healing on our side, and get out of the habit of making the other person the problem.

Note: We'll keep working with your conflict box in the coming chapters.

Person I'm in conflict with: *Bill*
What they did: *Lied to me*
The feeling I have when I think of this person: *Angry*
0-10 scale: *6*
Timeframe: *4 years*
My part in our unresolved conflict: *Is that I overpromised*

Diagram 4.4 Conflict Box Example of Ownership

Try not to make yourself feel like you've done something wrong if you feel like a victim or you point the finger outward at other people. This is all part of being human. Like you, I have a victim living inside of me who, at times, would prefer someone save me from my relationship pain so that I don't have to face it or feel it. For nearly two decades, I allowed my inner victim to run the show. Then my relationships became so painful that I couldn't keep pointing the finger outward.

I finally chose to be an author. Any of us can do this. We fall down, feel like a victim, have a fight, and get stuck in a dysfunctional triangle. But eventually we see how limited this is, so we rise up, look in the mirror, own our part, learn to fight differently, and move to the mountaintop of authorship with whatever lessons we've learned. Personal responsibility is one of the fastest ways out, or through, any fight, disagreement, or argument. In the next chapter, we step back in time to understand why this conflict stuff is so complicated. It all starts with where you first learned about conflict and what drives you to avoid it.

ACTION STEPS

1. Of the four steps to becoming a relational leader, where are you now? Which is the most difficult for you?
2. Share with a friend or accountability partner (but not a rescuer: make sure they're a challenger or a supporter!). Ask them to help you see another choice in a conflict you're currently in. Then imagine a third choice and a fourth. What are the other possibilities?

CHAPTER

5

Your Relational Blueprint

> Twenty years of medical research has shown that childhood
> adversity literally gets under our skin, changing people in
> ways that can endure in their bodies for decades. It can tip a
> child's developmental trajectory and affect physiology. It can
> trigger chronic inflammation and hormonal changes that can
> last a lifetime. It can alter the way DNA is read and how cells
> replicate, and it can dramatically increase the risk for heart
> disease, stroke, cancer, diabetes—even Alzheimer's.
>
> —Nadine Burke Harris

HAVE YOU EVER WONDERED WHY YOU GET SO DAMN ANXIOUS when a partner doesn't return a text? When triggered by a colleague at work or a partner, have you ever caught yourself thinking, "I feel like I'm back in middle school and completely tongue-tied—I don't know how to cope with this!" Or have you ever wanted to shut out the world and get away from people entirely—even those you love the most? These potent and painful experiences offer a window into some of the challenges that occurred in your earliest relationships. And these high-stakes relationships from when you were young shape how you relate to others throughout your life—

including how you connect and how you fight. In fact, all your relational experiences up until now shape how you relate to others, as well as how you do conflict. I call these past experiences your *relational blueprint*.

If your end goal is to get to zero with those you care about the most, it's important to look back in time and understand your relational blueprint. Reflecting on your relational history and making sense of it will help you feel less crazy, less alone, and more secure as you navigate conflictual interpersonal waters. I understand that if growing up you had no good examples about how to navigate conflict well, you might feel powerless to do it differently as an adult. However, by understanding how you were raised and what was modeled to you around conflict, you gain a sense of understanding that allows you to choose differently as an adult. In addition, this understanding will even help you empathize with and have compassion for yourself and those you are in conflict with.

Let's peek into your very first relationships. You came into the world dependent on at least one adult to survive. The presence of your caregiver was imperative to your survival because they met your physical and psychological needs (mental, emotional, relational). These caregivers were your attachment figures.* The nature of this primary relationship, known as an "attachment relationship," is the bedrock of your relational blueprint.

The term *attachment* comes from attachment science—a body of research in the field of developmental psychology that studies the relationship between caregivers and their child. Researchers look closely at how the parent–child relationship and their psychological bond impact human development throughout life.

---

* I use the term *parent* or *caregiver* to identify whoever raised you. I understand that some of us didn't grow up in two-parent households and that you may have been raised by many people, siblings, neighbors, or relatives.

SECURE ATTACHMENT

Consistent longitudinal research studies across cultures show that how well a child does in life, especially in their relationships, is determined by whether they developed a sense of security from having at least one caregiver consistently "show up" for them.[1] Author, professor, and psychiatrist Dr. Dan Siegel describes this sense of security as a "secure attachment."[2] Siegel reminds us that secure attachment is not about having perfect parents. It's about having parents who are willing to learn about themselves, learn about their child, and also repair the inevitable conflicts and disconnections between them (more on this shortly).

I describe a secure attachment as a relationship in which a child feels safe, seen, soothed, and supported (and challenged).* Think of these four "relational needs" as building blocks that create a stable foundation for your relational blueprint (as shown in Diagram 5.1).†

To me, feeling safe, seen, soothed, and supported and challenged are basic human needs. When each of these needs is met,

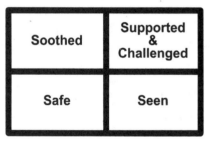

Diagram 5.1 The Four Relational Needs: Building Blocks of Secure Relationships

children feel good and they can develop in an optimal way. Not surprisingly, we have these same needs as adults. The difference between

---

* This is slightly different from how Dan Siegel describes secure attachment. One of his many definitions of secure attachment is when a child feels safe, seen, soothed, and secure. I'm replacing *secure* with *supported* and *challenged* to include what I see as a wider range that creates security.

† Throughout this book I will refer to these needs as "relational" needs although more accurately they are psychosocial needs. *Relational* is a little more user-friendly for the purpose of this book.

secure adult relationships and secure parent–child relationships is that in adult relationships the needs are mutually met, meaning we offer each other these needs in our high-stakes relationships, whereas in parent–child relationships, it's up to the parent to meet these needs for the child. Throughout this book, you'll hear me call these four needs the *relational needs* and the *Four Connectors* because they help us reconnect after a conflict or disconnection with another person.

If you had a secure attachment as a child, you learned to trust that relationships were a reliable, dependable resource for you. As you grew, you were able to make transitions from playing by yourself to being with other people without much inner conflict. Your authentic self-expression was listened to and received, which helped you develop and trust your voice. When conflict and disconnection happened, your caregivers worked with you to get to a good place again, and your confidence in relationships and yourself grew. According to the research, a secure attachment is the best predictor for how well kids do across many areas of life, including having higher self-esteem, better emotional regulation, better academic performance, better coping skills in times of stress, happier and better relationships with parents, stronger leadership qualities, more trusting and nonhostile romantic relationships in adulthood, more empathy, greater social competence, more meaningful relationships, and even more successful future careers.[3]

A secure attachment is a foundation from which to navigate the consistent challenges that life and relationships bring. As Siegel says, a secure attachment is like a safe harbor *and* a launching pad. When you get hit by the storms and waves of life, you come back to the safe harbor (your attachment figure) and regroup; then when you're ready to meet life's challenges, you "launch" out into the world, with your caregiver (and others) cheering you on. This "secure home base" is built when you experience the four relational needs being met over time.

If you've had problems with conflict, you might be thinking, "Well, secure doesn't describe me." If so, you may have had what researchers call an insecure attachment.*

INSECURE ATTACHMENT

If your parent or caregiver was too distant or too close too often, you might have formed what's called an insecure attachment. Perhaps your caregiver, for whatever reason, was inconsistent, unpredictable—or even worse, hurtful—and when any of your four relational needs went unmet, you might have learned that relationships are not reliable. You had consistent experiences of getting stuck in conflicts that weren't repaired well. Maybe you had the experience of feeling emotionally unsafe, ignored, or neglected. Or maybe, when you expressed yourself, you felt attacked, shamed, or criticized. You might then experience relationships as unsafe, and as a result, you shut down your emotions and become disconnected from your inner life. This in turn lets you doubt yourself further and feel confused and unsure about relationships. According to attachment science, insecure attachments with others "challenge our ability to be flexible, understand ourselves, and connect with others."[4] Insecure attachments can lead to a whole host of problems later in life, such as the inability to work through conflict in your high-stakes relationships.

Yikes! So are parents doomed to "mess up their kids"? And should they be present and available all day long? No. In fact, to imagine a parent can meet a child's every need is unrealistic. Parents are imperfect beings and they can't possibly meet a child's needs 100 percent of the time, no matter how hard they try. In a normal home, there will

---

* In many circles, people have heard these termed as attachment styles. And insecure and secure are two main attachment styles. Within insecure there are two subtypes known as anxious avoidant and anxious ambivalent and a third that some people consider its own category called disorganized. For the purpose of this book, I'm only differentiating between secure and insecure.

be thousands, if not millions, of disconnections when the parent, for whatever reason, cannot meet an emotional need or "be with" a child during an upsetting moment.

According to developmental psychologist Dr. Ed Tronick, who was the lead researcher on the "still face" experiment,* these disconnections, or "mismatches," as he calls them, between parent and child happen 70 percent of the time and are an essential part of child development.[5] What?! Disconnections are that frequent and normal? Tronick's research concluded that these mismatches are not the problem. In fact, they're part of a normal and healthy parent–child relationship. So, what's the big issue that creates the insecurity? The lack of repair and reconnection. That means the disconnection isn't the issue; it's the lack of getting back into connection that is stressful. His research shows that when disconnections don't get repaired and resolved it's stressful and dysregulating for the child, and the compensations a child must make to adapt to that stress lead to a host of other problems, the main one being insecure intimate relationships.

Thus, how parents respond and meet a growing child's needs and how they deal with the inevitable disconnections that occur in their relationship have a powerful and lifelong impact on the child's relational blueprint. To keep things simple, I like to think about secure attachment as being created through a cycle that involves connection, disconnection, and reconnection—with an emphasis on the reconnection part. Recall the Conflict Repair Cycle from Chapter 2. I want you to see this cycle as a normal and healthy part of secure attachments and good relationships throughout your life. (See Diagram 5.2.)

---

* The "still face" experiment led to many breakthroughs in the understanding of child development and children's relational capacities. If you have not seen it, I recommend searching for it on YouTube.

There are two important points to understand here: (1) disconnections (often created through conflict and misattunements) are a normal and necessary part of human relationships; and (2) reconnection is the most important part of the Conflict Repair Cycle if you want secure, agile, and great relationships. Feeling disconnected from a per-

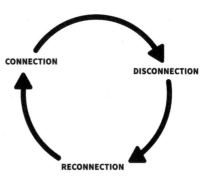

Diagram 5.2 Getting to Zero with the Conflict Repair Cycle

son who is important to you is normal, albeit painful. However, if you choose only one thing to focus on in this book, place your attention not on the conflict but on the reconnection. How you do the Conflict Repair Cycle today has been influenced by how the big people did it with you back then, but your willingness to learn and develop yourself now will determine how that cycle goes moving forward.

Something really interesting happens to a child in the space of disconnection. If disconnections don't get repaired and relational needs continue to go unmet, and if this happens too much or too often, the child begins to recruit resources and develop strategies focusing on keeping alert for threats, which takes away valuable internal resources that could be used for normal development and learning. Daily disconnections are not the issue. Daily disconnections that don't get repaired are the issue. Unresolved disconnections are detrimental to a child's developing brain, nervous system, and sense of self.

One of the main strategies children use to try to get their connection back is to modify their self-expression so they can avoid being rejected, left, or abandoned. One of our deepest fears as humans is to be rejected, to not be loved for who we are, to be cast out. When babies and young children feel emotionally unsafe, unseen, and unsupported, they develop strategies to avoid getting hurt, and usually they feel as if they have no choice but to change their behavior in the hopes that their needs are met. For children, it's life or death. We'll get more into childhood strategies and how to deal with those in the next chapter.

Remember, if a caregiver responds in a timely and attuned manner to disconnections and works to reestablish the connection, normal development resumes and the child feels that the world is okay and that "I'm okay" and "we're okay." At issue isn't the mistake, disconnection, or the "conflict" between the two; instead, it's all about how quickly and how well the disconnection is repaired.

The same can be said in your adult high-stakes relationships. How you do the Conflict Repair Cycle today not only gives you information about your history but also speaks to how secure or insecure your intimate relationships are now. The great news is the Conflict Repair Cycle is the same cycle as Getting to Zero, and you're about to learn it. I call it a cycle because, in my experience, it repeats regularly for the rest of your life, so you may as well get good at it. In this simple cycle, it's also very easy to see where your weak spot is. Do you struggle most with connection, disconnection, or reconnection?

Disconnections are impossible to avoid, so we need to put most of our attention on what happens after any disconnection: reconnection.

CHRONIC DISCONNECTION

We all prefer to feel connected to someone close, and it sucks when we feel disconnected from them. That feeling of being alone should be motivation to reconnect, but if repair and reconnection didn't go well as a child, you might have become used to the experience of disconnection. A chronic state of disconnection is not zero. Your baseline is likely a higher number. You might have a hard time seeing this because it's the water you swim in. For example, if you grew up in a household where you were left on your own a lot and the adults devalued relationships and never worked through conflict with you, you got used to going to your room and losing yourself in books or going out to play by yourself. Your baseline was one of disconnection and relationships didn't provide you with nourishment. It sounds simple, but many people who have never experienced how amazing it feels to reconnect after something went wrong can think that their chronic feeling of disconnection *is* connection.

In fact, many people live their entire lives thinking they are connected to other people because they have five hundred Facebook friends. But in reality, no matter how many friends they have, they may still *feel* disconnected. In other words, having friends or people close by doesn't guarantee the *feeling* of connection, which is where you are getting those four core needs met by another person: feeling safe, seen, soothed, and supported and challenged. So, if you're ever with a partner who doesn't seem to care or even notice when you feel alone and disconnected, it's probably their early relational blueprint talking.

Don't worry—your history doesn't have to be your destiny. Your brain is flexible, and you can rewire this process (it's called experience-dependent neural plasticity),[6] specifically in mutual adult relationships, by learning how to master the Conflict Repair Cycle. And if you can't remember or don't know about your attachment history because of trauma, neglect, or a bad memory? Don't worry, it shows up in your behavior in your closest relationships as an adult, especially when you are under stress and during conflict. Just think of that last time you acted like a five-year-old or chose to not tell the truth in your closest relationships. You can run, but you can't hide from your relational blueprint.

Scott and Roshni have three kids and were stuck in a big conflict. Roshni wanted Scott to relax and not be so uptight about the house rules and structure. Scott wanted Roshni to get onboard with the structure he'd established in the house. But anytime he tried to get her to comply, she felt controlled. She would judge him as too rigid, and then he would feel dismissed and disrespected. Seems like a normal fight, right? How would these two get to zero?

As we dug deeper, we found that Scott grew up as a latchkey kid in a blended family where everything was chaotic and unpredictable. So, naturally as an adult, when things felt out of control and chaotic (like in his current family with three young kids), he clamped down harder on his structure. He felt very alone, as if Roshni and the three kids were against him. Scott's relational blueprint was playing out in real time in his marriage, and when both Scott and Roshni understood this, everything began to change. Roshni finally could appreciate how scary it must have been for Scott growing up and how alone and out of control he felt. Scott started to understand why Roshni was so free-spirited and he could appreciate her parenting approach in a much more genuine way. After many hugs and tears, they both reached zero and felt more connected than they had in years.

ONE MORE LAYER OF SECURITY

We need to address one more essential factor in creating secure relationships. In fact, it might be the most important one—a parent's ability to self-reflect. The work of Dr. Dan Siegel shows that the single biggest predictor of secure attachment for a child is the parent's ability to self-reflect and make meaning out of their own relationship experiences.[7] You may not be a parent, but you likely want more rock-solid relationships. If that's true, then self-reflection is essential. The good news is you'll be doing a lot of self-reflection in this book, so you're exponentially increasing your chances of having secure relationships.

Whether you are a parent or not, the more you can learn about yourself, and make meaning out of your relational life, the more secure your adult relationships can be. This is true in my experience. There is no way in hell I'd have the marriage I have now without the tremendous amount of self-reflection and inner work I've done. In addition, my wife and our combined ability to self-reflect is what's helping us raise our kids in a secure way, year after year. Had I had children prior to working on myself, it honestly would have been a disaster. Not only would I have shamed my kids for being emotional, I would have continually run away from conflict with my wife.

THE DOWNLOAD YOU GOT

The final component of your relational blueprint is how conflict was modeled to you. How the grown-ups in your world did the Conflict Repair Cycle dramatically influences how well you tolerate conflict, whether you avoid or instigate, and how you reconnect after conflicts in your close adult relationships. For example, if you grew up in a family where reconnection rarely happened, you'll likely find yourself in an adult partnership where it rarely happens. This chronic sense of low-grade disconnection might feel okay for a while, but years of unresolved disconnections eventually erode the trust, strength, and security of the relationship. Furthermore, if you received external messages that conflict is bad or wrong and must be avoided at all costs, your own development and maturation will be stunted, and you will struggle in stressful high-stakes relationships. (Unless, of course, you practice being a relational leader.)

Hopefully, you can now appreciate why conflict is so difficult for all of us. Not only did we *not* learn how to do conflict, we got whatever download our families and communities modeled to us about conflict and repair. Please use that experience as fuel to upgrade how you do the Conflict Repair Cycle. Don't turn a blind eye to the reconnection process. Your well-being depends on it.

The Conflict Repair Cycle isn't about being perfect. Dr. Tronick's research makes it clear that we cannot always be or feel connected. There is no such thing as getting to zero and staying there permanently because conflicts and disconnections happen throughout our lives, needs go unmet, and traumas and injuries happen. Disconnections are impossible to avoid, so we need to put most of our attention on what should happen after any disconnection, which is repair and reconnect. This by no means justifies or excuses hurtful behavior. The better you do with the Conflict Repair Cycle, the more secure your high-stakes relationships will be and the more secure your internal sense of self will be.

Building off this relational blueprint, in the next chapter we'll explore one of the main outcomes of conflict gone poorly in our childhood: the inner conflict.

ACTION STEPS

1. Reflect on your relational blueprint and notice whether you feel like you had an insecure attachment or a secure attachment with your caregiver. How might that be impacting how you show up in conflict today? Are you willing to change your history in the present by making meaning out of your past relational blueprint?

2. Review the four relational needs. How many relational needs do you feel are currently being met in your most important high-stakes relationship? Can you see the correlation with how

secure or insecure that relationship is? Are you giving or offering the four relational needs to that person?

3. Draw a simple Conflict Repair Cycle diagram. Are you up for moving through this cycle for the rest of your life? If not, what beliefs or fears might stand in the way?

4. Share any or all of this with someone in your life.

Your Scared Animal

When you shut down emotion, you're also affecting your
immune system, your nervous system. So the repression of
emotion, which is a survival strategy, then becomes a source
of physiological illness later on.

—DR. GABOR MATÉ

D O YOU EVER WONDER WHY A CERTAIN FACIAL EXPRESSION ON
your significant other can raise so much stress? Or why the silent treatment from your best friend can be so upsetting to you? Ever wonder why you can't sleep at night because you feel so pissed at that person at work? When our scared animal perceives that someone else is doing something that threatens us, we react, and it's very hard to change our state until we deal with it. With any threat, our nervous system responds to help us address the threat. The challenge with conflict is that we often misperceive threats as being much bigger than they are, leading us to say or do things we later regret.

Chances are the most difficult experiences you have in life involve other humans. And unfortunately, we were never formally taught to work through conflict, even with the consistent stream of difficult people in our lives. Nor were we taught how to work with our own reactivity and the ways in which we are difficult too.

About once a week, I feel triggered by my wife. We've been together since 2003, so if I do the math, my wife has triggered me (by raising her voice, shutting down, being late, etc.) at least 886 times in the course of our relationship. I'm guessing I've triggered her in numbers way higher than that. Feeling triggered by other people is just part of being human, and like conflict, it's part of any good relationship. There's no way around this, so please let go of the fantasy that you can be like the famous spiritual teacher Eckhart Tolle and never get triggered. Every person has buttons, and other people will push those buttons. Don't believe me? Just move in with me for a few months or years.*

In order to understand our triggers, and more importantly work through them, it's essential we understand the brain and nervous system and how they work. Knowing how you are wired as a human animal will help you feel less crazy, less stupid, and more normal. Plus, it will help you get to zero sooner.

When you sense a threat, real or imagined, a very old alarm system fires to keep you safe. You run, you fight, you freeze, and in extreme cases you might faint or play dead without any conscious thought. Think of this threat detection system as the ultimate security system to keep the "home" of your body safe and sound. The challenge, of course, is that this system is always on, and there's no way to shut it off. It sometimes confuses a real threat with a perceived threat, which is what happens often in typical, everyday conflict.

For example, when I did a podcast interview with the man who came up with the widely respected Polyvagal Theory, author and scientist Stephen Porges, he described a real scenario between him and his wife, Sue Carter (who's done extensive research on oxytocin). It went like this: He woke up one morning, stood up too quickly, and almost fainted. This created a look on his face that he could not control because he was too busy trying to stay upright. A moment later, Sue

---

* I wish Eckhart would move in with me, seriously. I bet I could trigger that guy in just a few weeks.

saw his face and wondered if he was mad at her. What was happening to him and what his wife read were two different things. Although this might not seem like a big deal (these two later told each other what happened), these misreads can create conflict and can have detrimental consequences on your relationships, and even your health.

The sensitivity of the scared animal is both a blessing and a curse. If you are on high alert much of the time, your body will be more inflamed. The more inflammation you have in your body, the more your body attacks its own tissues, leading to disease and a variety of autoimmune disorders.[1] Yet your threat detection system is also a blessing because if you're walking alone in a parking garage at night and you sense someone is following you, your brain can literally save your life as it mobilizes your body to take action. This threat detection system is intelligent, and its job is very simple: to assess whether people are safe, dangerous, or life-threatening.* Your job is to learn its wiring and know how to use it to your advantage, because in the next few hours, days, or weeks, another person will "threaten" you, guaranteed.

YOUR TWO-PART BRAIN UNDER THREAT

To keep things simple, let's divide the brain into two parts.† I'm oversimplifying the brain into two parts here so that you can digest this complex material and apply it in a practical way. Throughout the book, you'll hear me use the terms *back seat* and *front seat* to describe the two parts of the brain, as shown in Diagram 6.1.

1. Back Seat

The back seat, or the scared animal, is the oldest part of your brain and is made up of your brain stem and your limbic system. Housed

---

* Stephen Porges calls this system *neuroception* and it's a part of his Polyvagal Theory.

† I know the brain is not really divided into two main parts. I'm aware of Paul MacLean's triune brain and many other models. However, I want to keep this simple and practical.

within it is the amygdala, which is the almond-sized part of the brain responsible for tracking threats of any kind and sending out a cascade of alarm bells in the form of hormones such as cortisol and adrenaline. The dispersal of these hormones throughout your body helps you mobilize and address the threat. Your scared animal has one job: to protect you. It doesn't think; it just wants to protect you from danger.

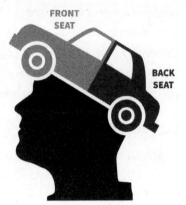

Diagram 6.1 The Simplified Two-Part Brain

2. Front Seat

The front seat is made up of the neocortex, sometimes called the frontal cortex, the front brain, or the PFC, and it is the logical or thinking part of the brain that separates you from the entire animal kingdom. As neuroendocrinologist and author Robert Sapolsky says, "The frontal cortex makes you do the harder thing when it's the right thing to do."[2] When you are in the front seat, you can "drive" a conflict to completion. You can drive your life responsibly and connect with others. When you're scared, the neocortex is the rational part of you that wants to build a case against the other person, and when you're settling a dispute, it can also take responsibility for seeing your part in the conflict. The neocortex also allows you to develop empathy.

Naturally, when under stress, your neocortex—your front seat— is compromised. When you get into a fight or are under some kind of threat response, your neocortex (logical, rational thinking) goes out the window and you are now operating from the more primitive brain regions, or the backseat brain, acting like a scared animal and still trying to drive. Once you are in your scared animal, you're less rational, more impulsive, and more likely to say or do stupid stuff. Think about it. Animals don't drive cars; people do. This primitive system has served humans for millions of years, but it can fire in an adult relationship the same way it would fire if a large carnivore was attacking you. This presents problems for family members or modern couples in long-term partnerships. Without knowing it, the person you love can trigger a very old survival system, and you lose your ability to recall how to work through conflict fairly. Depending on the trigger, your history, temperament, and sensitivity, you might quickly become threatening or unavailable to your partner or family member, or vice versa.

When you get your adult self together and get back in the front seat, the neocortex resumes steering. The neocortex allows you to calm down, bring back rational thinking, and make sense of what happened. You have the ability to pull the car over and take a few breaths. Soon, you'll learn many skills to help you come back into your front seat.

THE TRIGGER SCALE

Let's use a numerical scale to tease out the front seat from the back seat. I call this 0 to 10 number scale the *trigger scale*. (See Diagram 6.2.) Ten signifies the most activation, and 0 the least. Zero means that you have closure and you feel connected. We'll call the front seat a place where you are between a 0 and a 5, and the back seat is where your number is between 6 and 10. Remember how in the fourth section of your conflict box, you assigned yourself a number between 0 and 10 in relationship to the person named in the box; that's your trigger scale rating.

Diagram 6.2
The Trigger Scale

It's also important to note that there are two branches of the autonomic nervous system, sympathetic and parasympathetic, and these work in concert with your brain. As you move away from 0, up the number scale, because of life stressors or conflict with others, the sympathetic branch of the nervous system mobilizes your body to address whatever you perceive as dangerous or threatening. You become "triggered" or activated through an increase in heart rate, a tightening of the belly, narrowing of your vision, sweating, and many other body sensations. A 10 on the trigger scale puts you at the far edge of sympathetic activation. Keep in mind, during everyday conflicts with others, we rarely, if ever, hit a 10. Ten is a pretty extreme state when you feel intense fear, deep shame, or rage.*

For example, let's say you have a messy roommate. He always leaves his shit everywhere and hardly ever does the dishes. After months of living together, this will grate on you, especially if you are conflict avoidant. Your trigger number might be a 3 or 4. It's not that big of a deal, right? But if it keeps going and you continue to not say anything and he leaves his dirty socks on the couch again, especially if this catches you on a day where you're feeling grumpy, you might explode and say some pretty hurtful stuff. You might even threaten him. This is a moment when your scared animal in the back seat took over without a lot of choice or input from the front seat.

In everyday life, when you feel calm, safe, and secure, you are near zero in a predominantly vagal parasympathetic state sometimes known as "rest and digest." Your body is in a state when it can rest,

---

* What happens if you go beyond a 10 on the trigger scale? If you go beyond a 10, you move into a different category, an 11, which means the issue is now life-threatening, and you're out of the car entirely. A different part of your autonomic nervous system called the parasympathetic dorsal branch turns on as a way to help you not die. This is considered the "faint response," where your entire scared animal shuts down, all blood leaves the extremities and moves to your core organs. Your heart rate slows down, and you begin to conserve energy for when you get back up and need to fight or flee. The body is conserving all resources, so it expels unwanted and unnecessary resources. The body is doing its job, intelligently conserving resources so that when the threat has passed, it can mobilize again and get to safety. In everyday relationships, most of us are not going to experience something life-threatening, but it's good to know how our brain and nervous systems are designed to help us through conflicts of all kinds.

digest food, digest your experiences, and have positive social connections.* Zero is when you are connected to yourself (you have control of your mind and can feel the care and interest in your heart toward other people). Basically, it's the place where you feel good and available for connection. You're in what Stephen Porges calls your social engagement system.

When threatened, you leave zero and you mobilize into the Four Disconnectors—seek or avoid, posture or collapse—to protect yourself. The more serious the threat feels, the more your sympathetic nervous system takes over (see Diagram 6.3) and the more your number on the trigger scale increases. So, the moment you are triggered, you leave off the gas, let go of the steering wheel, and your ability to communicate effectively decreases. Your heart rate increases, and without knowing it, you hand over control to the scared animal. That's what happened when you shamed and blamed your roommate for leaving his dirty socks on the couch.

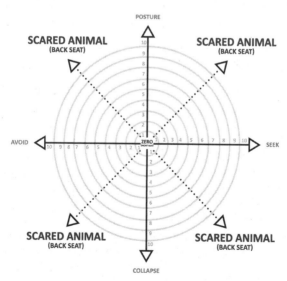

Diagram 6.3 When the Scared Animal Is Driving

---

* For the purpose of this book, I'm intentionally oversimplifying the nervous system. If you want to learn more, I recommend the work of Dan Siegel and Stephen Porges.

This movement from front seat to back seat can happen in nano-seconds. The most amazing part of your scared animal is that it will take over when something is dangerous or life-threatening without "checking in" with your front-seat brain. For example, if you've ever heard a loud *boom*, you might have instantly ducked or reacted before thinking you should do so. You act before you think. This threat detection system has our back, except when it doesn't. Very quickly we make meaning out of what's happening, but we often misread and misunderstand what's happening. Recall the example earlier of Sue misreading Stephen's face.

If you never learn to work with this incredibly sophisticated system, you'll delegate your getting to zero results to the scared animal, which doesn't care about getting to zero. It cares about surviving. Your main challenge during and after conflict is not only the other person and how they react but also how you work with your own scared animal.

BEING WITH THE SCARED ANIMAL

What if you could reframe your scared animal as merely a sensitive creature that has your back? It just needs a little mentoring from the adult in the front seat. In the context of conflict, most people judge themselves or the other person as "too much" or "not enough." You may have been told that you're "too sensitive," "too emotional," or "too needy." Or that you're not caring enough, not sensitive enough, or not appreciative enough. You may have also been told that the less you talk about conflict, the better. Typically, people are doing whatever they can to avoid the conflict and make it go away as quickly as possible.

Brandon did this his entire life. When his coworkers or partners brought up something difficult, Brandon would get triggered and try to hide it and smooth it all over as fast as possible. When Brandon was a kid, his parents called him "O.R.," which meant "overreactor."

What's a kid going to do with all those feelings? He went to his room and played video games for hours, doing his best to shut down his scared animal. He tried to develop strategies that were not so damned sensitive, because, after all, his "overreacting" caused problems in his family. Over time, he learned to ignore his feelings and sensations, even though he was triggered underneath his mask. In his perception, his parents had very little patience for his sensitivity, so with nowhere to go with his feelings, like a lot of boys, he stuffed his emotions. But stuffing them inside didn't do anything to help him resolve his conflicts and hurt feelings, especially as he got older.

By the way, when parents ask their children to stop feeling, they are asking their children to ignore and distrust their inner life, which is the opposite move to having fulfilling relationships that navigate conflict successfully. Parents who shut down their kids' emotions are likely people who have shut down their own emotions, which is why it's so hard for them to tolerate and build the capacity to deal with their children's emotions.

When Brandon dove into the Getting to Zero work, he saw that he could no longer keep using the coping strategies he learned growing up. He decided to own his sensitivity and start bringing it, and his true feelings, to his closest relationships. Brandon chose option C, and in doing so, he had to face all the conflicts he had been avoiding. It wasn't pleasant. But it started to weed out the people in his life who couldn't handle his sensitivity and he started meeting people who wanted more of it. Naturally, his intimate relationships became deeper and stronger.

To let your scared animal do its job—and learn how to better discern how it perceives threats and which responses are best—you must learn how to be with your scared animal. What does this mean? It means you have to learn how to be with everything going on in your inner experience: feel your feelings and sensations, breathe into them, and hold them like you would a small baby if it were crying.

LOOKING FOR THE NEGATIVE

Your brain has another interesting feature. Did you know your brain is twice as likely to avoid pain/threat than it is to seek pleasure/connection? That's right. It has what is called a negativity bias. During a podcast interview, Dr. Rick Hanson (an amazing researcher, psychotherapist, and author) told me that the brain is living inside of a carrots-and-sticks game where it tries to seek carrots (food and pleasure) and avoid sticks (threats and pain).[3] If you go a day without carrots, it's no big deal. But if you are not paying attention to the stick carried by other threatening people, then— *whack!*—you could die in an instant. So, it's much wiser to be on alert for sticks than for carrots. You also learn faster from pain than from pleasure so that your brain can help you avoid sticks in the future. Super smart, right? As Dr. Hanson says, "We're designed to be changed by negative experiences."

Even though we learn quicker from negative experiences, we move toward pleasure as our main strategy to get away from the threat of pain. This becomes an addictive cycle for many of us and why so much of modern society is self-medicating with sugar, Instagram, video games, and countless other distractions—to get away from negative experiences we perceive as uncomfortable and threatening. We are not so much a pleasure-seeking culture as we are a pain-avoiding culture through pleasure seeking. This is what the Buddha said was the root of all suffering.*

For example, in my twenties, I had low-grade emotional pain, discontent, and anxiety because of my inner conflict. But I didn't know the source of this pain. All I knew was that I didn't like feeling that

---

* Studying Buddhism helped me see that there is going to be suffering in life no matter what. And the root of that suffering is the desire for something "better" (seeking) and the ignorance of trying to get away from our suffering (avoiding).

way, so I'd drink and smoke weed and rock climb to get away from it. I was seeking pleasure to get away from the pain that I didn't know how to address.

When you seek to avoid your own pain and discomfort through pleasure, you rob yourself of any and all growth opportunities, you fail to take personal responsibility, and you shut down the deep learning that comes from working through conflict with someone you care about. This is why it is so paramount to learn how to be with your inner discomfort, disturbances, and sensations. To rise above your animal nature, you'll want to spend more time in the driver's seat learning how to handle the scared animal in the back seat. Doing this will help you handle conflicts and the stress that relationships naturally bring. In other words, we can learn to use our brain to manage ourselves.

THE COST OF LOW-GRADE STRESS

If you keep avoiding conflict, stuffing your feelings inside, and pushing away the discomfort and pain, is it really that big of a deal? Yes. The research is clear about the long-term health implications of this strategy. In a groundbreaking study in the 1980s called the Adverse Childhood Experiences (ACEs) Study, 17,421 people completed physical exams and confidential surveys regarding their childhood experiences and current health status and behaviors.[4] The researchers define adverse childhood experiences as physical abuse, sexual abuse, emotional abuse, neglect, exposure to domestic violence, substance abuse, mental illness, divorce, and other traumatic situations.* They found that unresolved conflicts such as these make life harder. The more adverse experiences people had, the worse their challenges later in life became.

---

* All symptoms of trauma and unresolved conflict.

> Childhood trauma increases the risk for seven out of ten of
> the leading causes of death in the United States. In high doses,
> it affects brain development, the immune system, hormonal
> systems, and even the way our DNA is read and transcribed.
> Folks who are exposed in very high doses have triple the
> lifetime risk of heart disease and lung cancer and a 20-year
> difference in life expectancy.
>
> —Nadine Burke Harris, MD, author of *The*
> *Deepest Well*, founder of Center for Youth
> Wellness, and Surgeon General of California

So, you can see that if we spent our childhood or decades in a state of disconnection with no repair or reconnection, it can be deeply damaging over time.

Minimizing Relationship Stress

When you report that you're "fine," and chronically thwart the Conflict Repair Cycle, you become accustomed to stress and learn to "tolerate" stress and "medicate" over your unresolved issues. In other words, some of us have adapted to living in a chronic state of low-grade stress and don't feel the cost until we are older. This is why stress is considered the "silent killer."*

For example, you may have grown up in a family system where the vibe in the house appeared fine or safe on the surface, but just below the surface, your nervous system was chronically on low-grade alert because in reality your four relational needs of feeling safe,

---

* In his book *When the Body Says No*, Dr. Gabor Maté writes about how chronic stress in childhood becomes detrimental later in life. He says, "The fundamental problem is not the external stress . . . but an environmentally conditioned helplessness that permits neither of the normal responses of fight or flight. The resulting internal stress becomes repressed and therefore invisible. Eventually, having unmet needs or having to meet the needs of others is no longer experienced as stressful. It feels normal." In other words, no matter how strong your coping strategies might be, the price tag for avoiding conflicts is high.

seen, soothed, and supported and challenged were not met. Your parents may have been proud to "never fight," and perhaps they swept anything difficult under the rug. But nothing ever got repaired and you could feel their tension, their resentment, and were left on your own, feeling unnoticed. You got used to the stress to the point where nothing felt overtly stressful. This is a situation where you felt safe physically, but not very safe emotionally because emotions were denied or discounted, especially negative ones. Your parents denied your negative emotions, didn't complete the Conflict Repair Cycle, and kept telling you, "It's fine; you'll be fine," or, "There's no need to be sad; there's nothing wrong. You should be grateful."

Children naturally adapt to this environment and tell themselves that, indeed, they are fine and nothing's wrong. This child grows into an adult who continues to deny negative feelings or experiences, and when things get difficult in their intimate relationships, they do what they've always done: blame or avoid, minimize, and compartmentalize.

When you shut down or repress emotions in relationship to unresolved conflict, your body secretes more cortisol. Cortisol, also known as the stress hormone, is vital and necessary for our well-being. However, too much cortisol, too often, creates an imbalance that has many negative long-term health implications.[5] John and Julie Gottman, pioneers in relationship health and researchers in clinical psychology who've studied more than three thousand couples, told me that couples that do conflict well live ten years longer than couples who avoid or struggle with navigating conflict.[6] In other words, how you do, did, or didn't do conflict might be taking a toll on your mental or physical health and well-being.

In my experience, and backed by loads of research, the stress caused by the inability or unwillingness to work through conflict is a major cause of failed relationships, divorce, and chronic health problems later in life.[7]

The High Side of Stress

It's important to remember that we need some level of stress (conflict) or we wouldn't be growing and evolving ("good" stress is called *eustress*). Consider that one benefit of relational stress is that people who challenge your values help you stay true to them. Stress ideally helps you face yourself and your pain so you can learn to work with it. With the proper tools, understanding, and support, you can view any stressful interpersonal challenge as a growth opportunity that makes you stronger, more adaptable, more resilient, and possibly more connected. Adversity builds character; conflict builds strong relationships.

The work you must do during interpersonal conflicts is to use your brain—along with other tools in this book—to move back into the front seat, back to zero, back to a place of reconnection. Conflict and our relationships shape who we are (literally) on a daily basis, and it all starts with the brain and nervous system, your perceptions of threat, and how you deal with stress.

ACTION STEPS ───

1. You are not your scared animal. But can you see the cost of not learning how to work with it? Write down the costs you may pay when you choose not to be the owner and take command of your scared animal.
2. The trigger scale: Use this every time you are triggered. Educate at least one other person so they start to learn about how upset you are.
3. Reflect on how you have historically done stress. Can you make a connection between unresolved conflicts and your well-being?
4. Connect with your practice partner and share what you learned about yourself in this chapter.

CHAPTER
7

The Price Tag of Avoiding Conflict

If you avoid conflict to keep the peace, you start a war inside yourself.

—CHERYL RICHARDSON

MOST OF MY LIFE I HAVE BEEN A CONFLICT AVOIDER. LITTLE did I know that by avoiding conflict I created more of it. What I learned the hard way is when you avoid an outer conflict with another person, you create an inner conflict with yourself. The inner conflict emerges when we are unable or unwilling to express ourselves honestly during or after a conflict. Sometimes we are too scared to speak the truth, and sometimes we're too young and the power differences in the relationship are too large. If you're a conflict avoider, you'll want to understand the origins and costs of whatever conflicts you avoid. Then, you can feel empowered to address them.

THE CORE INNER CONFLICT

I was a sensitive, emotional, and empathic young boy. If I saw an injured bird, a disabled person, or someone crying on the playground, my world would stop and my heart would ache. I felt, a lot. At times, crying got me in trouble with my parents. Sometimes my dad would say in response to my tears, "I'll give you something to cry about." If I cried on the playground, I risked getting teased or bullied. If I went to seek comfort from my mom in public, I risked being called a mama's boy.* I learned to bite the back of my hand to stop myself from crying (a strange habit I kept until my thirties).

My parents raised me well, with tons of love, care, and resources. I'm deeply grateful for that. I know, at times, my sensitive side was a handful. I demanded attention and affection. To them, I overreacted and even manipulated certain situations to get what I wanted. They handled me with the tools they had. But I still got the vibe that my sensitivity was a problem, so I eventually tried to bury it and hide it (which was almost impossible to do). I learned that being funny, charming, and athletic was acceptable and preferable to me being true to my emotional and sensitive side. This tactic worked better when playing sports, too. Over time I would trade my true self-expression (sensitivity, tears, negative emotions) for a modified self-expression (performance, achieving, acting tough) that got me belonging, connection, and acceptance. Like any normal kid, when I felt emotionally safe, I would express myself freely. When I felt emotionally unsafe or threatened, I disconnected and created strategies to cope.

Most children start to feel like they have two parts or personalities: one that feels innocent, wild, and free, and another that is more constricted based on mitigating threats and conforming to the rules of the environment. I call this rift between the two selves the *core inner conflict*, and for many people, it can last a lifetime.

I think it's useful to give these two parts a name. Keeping things simple, I call our authentic self-expression our *True Self* and our modified self-expression our *Strategic Self*. The authentic self, or True

---

* I find it interesting (and sad) that it's socially acceptable for boys and men to call other men "mama's boys," but when it comes to "daddy's girl," it's somehow cute and endearing. This is rooted deeply in misogyny and how boys are conditioned. I digress. Perhaps another book.

Self, is who children are at their core. The Strategic Self is who kids become based on how they witness conflict being dealt with and the complexity, messages, and demands of the environment over time.

I understand humans are not this simple. However, I find this distinction very helpful in explaining the inner conflict that most of us dealt with growing up. I split off from my True Self because, at times, expressing it caused me pain and rejection. I didn't want more pain or rejection, so I altered my self-expression and developed strategies to minimize anything that negatively impacted my connection with (attachment to) and approval of the people I relied on most.

Diagram 7.1 The Core Inner Conflict

Think of this inner conflict as a compass with two needles pulling you in two directions as shown in Diagram 7.1.

When we felt safe as children, we were in our True Self, and when we felt unsafe, we led with our Strategic Self. The gap between these two "directions" creates tension—the core inner conflict—that later contributes to something feeling "off" in your life.

And every conflict offers the opportunity for us to point our compass toward a true self-expression or to a strategic self-expression based on whatever we perceive will help us feel safe. During conflict, most of us tend to use strategies that rise out of the Four Disconnectors: We posture in blame, or we collapse in shame. We seek with charm, or we avoid in fear.

Reflect on your relational blueprint. Think of your childhood and the messages you received about your self-expression. Were you "too much," "not enough," or the "all-star" who couldn't do anything wrong? Did you space out and dissociate from your feelings, and go into fantasy and dream states instead? Or were you "a good boy" or "a good girl" because you never cried? Or did crying get you what you wanted? Were you judged as "naughty" when you didn't do as you were told? Did the grown-ups have your back, or did you feel completely alone, like a disappointment, an unwanted burden? What part of your self-expression—tears, rage, tantrums, sadness, silence, anger, joy, being slow, not following rules, feeling scared—was not okay, and what strategies did you adapt? Which of the Four Disconnectors did you employ? Did you move toward relationships or away from them?

You likely modified parts of yourself and developed strategies to keep your sense of belonging because you feared negative consequences such as hitting, shaming, ignoring, bullying, neglect, and rejection, just to name a few. Remember, to a baby and growing child, this feels choiceless. As you grow into adolescence, your strategies might feel more conscious—you may have rejected your family only to see that you then had to develop strategies to belong with your peer group. In social interactions, you kept things light, joked, or acted tough and tried on new behaviors that created less conflict and more external validation, acceptance, and belonging. If you traded your self-expression to avoid getting rejected or hurt, you likely created an inner conflict.

Kids take unresolved outer conflicts inward, and that is where they stay most of their life.

- "I can't be myself here."
- "I better not be too emotional or else . . ."
- "I don't want to be too joyful or playful here because . . ."
- "I'll just keep my mouth shut and keep to myself. It's no use; things aren't going to change anyway."
- "I will hate myself. That way, I'm the only person who can really hurt me."

Unless a child's self-expression has been cultivated and nurtured through secure attachment relationships (recall the four relational needs), the external messages around how to behave to maintain connection will dominate, and the Strategic Self will win out over the True Self because attachment is need number one.

My Strategies

As I grew into young adulthood, my Strategic Self won out: I became who I thought my parents and other people wanted me to be. My mom was a schoolteacher and then became a stay-at-home mom to raise me and my siblings. My dad was a three-time All-American ski racer turned businessman. Back in the day, he was one of the best ski racers in the world. He also played varsity golf in college, was an outstanding all-around athlete, and worked super hard to provide for his family. He was intense, and I looked up to him and didn't want to disappoint him with my sensitive, emotional, artistic side that preferred noncompetitive unstructured play in nature.

Although my dad always encouraged me to follow my dreams, instead I chose a strategy of playing the sports he and my mom supported: golf, tennis, and ski racing—because that's where the love, approval, and connection was. They paid for everything, showed up for games, and cheered me on. Like my dad, I was a very good athlete and was recognized for it, which kept my strategy going. Countless times, my Strategic Self was validated with comments from my parents and coaches like, "You're such a natural athlete" or "You're one of the best athletes, if only you applied yourself." Yet deep down, I couldn't care less about winning—or even playing—these sports. I never got excited to run laps around a tennis court, hit golf balls on the driving range, or put on a skinny one-piece downhill suit for a ski race, especially in a blizzard.

By the time I reached high school, I felt slightly more empowered to make my own choices. After my high school tennis team won the state championships, without me playing at all, I saw no point in continuing. My heart wasn't in it. I also quit golf in high school, and eventually I quit ski racing freshman year of college much to the dismay of my parents and coaches. To me, quitting felt like freedom, one of the signs you're letting go of a strategy that no longer serves you.

In my teenage years, I learned to find friends, belong, and gain acceptance, but I'd often do it at the expense of my true self-expression, which I buried deeper and deeper each passing year. After all, it worked: I got good at using my Strategic Self to get other people to like me. Yet my inner conflict was growing.

If you could rewind the tape and watch memories of your own childhood, no matter how perfect or messed up it was, you are likely to see that you traded parts of your self-expression for connection with others. Just ask yourself: "What did I do in my teenage years to belong?" Or think of a recent event, like the last date you went on or the last job you applied for. Chances are you held back your True Self so as to avoid rejection. We need some of our "strategies" to navigate our complex relational life. However, when our strategies become who we are, we compromise our own fulfillment. Over time, too much strategy leads to a pretty big self-betrayal and keeps the core inner conflict entrenched. For example, if you (or someone you know) followed the path that your parents or other influential figures wanted you to, you might have been able to live out their wishes for a few decades, but you never felt fulfilled, and you probably set yourself up for a midlife crisis. The turmoil of this inner conflict eventually catches up to you. It did to me.

I'll Go Wherever I'm Accepted

By the time I was eighteen, my inner conflict was getting bigger. On the first day of my freshman year of college, I met a kid who asked me if I wanted to get high. I had never smoked pot before, so I said sure. Within a few months, I was a full-blown pot-smokin' hippie. Had I met a jock on that first day, I might have become a jock. It didn't matter. I wanted friendship more than I wanted to address my insecurities.

I grew out my hair, started listening to the Grateful Dead, and almost got kicked out of college for taking bong hits in a friend's dorm room. After a shitty year of wake and bake, plagiarizing papers, getting Ds in my classes, I thought maybe it was the location of my school that was the issue. So I transferred and enrolled at a bigger university. With this fresh start someplace where nobody knew me, I rejected my hippie personality, cut my hair, joined a men's fraternity, and put on a coat and tie every Monday for pledge meetings. This was a chance to redefine myself and try on the behaviors of this group. Most of the guys drank—a lot. So I drank even more to keep up and fit in. When I drank, I felt more confident and secure. I felt pleasure and relief from my inner demons and confusion. We drank hard and hazed hard. The way we treated our pledges was deplorable, abusive, and unacceptable, and for years I felt ashamed at how I betrayed my integrity in the name of belonging. But because I was living my life from my Strategic Self, and because I felt lost, disconnected, and didn't even have my own back, I went along with it, participated in it, and did nothing to stop it. That is, until later. Typically, we can run our avoidant strategies for a very long time until something interrupts them.

During my fraternity days, a few of us would escape to the Utah desert to mountain bike, rock climb, and party. We often drank a lot and took acid or mushrooms. On one particular powerful mushroom "trip," I was walking with no direction through the desert, when I saw someone a hundred feet away who looked like me. As I moved closer, it turns out it *was* me. I instantly felt a deep sense of fear. How could I be in two places at the same time? Later, I would understand that I was seeing the core inner conflict between my two selves. It was terrifying and illuminating. It was my second psilocybin experience, and it began to shatter the façade of my Strategic Self. Later I would call this a "bad trip," but it turned out to be a pivotal moment in my life. Something had cracked and a little sliver of my True Self began to emerge.

Yet old patterns die hard, and I was now playing out my strategies with all the women I dated. One of my strategies was to charm them by trying to help them with their problems, which kept the attention off me and my insecurities. I acted sensitive on the outside, but hid my own emotions behind a mask and was "mysterious," which some women found attractive. This also impressed my male friends, and that gave me a booster shot of external approval. I also kept every one of my girlfriends at arm's length and avoided conflict. When they said things like "What's wrong?" or "Can we talk?" it felt bad, so I pulled away or pushed them away. I kept my vulnerability and truth locked behind a wall. My guess is that the women I dated could sense some kind of inner turmoil (my core inner conflict) and wanted to understand or help. They wanted the guy *behind* the mask.

It was the combination of my core inner conflict and my outer unresolved conflicts that led to a decade of failed relationships. Eventually, this pain was so great that it catapulted me onto the personal growth path. Whenever we're not being true to self-expression in an adult relationship, we feel conflicted inside and suffer feelings of anxiety, depression, shame, despair, or we feel just plain bad. In addition, if we look closely, we might see that below any unresolved outer conflicts with the people in our lives lies a deeper, older, and more entrenched inner conflict, where we struggle to be, or even know, our True Self.

This is why you see adults stay in hurtful or neglectful partnerships. Often one partner is choosing to hide their truth in the relationship because they'd rather stay with someone than risk speaking up, which could jeopardize the relationship, leaving them alone. This is also why people stay stuck in jobs they hate. Having a lame job where you can't express your truth but are collecting a paycheck is better than expressing your truth and getting fired.

This is an incredibly important concept. In any given moment, we all make choices based on what's going to give us more advantages than disadvantages.* For example, when you visit your partner's family over the holidays, sometimes it's better to keep your mouth shut because it's just not worth it to tell your mother-in-law that you don't really like the dinner she made or her political choices. Or you might strategize how you're going to quit your soul-sucking job but then decide you should stay on longer in order to receive that bonus you're expecting.

If certain needs continually go unmet, and the Conflict Repair Cycle doesn't complete, we adapt to keep the core attachment need met. Thus, we will use our strategies whenever we think they will help us more than hurt us. All of us have strategies to avoid pain and get what we want or fit in. And no matter how "healthy" we are or how good at conflict we become, sometimes we have to pull out a strategy to get through a difficult situation.

Marginalized groups have strategies to avoid prejudice and discrimination. For example, a person of color has strategies to avoid ongoing racism. A woman in a male environment might employ a strategy to avoid sexism. A gay couple might have a strategy of not holding hands in public to avoid hate. Those are strategies that help us avoid conflict, violence, and even death. Strategies come in handy. Our strategies are not right or wrong, good or bad, but we need to recognize them and know when they help or harm us and when they contribute to inner or outer conflict. The key factor here is choice. Most of us deploy our strategies without knowing it. For example, the term "people pleaser" says it all. A people pleaser tries to please people for some payoff. Some of us get turned off by people pleasers because their behavior feels disingenuous, like a strategy, which it is. Many people pleasers are not even aware of this habit. They act in a people-pleasing way without thought because they are entrenched in an old or outdated strategy from their childhood and because they

---

* An amazing concept taught to me by Dr. John Demartini.

may still be getting rewarded for it. Yet, strategies that served us as kids don't always serve us as adults.

When Sarah was a little girl, her mother struggled with depression. Her parents were physically there for her, but emotionally absent. Her father was often stressed and worked long hours. Sarah was the big sister of three younger siblings. She learned pretty quickly that her home felt best when she helped out. Instead of playing with the other kids in the neighborhood, she often helped cook dinner and clean up. She would even bring her mom food in bed. Sarah was praised with comments like "you're such a helpful little girl" and "I couldn't do it without your help." These messages reinforced her Strategic Self until it became the water she was swimming in. Sarah applied herself in school, thinking that it might help her mother get better and her father love her more. Everywhere Sarah went she was praised for how helpful she was and how good she was at taking care of other people.

As you can see, Sarah's strategy of being a good helper permitted her to experience less pain and more connection throughout her childhood. But as an adult, it started getting in the way.

Sarah studied to be a nurse, got married, and had her own family. Early on, the marriage was good, but after she had kids, she and her husband drifted apart, with both focused on work and the kids at the expense of their connection. Her husband had a habit of blaming her for their problems, and their parenting styles were often at odds. Instead of focusing on herself and her issues, she tried to change her husband, which only made their conflicts worse. He felt judged and would shut down, sometimes for weeks. Most of their conflicts were not resolved, and they began to pile up, year after year. She had big unaddressed resentments with her husband and grew short-tempered with him and the kids. Whenever her family asked what was wrong, she'd dodge the question and chalk it up to a stressful day at the hospital.

A lot of people are not aware of their core inner conflict unless— or until—they have an outer conflict that pushes it to the surface.

When Sarah contacted me, she had reached the end of her rope and was finally ready to do something drastic.

TWO SHITTY CHOICES

Part of the reason we stay stuck inside of our inner conflicts is because of how we approach the outer conflicts. Many years previously, Sarah's marital conflicts were set up as two bad choices, so she was immobilized by fear, not choosing either path. I call this concept *two shitty choices*. Here's how she saw it:

Choice A: Speak up and tell her husband the whole truth about her dissatisfaction with their marriage. If she chose this option, she feared it would make their marriage worse, her husband might pull away even further, and worst case, she would lose her marriage, experience financial stress, and end up alone. Yikes.

Choice B: Say nothing. Maintain status quo. Stay in the marriage and don't rock the boat. If she chose this option, she feared that nothing would change and she would feel bad and alone in a sexless, lifeless marriage. Ugh.

As I helped Sarah see this double bind, it started to make sense to her why she felt stuck. She had the situation set up as lose-lose. Can you see how not dealing with her outer conflicts with her husband was creating an inner conflict? When you don't deal with a conflict outside, you create one inside. Of the two choices Sarah could see, they both involved pain and discomfort that she didn't want to deal with. This is why we often stay stuck right where we are. The irony, of course, is what Monika in an earlier chapter discovered: she was already in pain. It's understandable Sarah was stuck because, seeing only two shitty choices, she was unwilling to embrace and face the most obvious conflict in her life. Turns out, she had a lot of choices; she just couldn't see them.

It was clear to Sarah that choice B was going to be more painful than choice A. With choice B, she'd have to live with lying to herself and her family, perhaps indefinitely.

But at this point, Sarah's pain was so intense that she decided to risk total rejection, financial burden, and humiliation by opening the door to a third choice, which led to a big breakthrough. I call this third option *choice C* for *conflict*.

Avoidance of doing the hard thing (conflict) creates more conflict and keeps you stuck and discontented.

I reminded Sarah that the only way out of her situation, which was keeping her stuck in the valley of victimhood, was to forge a new path, one that would involve discomfort and maybe even loss. Sarah wanted to be the author of her life, but she was living for everyone else, on their terms. If you recall, the movement from victim to author is a choice. And that choice involves conflict. Sarah would have to practice being a relational leader by learning how to do conflict. This meant she had to start expressing herself in her high-stakes relationships at home and even at work.

Sarah began telling her friends that she was indeed suffering. Prior to this, she had told no one about her marriage problems. She also started speaking up in her marriage and saying what she really felt. She let her husband know she was unhappy and really stressed inside. She learned about relationships. She learned to listen better. She started being okay with uncomfortable emotions. She got okay with discomfort in her body. Eventually, she said yes to conflict. At times it was painful and uncomfortable as hell for her to fight with her husband. But now, a year later, she realized a different outcome than either of those two shitty choices. All because she chose to be a relational leader (choice C) and lead herself out of the valley of victimhood and into a life she could author.

YOUR CHOICES

Now we get to go back and pull up the person whose name you wrote in the conflict box in Chapter 2. Chances are you are stuck, immobilized in a double bind, or blaming them. Let's examine your two shitty choices right now.

> **Choice A:** Speak up and say something—tell the truth, the real truth, and fear the worst thing will happen. The other person will react and the relationship may end (think of the worst-case scenario).

> **Choice B:** Continue business as usual—say nothing and keep the peace, trying not to make it worse. Stay stuck right where you are and never learn how to work through conflict or experience what a fulfilling relationship has to offer.

Which one sounds better right now? If you're not in enough pain yet, you'll choose B. If the pain is pretty bad, you're motivated to entertain choice A. You've probably had at least one experience of trying choice A and it didn't go well, so you are stuck, worried that if you do speak up, they will defend, shut down, explode, or, worse—end the relationship. But if you stick with business as usual in saying nothing about your issues, you'll feel the same inner conflict and dissatisfaction you've been feeling. Hmmm.

If you're like the rest of us, stuffing your truth (choice B) creates a kink in the hose of your self-expression. Whatever we are *not saying* has no place to go, so it builds up inside of us, often in the form of resentment (more on this soon). It can be hard to hold in our truth, and it begins to leak out in the form of gossip (triangulation), tension, complaints, sarcasm, and snarky comments. When conflict continues to happen and we keep withholding our true self-expression, at some point a dam will break and our truth will come spilling out, often sideways or in mean ways that can really hurt the relationship. So then, you have three issues to deal with: (1) the initial outer conflict that you avoided, (2) the inner conflict that the avoidance created, and (3) the new conflict you just created as your truth came spilling out. Instead of working through the conflict, you've compounded it. I call this *conflict creep*. Conflict creep means you're creating more conflict by avoiding it. In addition, the other person might feel hurt and angry that you didn't say anything sooner.

Can you see how avoiding the initial outer conflict creates more conflict, inside of you and outside of you with the other person? Gulp. Please don't blame someone else for putting you here. With choice B, you're the one choosing to stay right where you are.

Now what about choice A? Express your truth. We often try to wiggle out of expressing our truth and facing conflict because, let's be honest, it's fucking scary. Who wants to lose a friend, partner, or family member—or be judged, hurt, or criticized? Sarah can relate. She was playing "not to lose" instead of playing to win. With choice A, we've already made up our mind and predicted the future by saying things like, "I've already said something and it didn't help—it only made it worse. And that will probably happen again this time." Oh, got it, so you'd rather stay stuck in choice B, where you betray yourself and minimize things as "it's not that bad" or make the other person wrong by blaming them for how many more years? If you choose option B, just own it. Consciously choose that and stop complaining about it. If you want option B, which stands for *business as usual* and *betray myself*, be my guest. Say it out loud: "I choose B, avoiding the conflict and betraying myself. I'm not ready or willing to change this."

But if you want a different outcome, then let's explore the third option, the option that enables you to be true to yourself *and* get the kind of connection you want: choice C. Think C for *conflict* because it's the only way to be you, through some conflict. Choice C is achieved by moving from the stuckness of choice B to choosing choice A, as shown in Diagram 7.2.

Notice how choice B involves pain (inner conflict) and choice A involves pain (outer conflict). Hmmm. Pain or pain? Do you want the pain of staying stuck or growing pains? There are no workarounds that avoid pain. I don't care how difficult your current conflicts are; there is a way out and it starts with option C, embracing and learning how to do conflict. That's the way home! It's okay to be nervous about it; you're just afraid because you don't know how to

Diagram 7.2 Choice C

do it. No problem. Back to student mode, where you're going to move from victim to author and learn how to be a relational leader.

The Two Fears Stopping You from Seeing and Choosing Option C

As you explore option C, the new path, it's common for your fear to get pretty loud. Let's explore that fear. If you get really honest with the person you are in conflict with and try to work it out (again), what's the worst thing that can happen? What are you afraid of most?

Fear 1: They will likely get upset if you speak honestly with them, right? They might shut down, blame, humiliate you, reject you, or worse, cut you out of their life. Ouch, that all sucks for sure. But there's another subtle layer.

Fear 2: If all the bad stuff in fear 1 happens (they shut down, get defensive, cut you off, etc.), how are you going to feel? You'll likely feel some very uncomfortable stuff, right? And you prefer to avoid feeling uncomfortable because if you've spent a

lifetime repressing your emotions and running away from conflicts, that discomfort might feel like an underground volcano
about to explode out of control, and you like being *in* control. In
other words, if you upset them, you might feel pretty bad, right?

Here's an easy way to think
about these two fears. First, add
three more rows to your conflict
box for a total of nine rows, so
it looks like the box in Diagram
7.3. Leave row 7 blank for now.
We'll come back to it later. In
this new conflict box, fill out
rows 8 and 9.

Row 8: If you tell the person
the truth, what are you afraid
they will do (shut down, defend,
blame, cut me off, etc.)? Row 9:
If that "bad" thing in row 8 happens, what will you feel? Think
of emotions such as *scared, sad,
mad* and sensations such as *tense,
gripped, hard to breathe.* And use
I statements.

With her marriage, Sarah
was afraid her husband would
leave (or that she would leave),

Person I'm in conflict with:
What they did:
The feeling I have when I think of this person:
0-10 scale:
Timeframe:
My part in our unresolved conflict:
If I speak up, what am I afraid they will do (behavior, action, inaction)?
If that happened, what will I have to feel in myself?

Diagram 7.3 Conflict Box
Example of Fear 1 and Fear 2

everyone would find out (social humiliation), and her kids would
be permanently damaged from a divorce. If all of this "bad" stuff
happened, she would feel some really, really uncomfortable feelings, mostly fear, grief, and shame. It would also mean upending her
life, maybe having to sell her house and move or be less financially

secure. So her fear was beyond just having to feel emotions—there were real-life, practical issues at stake.

Filling out row 9 can be hard because we are so caught up in the other person's potential reactions and blame, it's hard to imagine how *we* will feel if the worst thing happened. Sarah was so focused on not upsetting everyone else that she ignored her own feelings. So, by exploring your fears thoroughly, you will see where you've been holding back because you don't want to upset anyone or feel the resulting uncomfortable feelings (listed in row 9).* By not speaking up (option B), you can keep a semblance of a relationship, blame them, and protect yourself. Read that again. *You get to protect yourself.*

Your fear, and the ways you protect yourself against feeling discomfort, is keeping you stuck. Own that. "I'm afraid and protecting myself." The sooner you can own this, the sooner you'll move out of the victim seat into the author seat and choose something different. The first step is to admit that you're immobilized in fear.

What's interesting is that *how* you're showing up with the person in your conflict box is strongly related to how you held back your truth as a kid. For example, Sarah grew up taking care of everyone else in her family and not needing anything, and as an adult she was still doing both. So, see if there's a connection to your childhood environment. Soon, you'll learn how to "be with" any strong emotion, including fear, which will empower you to consider choice C and move toward the heat instead of away from it.

CHOICE C AND BEYOND

Now that you see how choices A and B keep you stuck, you're ready for choice C. Choice C is the path to personal authorship *and* more

---

* We'll cover facing your inner discomfort in Chapter 9. It's time to learn how to be okay with uncomfortable feelings, cool?

connection. Yes, it's scary, to be sure, but it's also the way through your difficult situation. Start to equate choice B with self-betrayal. Say it like this: "I choose to betray myself by choosing choice B," and see how that feels. You can also say, "When I try to be who I think others want me to be, I have to betray who I am to keep connection." Start to equate choice A with being authentic and choice C as the path to get there.

Moving toward choice C is what this book is about. Choice C's declaration is this: "The only way to get the kind of relationships I want, where I can express myself, be myself, and get the kind of connection I want, is through conflict." With your relational leadership hat on and the ability to take ownership, you, like any of us, can learn how to work through conflict. And, no, there isn't some cute short-cut that allows you to avoid the discomfort of conflict. You've already tried workarounds, justifications, and shortcuts. It's time to get to the heart of the matter. And, yes, you might get burned because it feels like such a hot fire. But then again, you might not get burned and it might all be a mirage, an illusion that your fearful mind created. Choosing C is about closing that gap between your Strategic Self and your True Self through embracing conflict and telling the truth in service of yourself and the relationship.

ACTION STEPS

1. Conflict avoidance: Reflect and be honest about how you have avoided conflict in your life. Can you see how avoiding conflict has created or exacerbated an inner conflict?
2. Can you see your two shitty choices with the person in your conflict box? Write them down. Choice A and choice B. Then ask yourself if you are willing to choose choice C. Yes? Great. By when? Add some accountability around this and let a friend know when you'll choose choice C.

3. Finish filling out rows 8 and 9 in the conflict box (your two fears) using the instructions from the chapter.

4. Review these two fears—what you think will happen when you speak up and how you think that happening will make you feel. What are you most afraid of happening if you choose choice C? Are you willing to face that fear?

5. Share an insight from this chapter with a close friend. Name the feelings this chapter brought up in you. Let them see you in that.

PART 2 | DURING CONFLICT—
HOW TO GET TO ZERO

How to Resolve Your Inner Conflict

Do I live my life according to my own deepest truths,
or in order to fulfill someone else's expectations?

—GABOR MATÉ

OUR CORE INNER CONFLICT MIGHT JUST BE THE BIGGEST CON-
flict we experience. I felt mildly depressed and anxious for over
two decades until I chose to listen to those "bad" feelings and treat
them as feedback. I used my lack of fulfillment and pain to motivate
me to take the journey from being a victim in the valley to become a
truer version of myself.

The further from yourself you drift, the harder it is to achieve an
internal state of fulfillment. You cannot be fulfilled when you have
an inner conflict going on each and every day. And you can't expect
to be fulfilled or content being someone you're not. Nor can you
have a deeply fulfilling relationship. When you use strategies instead
of your honest self-expression to work through conflict, you'll have
a very hard time getting to zero. As we already discussed, this gap
between your True Self and your Strategic Self creates some level
of anxiety and depression, no matter how many friends you have. It
begins to look like the image in Diagram 8.1.

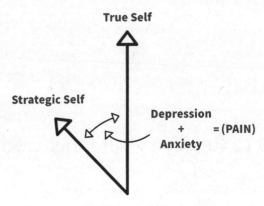

Diagram 8.1 The Cost of the Core Inner Conflict

GETTING TO KNOW YOUR STRATEGIC SELF

Before you integrate your Strategic Self into a truer version of you so that you can get the relationships you want, it's important to see how that Strategic Self is working for you. Remember, any strategy is serving a purpose. In fact, we all employ strategies every day. But we want to close the gap between these two compass needles and integrate them into one. How? By speaking up, telling the truth, and embracing conflict (choice C). The whole point of getting good at conflict is to help you see and experience the true power of being yourself and being in a great high-stakes relationship at the same time.

So, let's learn even more about the Strategic Self. I want you to consider that who you are, no matter how strategic or true you are, is built through a set of values. For example, my Strategic Self might value what you, or others, think of me. My True Self values me being true to myself, even if it means you reject me. If you're a conflict avoider, you probably value keeping the peace and not expressing yourself in certain scenarios. But this strategy keeps you disconnected from your True Self and over time affects what you value; surprisingly, it impacts the direction you go in life as well as how you show up in your high-stakes relationships.

For example, Phillip graduated from an Ivy League college and had no idea what to do after he graduated. He thought about taking a gap year to travel and figure himself out (True Self). But he felt the pressure from his family to get a real job. After all, each of his friends was getting recruited by start-ups and Fortune 500 corporations. Because he had majored in finance and his father worked for a large bank, he went to work for a big financial firm, thus following other people's values and his Strategic Self. The money provided a nice cushion to distract him from the inner turmoil he felt about what he really wanted to do with his life. For eight years, Phillip worked for this firm and received loads of outer praise and validation. This status and the recognition were of high value for his Strategic Self.

He started dating his girlfriend soon after graduation. At first things were great, but as the years went on, he became mildly depressed and distracted himself with booze and work. After all, if you work seventy plus hours per week, you can kind of avoid your issues. His girlfriend was his number one cheerleader and knew he was out of alignment with what he really wanted to do. For a long time, she tried to get him to quit his job, go to therapy, and get support. But she found this prodding made things worse, creating more conflict and disconnection. Whenever she tried to work through these moments of disconnection, Phillip minimized their problems and shut her out. He kept his feelings and truth bottled up inside. His strategy had always been to avoid feelings because, in his experience, they caused problems. Finally, she had enough—her resentment was too much to handle. With little notice, she broke up with him and moved out. Phillip was destroyed.

Up until this point, if we take stock of Phillip's values, we'd see that he valued status, money, booze, and fitting in; lower down on the priority list was his relationship with his girlfriend. But the sudden breakup changed his values. It didn't take long for Phillip to see clearly how he had botched his relationship by caring much more about status than his girlfriend. Because he hadn't valued his relationship that much, he was able to avoid his outer conflicts with her, and the booze served to numb his inner conflict.

Until your values around conflict change, you won't change, and it will be hard to "find" your True Self. Thus, it's critical at this juncture to get very honest about what you value and why because your values shape who you are, your choices, and what direction you go in life.

I call this direction your *compass*. A hierarchy of values dictates where your compass points. You navigate toward what you perceive is most important (and has the greatest advantages), and you avoid or move away from whatever you perceive is least important (and has the greatest disadvantages).

For the purpose of this metaphor, when you are being true to yourself and expressing yourself honestly (remember choice C), your compass orients to true north (even if you're wobbly). This of course is hardest in high-stakes relationships, where you have to navigate conflict and differences with someone else's compass that might be very different from yours. When you are not able to learn and work through conflict—like Phillip—your compass orients to magnetic north (choice B) and your true north is left at the mercy of whatever conflict-avoiding strategies you employ.* Typically, magnetic north shows up as you being and doing what others want you to be and do instead of you following your own heart and truth. Phillip chose to follow the herd and was operating by other people's values, orienting to his magnetic north.

When we are oriented to magnetic north, we conduct our lives without much thought, intention, or attention. It feels like we're on autopilot because we don't have to think too much or be too uncomfortable. We are "magnetized" to do whatever other people are

---

* On a real compass, true north is a fixed point and magnetic north aligns with the earth's magnetic field and is never static. I chose this metaphor because I believe our True Self is fixed and innate and magnetic north moves around all the time as we try to figure out, or find, our True Self. It's not a perfect metaphor, but I think it's useful.

doing or whatever we've been habitually doing. Phillip was magnetized toward status, money, and booze (external things). If we get enough validation and reward, we land in a zone of pseudocomfort and convenience that can last a lifetime. We also might stay stuck in the valley of victimhood, surviving and reacting and choosing instant gratification over the more difficult task of making the journey through conflict to become an author who is more aligned and has great relationships.

The more empowered you become around conflict, the more you begin to orient toward a true north that feels really good because you're telling the truth to yourself and others, even if it's uncomfortable at times. Your true north is where you are most fulfilled in life.

The question becomes: How can I be true to myself and be in this high-stakes relationship at the same time? This is the crux of any amazing high-stakes relationship. With any team, partnership, or family, people who have different values come together, and different values can create conflict. But the strongest partnerships and teams confront and resolve the outer conflicts and, in doing so, create fewer inner conflicts along the way.

The following compass exercise will help you identify your magnetic north (outside—who you think others want you to be) and your true north (inside—who you really are deep down). This exercise helps you see which direction your compass is currently pointing. It might clarify that inner conflict you've been feeling all these years. The compass exercise is inspired by and adapted from the Value Determination Process (VDP) of Dr. John Demartini.[*]

John asks a series of questions, which I've tweaked and shortened, that reveal your personal values. Your answers show you what you value and how you orient and travel in life. In this context, the term *value* does not describe things like "honesty" or "trust." Those are

---

[*] If you want a deeper dive into this subject, I recommend Dr. Demartini's book *The Values Factor*.

personal qualities you might admire or appreciate in yourself or someone. And, yes, in some circles those are considered values or virtues.
For this exercise, *values* are the things that matter most to you, that
you are pursuing, be it out of fear, frustration, habit, or inspiration.
Recall that Phillip *valued* status, money, and booze.

IDENTIFYING YOUR MAGNETIC NORTH— YOUR STRATEGIC SELF

A couple of tips before you start. Be honest. Think hard about what
your life really looks like. Think and reflect upon your daily choices
and actions. There's a difference between what you want your values
to be (true north) and what they actually are (magnetic north). Try
not to get confused. Initially, you write down only what your values
actually *are*, not what you wish them to be. This exercise comes in
handy as you work to resolve your outer conflicts.

Step 1. Think, Reflect, and Get Clear

Write only *four* short answers after each question below. You'll have
thirty-six words (or short phrases) total when you have completed the
exercise. Spend some time doing this exercise now.

1. How do you spend your time? (Example: working, family,
   scrolling news, working out, watching sports)
2. What do you spend most of your energy doing?
3. What do you spend most of your money on? Look at your expenses and what you buy most on Amazon and other places.
   Think of week-to-week expenses that make up your monthly
   expenses.
4. Which podcasts, blogs, books, magazines, movies, and articles
   do you read or listen to most, and when you surf the Web, what
   do you search for and explore most consistently?

5. Who do you spend the most time with?
6. Instead of working through conflict effectively, what do you do when you are stressed, scared, hurt, and frustrated by other people?
7. What are the themes, content, and patterns of your internal mind chatter? What do you think about all the time? What do you stay up late worrying about, thinking about, or fixating on?
8. Where in your life are you most trustworthy and organized, even when under pressure or stressed?
9. What does your spouse, family member, or the closest person in your life see as your top four values? What would they say is most important to you?

Step 2. Be Even More Specific—Clarify Your Answers

Let's say "working" turns out to be your highest value because you wrote it down eight times. Pin down exactly what about working you value. What does working give you? Status? Meaning? Leadership growth? A sense of purpose? For many people, working represents financial security, life purpose, freedom, or a certain kind of lifestyle.

If you wrote down something such as "family" as a value, make a distinction between family of origin, spouse, kids (parenting), and nuclear family (you, your kids, and your spouse). *Family* is vague. Be clear about what you mean.

If you put down things you do not like to do such as "cooking and cleaning" because you spend a lot of time dealing with them, for example, keeping the home in order for your family, clarify what that behavior represents or means to you. The deeper value in the activity might be "home," "being organized," or "parenting." Many parents understand that they will do a lot of unpleasant activities because they love their kids. Digging for the deeper meaning you find in that activity can help you own the value with less judgment and more neutrality.

Sharing the results of your life compass with a close friend can be extremely helpful. Ask this person if these seem right for you, given how you behave daily and who you present yourself to be, and get their feedback.

Step 3. Sort the Answers into Your Personal Compass

You should have thirty-six answers total. You'll notice certain ones repeat. Circle or put ticks by each answer and tally the ones that repeat. For example, if you mentioned "mothering" seven times and it is your most mentioned value, mothering is your highest value or the behavior you give the most priority. So, write "mothering" on line 1 of the pyramid in Diagram 8.2.

The next most mentioned value goes on line 2 and so on. For example, if "work" is mentioned six times, you would put "work" or "financial security" on line 2. You might need to lump a few related values together; for example, "health" might cover the less broad values of exercise, self-care, and healing your lower back injury.

At the point of the pyramid, like the arrow of a compass, is the value that is most important to you and where your attention is most focused and concentrated. And the wider part of the pyramid represents the stuff you do that's less important and harder to motivate yourself to do.

Your highest priority is that thing you spend the most energy on. You are most disciplined and reliable with that thing (even if you don't like what you're doing).

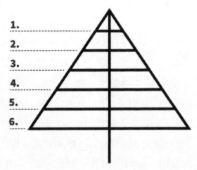

Diagram 8.2 Your Magnetic North

For example, Phillip placed a high value on status and money, so he was willing to put in seventy-plus-hour workweeks, even though he wasn't happy doing it. Olympic athletes don't need anyone to remind them to practice each day. Stay-at-home parents don't need anyone to tell them to cancel their plans if one of their kids is sick and needs to be pulled from school that day. They just do it without question because they value it. And part of the grunt work of parenting is all the cleaning, organizing, errands, and monotony at home.

Next, if you have a context or mindset you live your life by, a virtue or a way of being, list it along the vertical axis (the needle of the compass) or spine of the compass diagram. The spine is *how* you live your values. For example, the spine of my compass is "personal growth and development." Personal growth and development pervade all of my daily activities and how I approach my values. Growing and developing myself is a way of life, more than a value. Other examples are honesty, optimism, a religious view, a belief in a higher power, integrity. If you don't have a mindset that you approach your values with and that shows up in everything you do, don't put something on the spine. It's optional.

Let's look at Sarah's compass. As you may recall, Sarah is a conflict avoider. As we got deeper into our work together, I asked Sarah, "Who are you when you're not helping someone?" She drew a blank. Her strategy of helping others had become her identity, so much so that without it, she didn't know who she was. She agreed that even if her marriage was perfect, something would still feel off. No matter how many people she helped, or how much external approval she received, she had this strange sense of feeling empty and alone. In addition, she was experiencing new issues with her health. She wasn't sleeping well and she could only make it through her workday by relying on sugar and caffeine. Sarah couldn't even be with the truth of how alone she felt for more than a few minutes before she distracted herself again. More helping, more work, more busyness, more over-scheduling the kids' lives. When she did the compass exercise, she listed the following values:

1. Parenting
2. Work (part-time nursing that provided meaning and financial security)
3. Social obligations
4. Checking out with Netflix, TV, Instagram, news
5. My partnership with my husband
6. Health and well-being (yoga, walking, self-care)
7. Time in nature
8. Travel
9. Knitting
10. Other random stuff

Sarah had mentioned parenting eight times, work five times, and social obligations four times. As we moved lower down the list, it was less clear what she prioritized. Initially, she listed her relationship as her third highest value. As I challenged her in our work together, it became clear that, based on her actions, her marriage was fifth. She acknowledged that her friends and checking out were more of a safe haven than her husband. Interestingly, and maybe not surprisingly, she put her self-care and health below other people. Sarah wrote "being a good person" on her spine. Later we tweaked this to "altruism" because it's *how* she approaches her life. It's a guiding principle for her. By doing the compass exercise, Sarah was able to take an objective look at what she valued.

Step 4. Your True North

Now that you have your magnetic north compass in place, I want you to write down what you *want* it to be. Ask yourself, "What would my values be if I wasn't afraid and if I had my security needs taken care of?" Another way to tap into your True Self is to remember who you were as a child when no one was looking. What did you love doing when you were younger that you've lost touch with? As a kid, I cared about nature, belonging, and social issues more than I cared about sports. So it makes sense that later in life I spent a lot of time in nature and began to study relationships and myself. Eventually, my sensitivity became a real superpower as a relationship coach and teacher. The clues to your True Self are hidden within your most painful and pleasurable experiences in your life. Look for those highs and lows.

I'm going to assert that, like me, you have two directions in life, one is more fearful (magnetic) and one is more heart-based and courageous (true). Draw a new compass diagram, exactly like the one above, and write down what you want your values to be. Some readers might draw a blank on this part of the exercise. That's okay and makes sense because some of us have buried our True Selves and become so accustomed to our Strategic Self that it's the water we swim in. That was me for a long time.

Let's come back to Sarah. I had her fill out her True Self compass. "What would your values look like if you were not afraid and you could do exactly what you wanted to do?" After some back and forth, she got clear that her True Self compass would look like this:

1. Family/parenting
2. Marriage
3. Work
4. Self-care
5. Health

Observe how simple and clear it is. She noticed the gap between her magnetic north and true north and could clearly see her core inner conflict. For years she had been telling herself that she should quit her job and become a full-time mom. But her husband's job wasn't enough to afford their lifestyle, so she had to work, thereby missing out on being more involved in her children's lives. In addition, although she loved helping people, she was tired of getting so much praise and it not putting a dent in how she felt inside. Plus, her father was a doctor, and she felt pressured not to disappoint him by leaving the field of medicine. She'd thought about going into public policy to change healthcare, but she also didn't want a nine-to-five job that would take her away from her children.

She knew in her heart that all she wanted to do was help people grow and heal. She loved watching people change their lives, and this is part of what got her into nursing in the first place. So, though her Strategic Self was oriented toward nursing (pleasing her parents, fear of losing money), the intention and driving force behind nursing (helping others) was in alignment with her True Self. It turns out she wasn't that far off-center, so it didn't make sense to quit or change her career. The big difference for Sarah was that her Strategic Self was caught trying to help others who wanted rescuing so she could get approval and validation (remember her relationship with her depressed mother), which was leading to burnout. Her True Self wanted to help others because it was fulfilling. (No strings attached. No external praise needed. She just loved helping people grow.)

In her marriage, Sarah wasn't seeing how conflict with her husband could be *the* path to greater alignment. She was afraid he wouldn't be onboard with her desire to work less and prioritize family, so she had it set up as two shitty choices (discussed in the previous chapter): "Be myself and lose my job and my husband" or "Keep things the same and feel depressed and burned out." She couldn't see choice C (tell the truth to her husband about her marriage and career pain), nor could she fathom that conflict would be the way through her impasse.

HOW TO RESOLVE THE INNER CONFLICT

When there's a gap or inner conflict between what your values are in actuality and what you want them to be, the first step is to own that. Then look for the cost of your core inner conflict. Likely there's some pain there. Your clue is to see where you are in pain, where you feel dissatisfaction, or where you are longing. Finally, see why you've set it up so that you only have two shitty choices.

Now, recognize choice C.

You have to make a journey to close that gap between your Strategic Self and your True Self by telling the truth about yourself during and after conflict. This becomes a real hero's journey. Think about a good movie you've seen, where the hero has to confront the tension between who she is and who others want her to be.

Once Sarah had her two compasses in hand, we assessed how far she was from her true north. Seeing her gap, Sarah felt overwhelmed and shut down. This is a normal stage to go through; Sarah's collapse lasted about a week. She asked me, "What do I do?" I said, "Start fighting with your husband." We laughed, but she got to work. She was now clued in to herself and eager to set some goals toward changing her values to reflect her true north.

We began by dealing with the three values causing her the most pain and stress:

1. Her marriage
2. Her career
3. Her self-care

Each of these included an inner conflict. In her marriage, she had stopped telling the truth and was avoiding conflict with her husband. That avoidance created an inner conflict between speaking the truth and just trying to keep some basic connection going. Soon, they both said yes to conflict and began to transform their marriage. The inner conflict in her career? She felt torn between her love of helping others (True Self) and collecting a paycheck, pleasing her parents, and getting external praise and validation (Strategic Self). With her self-care, she was in an old strategy of helping others at the expense of herself, creating yet another inner conflict. I let her know that in order to change her hierarchy of values, she would have to become adept at conflict and that it would be a process, perhaps spanning six months to a year, before she would really see the fruits of her work with all three. Sarah was onboard. Soon she canceled her Netflix account, deleted Instagram from her phone, and put her time and resources into couples' coaching with her husband.

If you are honest, like Sarah was, and something you claim you care about actually falls lower on your list, it might feel uncomfortable to see that. You might think it "should" be higher, but as you look at it objectively and honestly, you find it's a lower value. Whatever results you see from this exercise are okay. Don't make any of it wrong. Be honest, whatever the information is. Then, if you don't like where your compass is pointing, commit to changing it over time.

Step 5. Identify Your Fears

Fear of conflict (fear of taking choice C) is the common root of inner conflicts (the gap between magnetic north and true north). If fear leads, you will justify and even defend your choices, lamenting that you "can't" because of X, Y, Z valid reason. "I don't have time." "I don't know how." "I don't have the money." These all could be used as excuses to stay right where you are.* You must begin to see that you are indeed choosing your direction every day. If you think it's not your choice, you have put yourself in a position to *not* have the power to change it.

Choice is *everything*. Even in your most painful moments in the valley of victimhood, your job is to find choice. Choice is the way out, and the way out starts with personal responsibility. "How can I get out of here?" "What is my first step?" Or, if you're still scared, "I choose to stay here until I'm better resourced."

---

* I understand that some of us have legitimate survival fears such as food, clothing, shelter. The assumption here is that because you're reading this book, those survival needs are taken care of at a base level.

Make a list of where you know you're not being your True Self. What is the context? Why are you holding back your truth? What is the cost if you stop hiding? Here's your prompt:

Context where I'm not being fully me	Work	Family	Partnership
Justification/reason	helps me keep my job	save face	keep relationship
Cost if I'm my True Self	I'd get fired	cut off from family	lose relationship

In the context of your high-stakes relationships, notice any valid reason you create about why you can't be you. On a blank piece of paper, write this: "I can't be myself because of _____." List all the reasons you can't be you. Then share this with a friend. Seriously. Try it. This is just another truth-telling practice. This way you get a few warm-up reps in as you begin to move toward conflict.

While you're learning to step into your truth and let go of other people's agendas about how you should be or who you should be, you will upset some people in your life. Some people might think you're weird or overreacting, or both. It might feel like you are being rejected or judged, and you might feel pretty damn lonely. Try to remember that you'll never be able to please everyone. You're opening your perspective to new options—and you don't know the outcomes yet. And, yes, one outcome may be that you let go of stagnant, conflict-avoidant relationships. That is uncomfortable, for sure. Yet, you have to see that by letting go of someone who doesn't respect your True Self, you make room for gaining new growth-oriented relationships that can handle stress and conflict—relationships that can handle the truth. Your relationships will evolve as you evolve. Relationships that can't handle conflict may end, and relationships that learn how to work through conflict will begin and deepen over time.

Closing the gap between your Strategic Self and True Self is merely the process of Getting to Zero—connection, disconnection, and reconnection. And the only way to get to zero is to learn how. The Getting to Zero process is so exciting because this is you learning about and reclaiming who you are.

HOW TO REARRANGE YOUR VALUES

How do you change your values and get moving toward true north? Remember this maxim I learned from a mentor: "People make choices based on what's going to give them the greatest advantages over disadvantages." If this is true, then to change we have to see certain choices and actions as more beneficial than others, or we won't do them and our values will not change. Make a personal commitment to tweak your magnetic north compass and give yourself a deadline. By what date will you have an updated compass that is more aligned with your true north? If you're not ready to make a huge career change, no problem. Start with changing how you show up in conflict in your high-stakes relationships. Define the support, challenge, and action steps you need to take to make that a reality.

For example, let's say you want to embrace conflict by telling the truth in one of your high-stakes relationships. But you don't say anything, which shows us how you really value avoiding more than self-expression. To change this, you need to see how telling the truth with this person will help both you and them. What are the benefits? Make a list. If you only see the negative, you'll stay stuck right where you are.

Maybe you want your application of the skills in this book to be a higher value, but you're overwhelmed with your work schedule (your highest value). You tell yourself you don't have time (the most common excuse we all make). To actually change, think how investing time, money, and energy into learning how to work through conflict will serve your career. List ten to twenty ways in which learning these skills and tools is going to help you be a better employee at your company. Maybe it will help you get a raise because you learn to be a relational leader and your boss values people who are mature enough to work through conflict. Perhaps you move into a new management position because people begin to see you as the competent one when it comes to communication and team dynamics.

Sam made a similar value shift years ago when he was struggling with prioritizing regular exercise. He changed his values, worked through some blocks, and hasn't looked back. Sam had to see how regular exercise would help him release some stress and tension he was holding in his body. Less tension meant he would feel better mentally, which would make him more pleasant to be around. Exercise also helped him avoid that midafternoon lull, which in turn increased his productivity. All of this helped him be a better leader, boss, partner, and friend.

Hopefully, you're beginning to understand why you have a core inner conflict playing out in every outer conflict. No matter what life steps you take—getting married, adopting kids, moving in with a friend, or going into business with someone—conflict will happen. If you embrace conflict, it'll be the path to transforming who you are from the ground up. As you practice getting to zero with other people, your magnetic north and true north will align over time.

ACTION STEPS

1. Write down three strategies you used as a child to keep connection. If you don't remember your childhood, look at your current or past high-stakes relationships for patterns.
2. Complete the compass exercise for both magnetic north and true north.
3. See your core human split and reflect on how this feels. Journal about it.

4. Begin the process of changing your values if you are unfulfilled. Start with making "learning conflict" a higher priority by seeing how many benefits you can list to your highest value.
5. Take a risk and share your answers with a friend. See if you can share this information vulnerably without censoring anything. Own where you're at and what you're committing to changing about yourself.

How to Be With *Your* Triggers During Conflict

As every therapist will tell you, healing involves discomfort—but so does refusing to heal. And, over time, refusing to heal is always more painful.

—RESMAA MENAKEM

DURING CONFLICT, YOU MAY THINK THAT YOU KNOW HOW TO handle yourself, but just look at your track record. If you examine it, you'll see that you're as difficult as those you are in conflict with, just in different ways. While your partner might not return your texts when in conflict with you, you might give off a negative vibe, raise your voice, or blame them for your problems. I've interviewed dozens of the world's leading experts on relationships and we all agree on a few things, one of which is this: relationships fail when people are unable and unwilling to learn how to work with their own reactivity and the other person's reactivity during and after conflict. It's that simple. Said in plain terms: people don't know how to work their shit out.

Look at your own relationship life. Your relationships that went south likely did so because your scared animal took over or the other person's scared animal decided to drive the car. And neither of you knew how to manage yourselves or the other person and adequately recover. In my experience, most of the time unresolved conflicts boil down to each individual struggling to "be with" all of the uncomfortable stuff that gets triggered during conflict. Uncomfortable stuff like emotions, body sensations, and fearful thoughts. Thus, learning how to be with your inner experience is an essential first step in working through conflict effectively.

When you're disconnected from yourself and from the other person, you're operating from a primitive part of your brain—the scared animal is in charge. Remember what you did as a kid when conflict happened or when you were upset by other people. Whatever you did, I'm guessing you didn't learn how to be with your inner discomfort and pain. Instead, like me, you probably shut down emotion, distracted yourself, or dissociated into daydreams and pleasanter feelings. Or you internalized the conflict and felt it was your fault and that you were somehow a bad person as a result. Or you bent over backward to try to end the conflict, feeling like your role was to be the peacemaker at all costs. The truth is, very few people know how to be with their inner pain and discomfort. But the good news is you can learn how, and it will go a long way to resolving conflict in your life. Let's focus on learning how to be with the uncomfortable stuff inside that conflict triggers.

OUTSIDE IN VERSUS INSIDE OUT

Let's say a conflict is under way and the other person is moving away (too much distance) or acting aggressive and blaming you (too much closeness). Your scared animal senses a threat and you disconnect (using one of the Four Disconnectors: posture, collapse, seek, or avoid).

It feels intense and you want all of it to stop. The first thing you have to understand is where the threat is. Is the threat outside of you, or inside of you? How do you know the difference?

To answer this question, let's remember Ted Striker from the movie *Airplane*. Ted is a war veteran turned cab driver, who has to fly the plane when the pilots pass out. The plane is about to crash and Ted begins to experience huge amounts of fear, flashbacks, and self-doubt to the point where he vacates the pilot's seat and places a blow-up pilot doll in the seat, saying, "I can't take the pressure." He nearly quits trying to help land the very plane he's supposed to save. Is his stress outside or inside of him?

Most people think that the stress they feel during conflict is outside of them, because when the plane has landed and the storm has passed, they feel better. People conclude that it was the plane and the bad weather, when in reality, those were the triggers and not the root cause of the underlying issue. In other words, you might think the other person is the problem instead of all that uncomfortable stuff they trigger in you. Most of us were taught that other people "make" us feel a certain way, which is only partially true. Other people's behavior impacts us, yes. They trigger all kinds of feelings in us. But it's our responsibility to deal with our triggers because they are inside of us. Most conflicts are a combination of inside and outside threats, so it's critical to know how to get to zero alone and together if the other person is willing to collaborate.

Ted Striker couldn't handle the flashbacks, the sweat dripping down his face, and the overwhelm he was experiencing inside. It was too much. We've all heard countless real-life stories of near plane crashes, but the difference is that these pilots remained calm enough (inside) through the storm (outside), and as a result they successfully landed the plane (which Ted did too!).

Although our conflicts might never be as ridiculous as those in the movie *Airplane*, they are stressful to the point of us wanting to hit eject. But doing so, instead of working to resolve the conflict, is to create more stress in you and in the relationship.

THE EMOTIONAL DISCOMFORT THRESHOLD

How much internal emotional discomfort you can handle is what I call your *emotional discomfort threshold*, or EDT.

In my twenties I was a pretty "tough" guy, but my emotional discomfort threshold was low. The moment a woman brought some need or emotion to me, such as "Hey, I'm feeling disconnected and want to talk about it," I didn't like it and I didn't know what to do. So, I would "fire" her from the role of my girlfriend—ah, sweet relief! No more emotional discomfort. The deeper truth was that her need and emotions triggered uncomfortable feelings in me that I couldn't handle. My EDT was the size of a Matchbox car. Ironically, as a wannabe extreme athlete, I could handle all types of discomfort in other areas of my life—such as sleeping on the ground in the middle of the wilderness for months on end, climbing without ropes a thousand feet off the ground, and bombing down chutes at my local ski resort. But interpersonal emotional discomfort was a completely different animal.

If we aren't trained or don't develop skill in feeling our emotional discomfort, our relationships will start to get messy and spill out sideways, and our emotions will come out as blame and shame. Mistakenly, most of us misplace the source of the discomfort and do what I did: "You are making me feel this way and it's your fault." Then we either try to change the other person, or we move away from difficult people. Understandable. But in doing so, we miss the lessons, and our EDT stays the same. We never grow.

The issue is not the difficult people in our lives. We are all difficult, including you! The issue is the uncomfortable stuff that those difficult people bring up in us that we don't know how to deal with. Rather than asking the other person why they are making you feel this way, ask yourself, "What feelings does this person trigger in me that are my responsibility to deal with?"

To increase your emotional discomfort threshold, you need two things: (1) self-regulation and (2) self-reflection. Both help you be with your inner experience like a champ. These skills can be incredibly empowering because you can learn to feel better without avoiding any discomfort and without the other person doing anything different.

Learning how to be with your experience, emotions, pain, stress, and upset is crucial for good brain development and great for relationships.

> Learning how to be with your experience, emotions, pain, stress, and upset is crucial for good brain development and great for relationships.

Years ago, I joined a Buddhist community, partly because I wanted to study Eastern psychology and practices, and partly because I needed to learn how to be okay in my own skin. At the time, I was pretty disconnected from my True Self. Meditation finally taught me how to be with my inner experience and expand my emotional discomfort threshold. I slowly learned how to feel my emotions, my sensations, and observe my thoughts with less and less judgment. Before meditation, I had no language for what in the hell was going on inside of me. For six months, my very first therapist asked me how I was feeling, and my consistent answer was "I don't know" or "Nothing" because I had spent almost three decades repressing my emotions. In time, I learned how to feel, cry, rage, to label and express myself and the entire range of my emotions. It was a huge breakthrough and gave me the ability to connect with people in a much more powerful way. Up to that point, I didn't know how deep you could go in a relationship when you shared real emotions, especially in the moment. Once I learned how to *feel*, my relationships vaulted to the next level.

THE NESTR MEDITATION

You might be asking, Well, how do I increase my capacity to feel? After years of learning about meditating and becoming a meditation instructor, I eventually developed a basic meditation that was all about self-regulation and self-reflection. I call it the *NESTR meditation*. I like the metaphor of a nest because a nest is a safe place for an egg to grow, develop, and hatch. Using NESTR, you will learn how to be like a nest holding your inner experience (the egg). Instead of focusing on the breath, like many meditation traditions do, in the NESTR meditation, you make the object, or focus, your pain and discomfort. You learn how to "hold" that intense emotional and sensory discomfort that is inside your heart, mind, and body. NESTR helps you learn how to stay in the front seat while observing and containing the freakout happening in the back seat. Here's what the acronym means.

N—**Number**: Use the trigger scale and pick a number from 0 to 10; 0 is your safe home base, where you are in the driver's seat and feel great. Ten is when you are in the trunk, feeling enraged or barely able to hold it together.

E—**Emotion**: Label your experience with an emotion, such as *happy, sad, mad,* or *afraid*.

S—**Sensation**: Notice the physical sensations you experience, such as sweating, heat, cold, tingling, aches in your low back, or tension in your neck.

T—**Thoughts**: Notice where your mind is and what you are thinking about.

R—**Resource**: Use your front-seat brain to find a place in your being or body that feels grounded and okay, a place where you feel adequately resourced and good right now.

When you do this short meditation, it sounds like this quietly inside your head. *I'm noticing I feel triggered at about a five (N). I feel hurt and a little sad (E). I feel some heat in my low back and my left knee is pulsing (S). I'm thinking about my sister not coming home for the holidays (T). And I feel strong and good with my feet on the ground (R).* The NESTR should take about five minutes or less. If you get lost, download the guided meditation (see the resource guide at the back of the book), and practice every time you feel triggered. With practice, your number should move toward zero as you get more and more okay with feelings and sensations.

Let's increase that emotional discomfort threshold and dive deeper into each part of this meditation so you have better understanding and more incentive to practice.

Self-Regulation

Psychology nerds like me like the term *self-regulation* as the name for how to be with your feelings, sensations, and inner experience. Many people confuse stuffing their feelings with self-regulation. These are definitely not the same. Stuffing feelings has a place and is a great life skill, such as when you are competing in sports or focusing at work or when you disagree with your neighbor's choices. Better to act kind than come out swinging with all your feelings and judgments.

Self-regulation is a process, much like surfing a wave, whereby you "ride" the emotions and sensations until they pass. For the purpose of this book, self-regulation is different from being calm. Being calm is what it's like after the storm has passed. Self-regulation is staying with yourself in the midst of the storm and riding the waves of sensations and emotions no matter how big the waves are. Self-regulation is the ability to stay present and be with your experience in the midst of any external or internal storm. Self-regulation is an incredibly valuable life skill that all of us should know how to use. It's vital to know what's going on internally so you can soothe the scared animal and really show up for yourself. Using the NESTR meditation, we learn to regulate three internal factors: our emotions, sensations, and thoughts.

Being With Emotions

Most of us were offered a very narrow teaching, if any, around how to be with our negative emotions, sensations, and discomforts, especially in the context of close relationships.* If your parents were not good at helping you with your feelings, it will be hard for you to be good at handling your feelings as an adult. If you stuffed down or avoided feeling emotions as a kid, you won't be able to handle your emotional life or "emotional" people as an adult. Instead of seeing other people's emotions as information that can help you understand yourself and them, you'll see them as threats. But the danger of this strategy is inside: you won't feel known or understood by others because *you* won't know what's going on inside, let alone how to share it.

> Emotional competence is the capacity to stand in a responsible, nonvictimized, and non-self-harming relationship with our environment. It is the required internal ground for facing life's inevitable stresses, for avoiding the creation of unnecessary ones and for furthering the healing process.
> —GABOR MATÉ

When you learn how to be with your emotions, you'll have a lived experience of conflict going well and can relax, knowing things can always get worked through. You'll appreciate that emotions come and go, like the weather. You'll value other people's emotions and be able to empathize with, and validate, what they are going through.

Being With Sensations

A sensation is something you feel inside your body. Most of us can recognize simple sensations, such as sweat trickling, heat, cold, physical pain, and soreness after a hard workout or accident of some kind.

---

* Many personal growth types say there's no such thing as a negative emotion. I can get with that, but because most of us don't like to feel anger, fear, frustration, rage, despair, disgust, hurt, etc., we tend to label these as negative. I think that's understandable.

Most of us don't like painful or uncomfortable sensations, which is why we reach for anything that will take the edge off a painful sensory experience. If you've ever been on the receiving end of a sudden breakup or have been terminated without notice, you know what it feels like to have a pit in your stomach, how your voice gets shaky, or how your heart aches. When you "get okay" with uncomfortable sensations, you'll be able to ride the waves of discomfort without making any of it a problem. You can feel yourself shaking and stay with it without needing it to stop. Although it can feel scary and uncomfortable, the body's movements are to be trusted because they are one way it moves stuck energy. With practice, you'll increase your emotional discomfort threshold, which ultimately makes you stronger in conflict.

Being With Thoughts

Being with the thoughts that arise when emotions and sensations get intense is another layer of being "with" your experience of staying with the scared animal. Some meditators call the chatter of our thoughts the "monkey mind" because sometimes it feels like an out-of-control animal jumping from one topic to the next, unable to truly focus. During conflict, your mind (often triggered by the scared animal) can jump to conclusions, fast-forward to the worst-case scenario, and completely forget what you wanted to say. For example, it's very common for us to envision different scenarios when someone doesn't return a text in a timely manner: "They don't care about me" or "They're mad at me." This is why it's so important to train your mind so you don't leap to any conclusions, which is one of the core objectives of meditation. Any meditator knows that a central starting point of meditation is to simply notice and observe the endless chatter of your thoughts. Part of training your mind is directing your thoughts to the task at hand—getting to zero. We can do that through self-reflection and self-inquiry.

SELF-REFLECTION AND SELF-INQUIRY

Attachment scientists have found that the more you can reflect on your past and make sense of it in an ongoing way, the more you can create secure relationships in the future. In fact, when parents can self-reflect in an ongoing way, it's the biggest predictor of whether or not they will raise securely attached children.[1]

The more self-awareness you have, the stronger the likelihood you can handle yourself and the more "other-awareness" you'll gain.* And the more you will become an author, leader, and anchor in your community.

Self-Inquiry Practice

Whenever I'm triggered, feeling riled up or shut down, distant, or disconnected, I pause the conversation and ask for a little space. Then I dive into a *self-inquiry* practice. Basically, I ask myself a series of questions so that I can learn and make adjustments.

This self-inquiry practice can be done during your basic NESTR meditation or it can be done after the NESTR on a short walk in nature. One of my favorite places to do self-inquiry practice is while walking. Sometimes I even put on what I call "thinking music" (music with no lyrics or words) that helps me go inside, move my body, and think. If you prefer silence, don't use music. Whatever helps you hear yourself and your thoughts. Next, mentally draw a conflict box like the one in Diagram 9.1 because it will help you orient on what to do next.

---

* Of course, this isn't always true. I know plenty of personal growth junkies, meditators, and yogis who are horrible at conflict and their relationships don't improve. My take is they are not learning and applying direct, practical relationship skills. Their "self-study" has given them a lot of good concepts but has done little to change their ability to be with their activation during conflict with other people. Just because you are self-aware doesn't necessarily translate into being good at relationships.

Get clear about these five rows. If you can't own anything in row 4 and try to put yourself in their shoes in row 5, don't proceed until you can take ownership of something. You might call a friend or coach and have them challenge you to find your part in the dynamic. When you're stuck in the back seat with the view that you're

Their Name
What they did
Impact on you
What you did
Impact on them

Diagram 9.1 The Conflict Box for Self-Inquiry

"right" and they're "wrong," it just means you're having a hard time thinking or seeing clearly. No problem—you can always ask the person you're in conflict with what your part is. I'm sure they won't have any trouble pointing out where you messed up.

Self-inquiry requires deep listening. Can you listen to yourself until you feel that you understand what happened? If you can make sense of that issue that raised conflict, you'll begin to calm down. If you can get all five rows completed, move on to the following self-inquiry questions and feel free to add more if they help you gain insight into your part:

- ◆ What am I scared of right now?
- ◆ Is this conflict new or repeating?
- ◆ Is the feeling associated with the conflict new or repeating?
- ◆ Is this feeling I'm experiencing going to kill me?
- ◆ Am I willing to be with this discomfort, without distraction, until it passes?
- ◆ Have I ever felt like this before I met this person?
- ◆ Who does their behavior remind me of?
- ◆ Am I expecting them not to challenge me and my values?
- ◆ Am I expecting them to live like me or do it my way?

+ Did we have agreements about this issue, and if so, did I break any of them?
+ Why is this so upsetting to me and what is it really about?
+ Am I willing to stay in relationship and work through this?
+ What is my next step? (See below.)

We can make serious progress with even the first question: *What am I scared of right now?* This question allows you to find the exact trigger point of when you started feeling this way. Once you locate that, you can get more traction and return with more self-awareness to whomever you had the conflict with.

Frida was anxious. She had a huge unresolved money conflict that involved five family members and her parents' will. Her father had died many years ago and her mother had Alzheimer's. The family had never resolved the financial inheritance conflict. It all fell on Frida's shoulders because she was the "responsible one." But the pressure was almost too much. The stakes were high. Before we went in to navigate the conflict with her brother and sister-in-law, I guided her through a NESTR meditation. When we started, her number on the trigger scale was a seven, going on eight. She was super tense and nervous. But as she went through the meditation and stayed with all the emotions and sensations, her number began to decrease (by the end of a NESTR meditation, your number should decrease). Soon, she was back in the front seat at a three. The meeting went well and she was able to lead the family to a better place.

There are numerous side benefits to using NESTR meditation outside the domain of conflict, including strengthening impulse control (Do I really need to eat those cookies in the pantry?), social awareness, and leading and managing other people. If you're a parent, being with your upset and discomfort will allow you to respond versus react when your children trigger you. When you choose not to learn how to regulate your emotions, sensations, and thoughts, you're coming into the game of conflict with a serious disadvantage and a scared animal who will most likely lead the charge.

UNDERSTAND YOUR RESOURCES (INTERNAL AND EXTERNAL)

When you are scared, you become hypervigilant, looking to protect and defend, and your options seem to narrow. This is why it's so important to have consistent, reliable resources at your disposal. Think of a resource as a stable surfboard that helps you ride the waves of your experience. It's the thing you reach for when you feel like you're drowning. A resource is meant to support you and help you come back to the driver's seat. Ideally, you have both internal resources and external resources to reach for. An internal resource might be your kind heart, your butt in the chair willing to do what it takes, your mind and thoughts to help you navigate your way through, and your spine as you stand or sit up tall. It can even be your breath—taking a few deep breaths, feeling your chest rise and fall, can help you move from your scared animal to a calm driver.

An external resource can be the soft earth under your feet, a bed, another person's hand or gentle touch, or a loyal pet you can cuddle with. Most of us have something outside of us that helps us be with our experience and that calms us down even when our experience is upsetting. Whenever you're adrift in reactivity, reach for the resource that feels like an anchor.

Finding an Internal Resource

Here's an exercise that will help you find where your internal resources are. (If you want me to guide you through this so you can really close your eyes, go to More Resources on page 301.) Close your eyes or look down with a soft gaze (whichever helps you see pictures in your mind), and call to mind a rough moment in your life that you got through. It could have been last month, or maybe it was twenty years ago. Briefly see yourself going through the hard thing. Now, see yourself on the other side of it. You got through it, yes? Feel the truth of that. Locate that feeling in your body right now. What does it feel like that you got through something difficult? Feel that feeling now. Perhaps it's a feeling of your shoulders relaxing, your heart and chest lifting, or your back feeling solid and strong behind you. Where does this resourced part of you live? Was the resource your heart, your mind, your breath? What internal resource helped you get through it? Maybe it was your body lifting weights after getting bullied as a kid. Maybe it was the intuition and smarts you developed from growing up in an unpredictable home. Perhaps you told yourself, "I can get through this." Maybe you dug deep and had to learn something about yourself. Write down whatever thoughts or beliefs you created to get you through it. All of these are internal resources.

Finding an External Resource

Now look closely to see what external resources got you through that difficult experience. Perhaps a coach, a therapist, or a friend was there for you. Maybe it was a pet, walks in nature, working in your garden, or the sound of the ocean. Who helped you? What helped you? I remember when I was really upset as a kid, I'd go outside to climb a sixty-foot-tall white pine tree. I would climb as high as the tree would let me. There, up near the top, the limbs would sway in the wind. It was like they were rocking me, comforting me. Nature, the gentle breeze, and that tree were external resources for me.

Be sure to write down your internal and external resources. These are guideposts for when you are under stress. If you struggle to find resources, then your job is to start creating them now: hire a relationship coach, go for a walk in nature, start meditating, and remember the gift of regulating your breath.

In my experience, the best external resource is another capable and resourced human. We are built to help each other through difficult emotions and experiences. Nothing else in the world can do that.

Nothing will help regulate a scared animal faster than a safe human. Though a dog is good, another person is even better. Dogs can't provide you with the Four Connectors of feeling emotionally safe, seen, soothed, and supported and challenged. Yes, they accept you, but they don't have the capacity to know your internal world and validate it. Only a human can meet all of those needs.

Being an Anchor to Yourself

When the inevitable conflicts of life hit, sometimes we don't have another solid person at our side. Or the person we thought was solid is now the "enemy." All the more reason to show up for yourself and learn new ways of being with your experience.* Sometimes your scared animal might feel more like a scared child. That's okay. Go there. If you feel like a scared or hurt little boy or girl, help this part of yourself out. Show up, and be there, just like you would if I handed you my crying son or daughter. Sit down in a safe place, put on some peaceful music, close your eyes, and put your hand on your heart. Breathe right into the pain. Feel. (Download the Hurt Kid meditation. See the resource guide at the back of the book.)

Hitting the Pause Button

Sometimes, we can't locate a resource because the "threat" is still in our space: the same home, the same car, the same job, with the same person. The conflict isn't improving because our scared animal is driving around in a circle and it feels like the other person is in the car with us. If we are getting pounded by wave after wave of triggers, we'll need to seek an island, another boat, or a safe place to regroup and collect ourselves.

In a situation like this, what's needed is space and distance. I call this "hitting the pause button." The word *pause* implies that I'm

---

* At times, you'll hear me use the term *anchor* to describe what it's like to really be there for another person. In his book *Together*, former surgeon general Vivek Murthy uses this word in the same vein.

going to hit Play or Resume again soon. The pause is a type of boundary that says simply, "I need a break to collect myself." It's a chance to show up for ourselves, relax, zoom out, and get clear on what's going on. Ideally, in your high-stakes relationships, you both agree that pausing is allowed and even encouraged, especially if things are escalating or going nowhere.

In your pause, focus on what you can control, which is yourself. Although your pause might also benefit the other person, it starts with first meeting a need you have. For example, when I'm making things worse or when I need space to calm down, I need to hit the pause button. I might say, "I'm overwhelmed and need a pause." Or, "I need to hit the pause button right now so I can gather myself and then come back with my rational mind." Even though you are getting space from the other person, your pause is really for you to take good care of yourself, get centered, and listen better.

When asking for a pause, it can be helpful and considerate to speak to the other person's fears as well. You could say something like, "I know me taking space scares you and upsets you. I'm not running away. I just need a pause so we can both feel better as soon as possible."

It's important to understand that we are not giving the other person a pause, even if we think they need one and we don't.* The pause is always for us to take time and space so we can collect ourselves or get a break from the uncomfortable stuff we are feeling.

Remember, during or immediately after conflict, your job is to figure out what is going on inside you and what you can own. Doing this act will save you vast amounts of wasted time and energy later. If

---

* This is very different from most conventional parenting models that encourage "time-outs" for kids who are misbehaving or in conflict. One hundred percent of the time, it's the parent that needs a time-out more than the child. If we move to "hitting the pause button" instead of a time-out, perhaps parents will come to understand that you can't pause another person, you can only pause yourself.

you skip this step, you run the risk of letting your scared animal do the speaking, and we all know what it's like to regret something we've said or done in the heat of the moment.

During interpersonal conflict, we struggle in a variety of ways, but mostly we struggle to be with our own scared animal. If you get in conflict and have yet to practice what's outlined in this book, you will struggle to self-regulate and be with your experience, and you will "act out"—blaming, shutting down, and triangulating. The work is to learn how to handle your triggers, judgments, and reactions and increase your discomfort threshold. Once you learn how to be with anything going on inside your head and body, you automatically increase your capacity to work with difficult things on the outside, like other people. Not to mention, this helps you reconnect to yourself.

ACTION STEPS

1. Self-reflection
   A. Find your resources
      i. Complete the internal/external resource list. Be sure to list two of each type of resource.
      ii. Flag the most inspirational and positive memory you have of getting through something hard. Notice, in great detail, how you got through it by identifying the internal and external resources you used. When you get lost, bring up this memory.

2. Self-regulation
   A. Do a NESTR meditation the next time you're triggered to increase your discomfort threshold.
   B. Download and practice the guided NESTR meditation at http://gettingtozerobook.com.

3. Hitting the pause button
   A. Practice hitting the pause button in your next fight and make an agreement with the other person around it. (Refer to Chapter 15 on agreements if you need help.)

4. Share all of this with a friend.

10

How to Be With *Their* Triggers During Conflict

> I cherish my own freedom dearly, but I care even more for your freedom.
>
> —NELSON MANDELA

IMAGINE FOR A MINUTE THAT YOU ARE IN A SMALL BOAT, A DINGHY, way out in the middle of the ocean. In the dinghy, there's only room for you and your bags (the baggage represents all the relationship traumas and pain you've been through). You've decided you don't want to be all the way out there alone. You understand that it might help to have someone close by, so you buddy up with someone. The two of you decide to tie your boats together. (See Diagram 10.1.) Two boats tied creates a relationship. It takes you a while to figure out the best knots to use, but pretty soon, you're both feeling

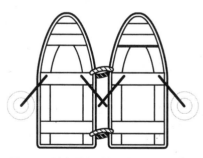

Diagram 10.1 Tying Your Boats Together

stronger together than when you were out there alone. You share resources and ideas. You learn to communicate about which way to go and how to get there. You choose to stay together.

You've put in a little time to figure out the basics of traveling together. Previously, you didn't have to check in with anybody. Now, you're checking in all the time as you learn new skills that involve collaboration. Although you both have your own boats that you can steer anyway you choose (which symbolizes your independence), you are choosing to keep your boats lashed together because you think that is better than traveling solo. This is why we partner or join a team: strength in numbers, right? Two minds are smarter than one. The other person or people might see threats, dangers, and possibilities you don't see.

With your boats tied together, you learn that although collaboration is great, it's inherently harder than being alone because it's impossible to avoid impacting each other. This challenges your independence and forces you to be less selfish and more considerate, keeping the other person in mind regularly. If they get upset and rock the boat, you feel it. If they fall in the water, you have to haul them out. If you lean too much to one side, they feel off balance. If they stop paddling, you're affected. If you're having a bad day, they feel it. In high-stakes relationships, we impact each other continuously.

Without realizing it, most people underestimate how freakin' hard it is to travel with another person through the vast ocean that is life. To cope, many people resort to asking the other person to change (posture and seek), or they go inward (avoid and collapse) and stop speaking up, stop telling the truth, and go along with the direction the other person wants to travel. They don't want to rock the boat. After all, they think, *Someone has to compromise.*

But you know now that habitually seeking or avoiding confrontation adds more stress to the relationship (conflict creep). Resentments build and your boats become more unstable. Now the "vessel" of your relationship is at risk. And when the storms come, you're no longer a team, but at odds with each other.

When the stakes are high, such as when we are raising a family, starting a business, or joining a team, we are automatically playing by different rules and forced to think of the other person or other people. If they act like a complete jerk or decide to go AWOL, get addicted to drugs, stop pulling their weight, stop paying the mortgage, or stop taking care of the kids, it impacts you, right? And vice versa. In fact, everything they do affects you. If I do all the work in our relationship, including paddling for both of us, and you sit on your ass, we will go in circles and never reach our destination, as shown in Diagram 10.2. And I will eventually get frustrated and angry.

To get the most benefit out of our mutual relationship, we both have to practice what's called *mutuality*.

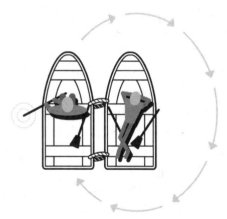

Diagram 10.2 Lack of Mutuality

Mutuality means we both pull our weight. We both paddle to get to where we want to go. We both take responsibility for our part in getting the boat from point A to point B. When we choose a mutual relationship, we choose a vibe of connection over disconnection. Disconnection feels bad to both of us, so we work to stay connected and work to stay at zero.

To survive and ultimately thrive on the journey ahead, we must remember how deeply dependent we are on other people. Just look at how many people you depend on to provide you with fresh food from stores or fast internet at home. As we grow and move toward interdependence, learning to collaborate becomes an essential life skill. Interdependence is a two-way street where we depend on each other and practice mutuality. For example, in a business, the sales team depends on the marketing team to provide new leads and marketing depends on sales to keep the lights on. These two departments are interdependent. In high-stakes relationships, many people get stuck seeing dependency as somehow a bad thing. But it's impossible to be in a partnership without dependency going both ways. Hence the term *interdependence*. In fact, partnerships that embody interdependence are the strongest partnerships.

FIVE WAYS TO BE WITH THE OTHER PERSON'S SCARED ANIMAL

Although these five tips can apply to any high-stakes relationship, they are especially suited for an intimate partnership because in my experience an intimate partner is the hardest person to handle over time. Either way, it's essential to know how the other person experiences a conflict. It's in your best interest to learn about what makes the other person tick so you can help when that person's scared animal comes out, which helps you and then helps the two of you when things get difficult. We can learn a lot of different ways to be with another person's scared animal. Here are five of my favorites.

1. Offer the Four Relational Needs

If you feel disconnected from the other person, part of the problem is that you probably didn't handle the conflict very well and you might not have handled them, their feelings, and their scared animal very well. Or maybe your story is that they didn't handle *you* all that well. Either way, it's okay. To start repairing your disconnection, consider the four relational needs questions below and apply these Four Connectors that will help you get the connection back:

Do they feel emotionally *safe* with me right now?
Do they feel *seen* and understood by me right now?
Do they feel *soothed* by me? Am I demonstrating that I'm willing
to work through this and get to zero?
Do they feel *supported* and *challenged* by me to reconnect?

It might help to imagine the other person as a scared little kid who's been hurt, and you're the only person around who can help. You'd want to offer the Four Connectors to that kid. Ask them the four connector questions. If they answer no to any of the questions, you have more work to do. This is a test of whether you can show up for them. First give that which you want to receive. Offer to meet these four relational needs. Over and over, conflict after conflict. As they feel more emotionally safe, seen and understood, soothed, and supported and challenged, they move from the back seat to the front seat and from the scared animal to the adult—back to zero.

Remember, we can sometimes be the one who feels disconnected from ourselves and from the other person. But if you are more connected and resourced than they are, then show up for them. If you're the one who's upset, ask them to show up for you, and then once you are resourced, reciprocate and show up for them. Someone has to start. Otherwise, you're both sitting in your own little boat pouting and waiting for the other person to make the first move.

2. Stand for Three

When you join boats with someone, you're taking on three problems: you, them, and the vessel that holds you two. Therefore, you have to consider all three. I call this context or framework *Standing for Three* because it serves as a reminder that to be successful in any high-stakes relationship, all three items have to be considered and handled well. It looks like this:

1. Standing for yourself
2. Standing for the other person
3. Standing for us

Let's break down each one.

Standing for Yourself

Under stress, most of us disconnect and go into self-preservation mode. We protect and defend. This isn't standing for yourself. When you take a stand for yourself, it's an empowered move that comes from a base of self-connection and self-respect. The attitude here is "I'm going to take a stand for myself because more is possible when I have my own back. Not to mention when I stand for myself, it's good for the relationship." Do the work required from the previous chapter to get better at standing for yourself.

Standing for the Other Person

Now it's time to take a stand for the other person.

Taking a stand for someone else means that we act as an anchor for them. This means that not only will we be there in a time of need and support them but also we will challenge them to be true to themselves and their life. We become a clear advocate and champion for them to reach their goals and dreams.

My wife and I joined boats almost two decades ago. At first, I was reluctant and did my best to weasel out of tying up our boats. It was too big a commitment. I liked keeping my options open, and I didn't want to be "tied down." The truth was—I wasn't ready to be there for another person. I was too self-absorbed and too scared. When I made the commitment, I took a stand for my wife, my kids, and my close friends. I realized I wanted each of these people to follow their true north, and so I behaved in a way that reflected that.

The closer your relationship with someone is, the more advantageous it is to be there for them when they are upset with you. This might seem counterintuitive because when you and another person are in a conflict, you lose sight of the fact that you're a team working toward a common goal. Instead, it feels like they are in the way or they are the enemy. Why would you want to be an anchor for them when they are the person "making" you upset? It's simple: You are linked to them. You chose this high-stakes relationship. Your boats are bound together until you decide otherwise. That should be enough incentive to work out any conflicts because it sucks to be so close to someone yet be on shaky ground, day after day after day.

The more adept you are at conflict, the more genuine your anchor behavior will be and the more trust you will build into the relationship. By staying in relationship even when you're mad at the other person, you send the message that *they* matter and that *us* matters.

If you feel resistance to what I'm suggesting, it could be that you are the type of person who hasn't stood up for yourself or prioritized your own needs; therefore, it can be hard to prioritize the other person. Perhaps no one looked after your needs as a kid and you spent your life prioritizing others; you might be exhausted with putting others first. Or it's possible you may have a habit of collapsing or avoiding and pretending like you don't need anything. Whatever the case, you need to learn to prioritize the other person in a way that works for both of you.

Standing for the other person means that you behave in a way that enables them to feel like they are a priority to you. Truly prioritizing someone you care about is harder than you think. For example, my wife is the number one person in my life. She's my rock, my anchor, my best friend, my co-parent, and so much more. Sometimes I claim she is a priority to me, but . . . if I dive into work after the kids go to bed instead of connecting with her, it's pretty clear that she's not the priority that night. I could defend myself here, or I could submit to the idea that her experience is valid and course-correct to create a new agreement about what happens after the kids go to bed. Although having an agreement about what you do in your free time might feel controlling to some, I find it allows for more freedom for both people.

Follow up your words "I'm standing for you" with behaviors that align with that claim, which strengthen your capacity to lead, handle conflict, and stay in the driver's seat of your reactivity. You might say, "You are important to me, I want to work through this hard conversation with you, and I'm willing to learn." Then stick with it.

Standing for Us

The third element of the Standing for Three principle is the boat. We have to pay attention to the relationship itself and take a stand *for us*. One of my podcast guests and founder of the Collaborative Way, Lloyd Fickett, introduced me to the phrase *for us*, which refers to the idea that whatever we do in our boats, and wherever we go, it has to be good for both of us. Otherwise, why do it?

If in the boat metaphor we are far out at sea, we have to attend to ourselves, to the other person, *and* to the boat. After all, the boat might get a hole in it. The sail might rip. The motor may conk out. So, taking a stand for the boat, for the relationship itself, is the last piece we take a stand for. If the boat sinks, neither you nor your partner makes it, no matter how much you stand for yourself or the other person.

When I chose a life partner, I signed up to take onboard her baggage, pains, and dramas. And she went into the relationship consciously saying yes to mine. We both saw that partnership would be better than nonpartnership, so we went for it. As a result, we prioritize each other and the boat we are riding on, Standing for Three. People in great relationships understand a simple principle: if it doesn't work for you, it doesn't work for me, and thus it isn't going to work for us.

People in great relationships understand that if it doesn't work for you, it doesn't work for me, and thus it doesn't work for us.

I'm not going to lie; collaboration is very hard sometimes. In fact, it's much harder than rowing your own boat wherever you want. Collaboration and cooperation are complex. You have to think of yourself, the other, and the partnership. Because you take a Stand for Three, you understand that conflict is part of the territory of being a good team. There is absolutely no way around this in a good high-stakes relationship.

Another one of my podcast guests and fellow relationship teacher Pete Pearson taught me the concept of TEAM: together (T) we (E) can accomplish (A) more (M). Great relationships are just like great teams because they hold a "for us" context. Great teams recognize that the team is more important than the individual. Although LeBron James knows that he's going to get the ball more than anyone else on the team, he understands that without his team, he'd be nothing. No world championship basketball players play alone. Championship basketball players are created inside of teams. Tom Brady, arguably the world's greatest quarterback of all time, is no different. He plays well because he's in it for the team as much as he's in it for himself. These players also understand that playing for a team in some ways is much harder than playing as an individual. Tom Brady deals with more unknown variables—other people—than Tiger Woods does.

Standing for Three ensures that you are committed to handling all of you: your scared animal, their scared animal, and the boat you both rode in on. If I stand for you but neglect myself, our ability to be a team will be compromised. Likewise, if you stand for me, but not for you, it starts to feel win-lose. Someone gets their needs met, but someone doesn't. You can't Stand for Three unless you take a stand for you, them, and the relationship.

3. Agree to "Handle" Them and Be With Their Triggers

Back in the day, my girlfriends would get emotional from time to time. They might have felt scared, wept, or gotten super frustrated by me. My response? I would sort of listen but would change the subject as soon as possible or walk away. In doing so I was blocking more of their feelings from coming out because I was blocking my own feelings from coming out. It wasn't long before they got the message that they couldn't bring their upset or pain to me. I just couldn't, or wouldn't, handle it. At the time, I didn't know that the problem was on my side. Think about it this way: If you're sad and I've never dealt with my own sadness, your sadness is going to make me uncomfortable and I'm not going to know what to do with it. But if I've been sad and felt sadness before, I can relate. I know what sadness is like and now I can be there for you.

In graduate school, I learned that if I wanted my clients to feel safe to feel their feelings, I'd have to start feeling my own, which soon increased my capacity to be with other people's strong emotions.* One of my first mentors said to me, "Jayson, you'll never be able to handle someone else's rage if you can't handle your own." This was true: During my previous years of working with angry teens, I never knew what to do. When the boys would get angry, I'd just stare or tell them to calm down. I had never touched my own anger or rage, except when I was belligerently drunk in college. But in those moments, I was disconnected and raging, which is different from *being with* my rage. It's a big difference.

---

* If you want any relationship to deepen and continue, one of the greatest gifts you can give is to be there for them emotionally. As you are learning to be with your own upsetting feelings, you're also increasing your capacity to be with someone else who is upset.

If you're not yet comfortable enough with other people's emotions, instead of reacting, own up to the fact that your emotional discomfort threshold is very small and you're not sure what to do. At the very least, this is you practicing being honest and being your True Self.

Most of the time, you'll be dealing with a person who is in pain about something you've done. Think, *What are they feeling and how can I help make this right?* You can even ask them: "I see you're upset. What can I do to help?" Or, if you know them really well, you can do the very thing that you know helps them. When we know the inner workings of the person we claim we care about, it helps us be a better teammate and we can behave in ways that help them and lead to connection sooner rather than later.

4. Offer Reassurance

If we feel resourced enough, another thing we can do with our boatmate is to reassure them. But how do we do that if we don't mean it? Or how do we do that and not sound condescending or patronizing? Reassuring someone you care about has everything to do with who they are and what helps them. For example, if you are partnered with someone who has abandonment issues, you'll want to let them know that you're there and not going to leave (but only say that if you mean it). If you are with a business partner who is afraid you'll quit, you can reassure them that you're committed to the end. Anytime another person's scared animal is in charge, send the message it needs to hear so that the person can calm down.

One way to get to know the other person and what they might need is to have them reflect on which messages they would have liked to hear growing up that they likely didn't hear. You can ask them this question: "When you were hurt as a little kid, what would you have liked to hear from an adult that would have helped you feel seen, supported, and safe?" Use those messages to reassure them the next time they get stuck, shut down, or upset. Give it a try when things are not at their worst. Practice and refine it. Do this for each other. Know each other's reassuring statements. If you never received reassurance as a kid, it can feel awkward to offer it to someone else. Here are some examples of what to say when the other person is in pain or feels disconnected from you:

"I'm here."
"I'm here and I care."
"I won't leave" or "I'm not going anywhere."
"I see you're upset and I'm here if you need anything."

Ask yourself, "Is my reassurance followed by actions that undermine it?" Do you really mean it, or are you just trying to get out of the conflict quicker? If the other person is looking to you to "fix" them by saying all the right things, that won't work either. The objective is for you both to work together to soothe each other's scared animal.

5. Remember Your Why

Let's be honest, there is a reason why you chose this particular relationship. There's a higher purpose than just avoiding being alone. Dig deep and find the reason this relationship matters to you and be willing to fight for it. Nelson Mandela fought every day with his people for his people and for all people. He never lost sight of his why, even on the darkest of days. If you can get behind the higher purpose of what this relationship stands for and is all about, when things get hard, you will be able to hang in there through the tough times.

What's in it for you? If you're honest, as a social mammal, you'll see connection, friendship, growth, becoming stronger, companionship, love, acceptance, respect, and that deep purpose that only you can feel and know inside. If any of these whys are true, then you'll work to help the other person because it also helps you get what you want. Because when things get hard in conflict, you are vulnerable to losing contact with your why.

---

*Be willing to first give what you want to receive. Why expect
to get something you are not willing to give?*

WHEN IS IT NOT YOUR JOB TO HANDLE
THEIR TRIGGERS OR SCARED ANIMAL?

*Yeah, but when is it not my job to handle or be with the other person
and their emotional reactions?* Once you choose to have a relationship with an intimate partner, you're signing up for learning how to
handle them, like it or not. In an intimate partnership or friendship,
it's the job of both people to handle each other because the relationship is mutual. It's what we do for each other. However, we all have
limits. If someone crosses the line into what feels like abuse or if the
person is not living up to your collective agreements, you can make
choices accordingly about what you are willing to tolerate or not.

In a high-stakes friendship or work relationship, handling the
other person means that you won't run away if they get reactive because you understand that emotional reactions are part of relationships. If you shut down because you suddenly become scared or feel
hurt, then take a pause and come back at a time that works for both
of you. Remember, your boats are tied together. Do you really want
to help only yourself and push them to help only themselves? Is that
the most efficient way to travel? Not in my experience. Being a team
requires collaboration, listening, adjusting, and constant tweaking to
ensure the relationship is working for both you and the other person.
There will likely be something that you need that won't feel conve-
nient for them, but if they know it's meaningful to you, they'll stretch
themselves. Likewise, they might need something that feels annoying
to you, but you will step over your resistance and show up for them.
When you both show up for each other, over and over, conflict after
conflict, you cement the strength and power of your connection.

But remember, handling them is just one of the keys to being able to work through conflict effectively. Work toward being an anchor in troubled waters. In doing so, you'll set yourself up for more smooth sailing.

ACTION STEPS

1. Are you up for "handling" the other person's scared animal? If you're not answering with a full yes, this is something to deal with before you move on.
2. Standing for Three: Have you ever taken a stand like this? What would be possible if you did? Out of all three (me, you, us), which is your weak spot? What are you going to do about that?
3. Are you offering the four relational needs in a consistent and reliable way?
4. Practice reassuring the person in your closest adult relationship after learning what is reassuring to them. Share reflections on what it was like.
5. Journal about all of this and share at least one part of this with the person closest to you as a way to be seen.

11

How to Listen During and After Conflict

All criticism, attack, insults, and judgments vanish when
we focus attention on hearing the feelings and needs
behind a message.

—MARSHALL B. ROSENBERG

EARLY IN MY RELATIONSHIP WITH MY WIFE, I FELT LIKE I WAS A
pretty damn good listener. After all, I had just received a master's degree in psychology. I was a therapist and getting paid to listen
to people all day. But like any normal person, I resorted to getting
defensive in my fights at home. Here's an actual dialogue with my
wife about her friend Teresa:

> Me: [*thinking I have the answer to her problems*] You
> asked for my help, didn't you? I think you need to
> confront Teresa.
> Her: You're not really listening to me. That's not what I said.
> Me: I am too listening. I'm here, aren't I?
> Her: [*arms now folded and turning away*] Yeah, but I
> don't feel understood. You're not getting me.
> Me: I am too. I totally understand you. I know exactly
> what you said.

Her: [*about to shut down and give up*] Well, never mind,
I'll get support elsewhere.

Me: [*growing more anxious*] Wait, honey, let me try
again. I swear I understand you.

Yikes. Sometimes when my wife was upset about something, this was how I listened. As you can imagine, it was pretty painful. I kept wasting time defending myself, trying to convince her that I really did understand her—without actually understanding her. Then one night after a long fight that wasn't resolved, she went to bed upset and withdrawn. I stayed up. I was pissed. Pissed at her and pissed at me. I wanted to punch something, anything, but sat myself down on my meditation cushion instead. After blaming her thoroughly in my head, I kept asking myself what my problem was. I knew I was missing something. I was in a loop, a repeating pattern of defending myself. Defending what? What was I protecting?

People who suck at conflict also suck at collaboration.

Eventually, I found it. I was protecting myself from feeling shame, feeling inadequate and incompetent to help her. *Clearly*, I thought, *something is wrong with me.* This brought up old feelings from the past when I didn't get it right for my parents, coaches, and teachers. Instead of feeling my shame and listening to it as feedback to course-correct, I postured over my shame. The last thing I wanted to have happen was for anyone to *see* me in my shame. But that night I sat with the feeling of shame and the insight it brought to me. Tears ran down my face.

I started to see what I was missing. I started to see a way out. My solution was so simple that I created a new rule for myself with my wife: *I don't understand her until she says she feels understood.* So rather than it being up to me to know if I'm understanding her (which doesn't include her experience), I'll leave it up to her to tell me if she's understood. Duh! This was a big turning point for me with my wife. Our fights shortened because she didn't have to fight to feel understood. It pushed me to stay curious longer and forced me to set down my narrative, ideas, and solutions until she had spelled out what was happening for her.

Soon I started teaching this to the couples I worked with, and my results helping them navigate conflict turned a corner. Over time I turned this into a tool I call *LUFU*. It's a commitment that means I'm going to listen (L) until (U) they feel (F) understood (U). I've taught LUFU to hundreds of couples and thousands of people all over the world. When done well, this skill can completely change and accelerate the reconnection process. And for the parents I work with, it completely changes how safe and seen their kids feel, which in turn strengthens their family dynamic.

LUFU is the ability to help someone feel you understand them with anything they are sharing or experiencing. As you listen well to them, they move closer and closer to zero, the place where your connection feels best.

As spiritual teacher and author Byron Katie reminds us: "No one can ever fully understand you."[1] But we do our best to get as close as we can. I mention this because we want to be realistic about understanding what it's like to be another person. We'll never really know, but we want to listen so they feel *mostly* understood in a way that helps us get to zero.

LUFU can change the course of any relationship. Why? When people feel understood, they don't have to fight, the scared animal relaxes, they soften, they feel seen, and their heart opens more. LUFU offers the speaker the sense of being seen and known, which is such a good feeling. Consider this a daily practice for the rest of your life. Trust me, you'll be a better family member, parent, friend, coworker, boss, and lover.

A quick rule of thumb before you start: The most resourced person in any given moment goes first. Whoever is able and willing to listen first sets their own shit aside and focuses on the other person. Likely, you will be the one to use LUFU first because you are reading this book.

THE EIGHT STEPS TO LUFU

There are eight basic steps to LUFU. Once you learn them, the process becomes fluid and second nature. I've watched countless students adopt LUFU and now it's a natural part of how they communicate. They report that their ability to navigate conflict is completely different because they have become a better listener. I recommend practicing LUFU at first in low-stress situations because then you're more connected to the front part of your brain and less triggered. As your LUFU reps increase, you'll feel ready to handle the higher-stress conversations at work, with family members, or with an intimate partner during conflict.

All steps in LUFU are fluid and nonlinear, but for ease of adoption, do your best to stick to the order until you are comfortable with the process, then you can riff off this framework. You'll always come back to step 1—curiosity—for maximum results. When you lose your way, also come back to step 1.

Here are the eight steps to LUFU:

Presence
1. Curiosity
2. Reflective listening
3. Same-page questions
4. Active listening
5. Empathy
6. Validation
7. Own your part
8. Completion through shared reality

Presence

Before I describe the eight steps, let's briefly discuss *presence* as it's the foundation of LUFU. Many books cover the subject, but here's the definition I use: Presence is your ability to be with yourself and someone else on a moment-by-moment basis. If "completely checked out" is on one end of the spectrum, presence is on the other. On the disconnection scale discussed in Chapter 1, zero represents *very present* and 10 is *not present*. The more present you are, the better listener you can be because you're using more than your mind and cognition to listen. As you gain skill in staying present through the listening process, you begin to use all your senses to listen.

Presence includes being aware of your thoughts, feelings, sensations, and perceptions as they move through you. Becoming more present can be a lifelong practice. Countless spiritual traditions are devoted to practicing presence. I understand presence might be a new concept for you and seem esoteric or vague, but my guess is you've experienced presence many times in your life. Playing sports, sex, dancing, breastfeeding an infant, or playing music are just a few activities in which people enter into a flow state, where they lose a sense of time and space and feel completely in the present moment. Likewise, we can experience presence when we play with a child, immerse deeply in a work project, or mountain bike, rock climb, or walk in nature. The cool thing about LUFU is that it's designed to cultivate presence. You don't have to know how to do presence. The very process of LUFU helps you be present.

I totally appreciate how hard it can be to stay present when you are triggered and the other person is blaming you. This might happen when you're listening, and you hear things that trigger you. Set them aside and stay focused on the other person. LUFU forces you to stay with them and their content.

While you stay with them, I also want you to stay with yourself. When you are present with someone, it means you are really tracking them, their tone, their vibe, their way. At the same time, you are able to notice what you think and feel, too. Pay attention to what you're communicating nonverbally through the entire connection, disconnection, and reconnection process. Your scared animal and other people's scared animals are sensitive to nonverbals.

When I do the LUFU exercise at live events, participants often report that, although they have a lot of good relationships, the total stranger they just met who is practicing LUFU with them listened better than any of their friends back home. It goes without saying that the more present you are, the better your relationships will be and the better listener you will become. Presence is also the key to healing and integrating traumatic and challenging life experiences.[2]

Step 1. Curiosity

We are all naturally curious, especially as children. As adults, we know how to be curious about the things we're interested in, but we probably suck at being curious toward the person we feel triggered by. The moment you lose curiosity, the conversation is compromised.

Slow down. Stay present; stay curious. Be curious about everything the other person is saying, how they are saying it, what they are not saying, what the storyline is, and so on. Stay in there and track as much as you can. Most of us listen by waiting for our turn to defend, rationalize, and justify why we're right and they're wrong. Waiting your turn = you've already lost curiosity = being stuck. Set this habit on the shelf, knowing that later in the conversation you'll get a chance to unpack your side of the story because that's what is fair and reasonable in a good high-stakes relationship.* Come back to your curiosity that is trying to make sense of their story.

---

* If you *are* given a turn, that's really good information about the kind of person you're choosing to be in a relationship with.

Step 2. Reflective Listening

Reflective listening is a tool borrowed from the counseling and therapy world. We merely reflect, or repeat back, what the person is saying. A great way to reflect back is to use word combinations such as these:

- ◆ "It sounds like . . ."
- ◆ "I hear you saying . . ."
- ◆ "What I'm getting is . . ."

When your boss says, "I'm annoyed at you for not paying that invoice on time." You can say, "It sounds like you are irritated with me because I didn't pay the invoice by the due date."

Although this sounds super basic and generic, it does something simple and powerful. It tells the person that you are interested in, and tracking, what they are saying. It communicates: "I'm with you. I see you and I hear what you are saying." That message goes a long way. And, yes, initially some speakers will feel annoyed with your reflection, like you are using a technique on them. If the other person feels "therapized" by your reflective listening, validate their feeling (see step 6) and say something like, "I hear you. That makes sense. I'm trying to learn how to be a better listener and want to make sure I fully understand your point of view."

But as you practice reflective listening and your responses become more fluid, others will feel like you understand them better. That will feel great for them because here is the alternative:

Boss: I'm annoyed at you for not paying that invoice on time.
Staff: Why are you overreacting? It's only a day late.

Which approach would work better for you?

Step 3. Same-Page Questions

During conflict, getting on the same page and staying there is half the battle. Sometimes people are not even fighting about the same thing (as you will learn in Chapter 13). So it's essential as a listener to confirm that you have a shared understanding as the other person speaks or tells their version of the story. Same-page questions are an amazingly simple way to clarify what they are saying, thinking, and feeling. You may ask these questions once or many times throughout the conversation. Ask these questions right after you've reflected back what they are saying. The message you're communicating is "Are we on the same page?"

Here are sample same-page questions:

- "Is that right?"
- "Am I following you so far?"
- "Am I with you?"
- "Do I have that right?"

Here's how reflective listening and same-page questions go together. Note the same-page questions are underlined:

- "Sounds like you are irritated with me because I didn't pay the invoice by the due date. Is that right?"
- "I hear that in your experience I didn't return your text, so you got mad at me. Am I following you?"

During college, I was too hungover and too scared to ask the professors to clarify issues I didn't understand, so I didn't learn that much. I also didn't care. In graduate school, the classes were smaller and I had more genuine interest in what I was learning, so I began to ask questions if I didn't understand something: "Is this what you mean?" or after summarizing my understanding, I would ask, "Do I have it right so far?" As a result, I learned more, especially if I reflected back what I was learning in my own words. I notice that when I'm learning something new, I now need to summarize or rephrase the item in my own words so that I can better understand. Then I ask my mentor or teacher, "Am I getting it right so far?" This is how engaged students learn. Be an engaged student in your relationships, especially during conflict.

Step 4. Active Listening

My definition of active listening is different from the one normally taught. My style involves an uncomfortable interruption to make sure I am digesting and understanding what the other person is saying. That's right, just like hitting the pause button, I interrupt the speaker. Why? Because it helps me listen better and helps them feel understood.

So, if the person goes on and on with a lot of content and storyline, or it becomes a venting session about their anger toward you, then your job is to interrupt them so you can stay present. You don't interrupt them to get a word in or defend yourself. You interrupt only to stay present.

When people go off on a monologue for many minutes, most normal listeners can't hang on and instead start to check out. When this happens, you become a "captive audience," a by-product of losing your agency as a listener.*

It's your responsibility as the listener to not allow someone to hold you *captive.* I don't know about you, but when I'm in conflict, I want another present person, not an audience, and vice versa. It isn't a TED Talk. Thus, you have to do something uncomfortable to take your agency back—interrupt them.

---

* "Captive audience": I love this term! I learned it from my friend Decker Cunov at a workshop I attended in 2008.

This will be hard for some of you because you have been taught that being a good listener is to be quiet and still, like good boys and girls. This is also the socially accepted norm for being polite. Contrary to popular belief, being quiet and polite has absolutely nothing to do with being a good listener. I don't know about you, but when someone talks to me more than a few minutes without my participation and without natural pauses, I check out. I can't hang with a monologuer.*

When you sit passively on the sidelines being quiet and nice, you allow the other person to run their story with the assumption that you are following their every word and that you understand. Have you ever had the experience of being at a large family gathering when Uncle Jack "hogs the mic" at dinner? It's like he's the only one talking and no one says anything because "that would be rude." Or how about when you meet a friend at Starbucks and they talk the entire time without asking you a single question? If you find yourself in any of these situations, stop blaming them. It's your responsibility as the listener to get out of it. This puts you in charge of understanding them, rather than in the passenger seat allowing them to be responsible for your level of understanding. Major difference. Active listening keeps you engaged. Here are a few options of how to interrupt:

- "Excuse me for interrupting, I just want to make sure I'm understanding you."
- "Hold on. I need to interrupt you so that I can follow you. Let me make sure I'm with you so far."
- "Wait a sec, my bad—I need to pause you because I want to understand. Are you saying X [*review the content so far*], or are you saying Y?"

---

* A monologuer is someone who likes to hear themselves talk or is no longer present. Think about it. When someone keeps talking at you, they're not in connection with you. There's no exchange. It's one-way. They aren't present enough to track that you're checking out.

Then use a same-page question:

* "Does that sound right?"
* "Did I get it right?"
* "Am I understanding you?"

You can add something like: "Okay, carry on, thank you. I just wanted to make sure I had it right so far." You want to actively listen so the very moment you get lost, you can stop them for clarification. You can also give a quick summary using reflective listening.

If they ask why you are interrupting them, tell them that your limited attention span needs small chunks of information at a time, which helps you follow their story. Telling the other person this helps you do a better job of staying present and understanding what they have to say. Continue to make sure you are on the same page (using same-page questions) to express your care and desire to "get" them.

Think about it this way: As a speaker, would you rather (a) have someone be polite, quiet, and check out while listening to you, which means you don't feel understood? Or would you rather (b) have someone interrupt you and then have the feeling of being understood? That's what I thought! You'd be surprised at how many professional therapists and counselors take your money and let you ramble on while they nod as if they were "active" listeners—this is not a good way to practice therapy.

Note: If you are interrupting to *counteract* or dispute what they're saying, that's not active listening—that's defending and arguing. I'm talking about staying in the leadership seat of being a present, engaged, and curious listener.

Step 5. Empathy

I define empathy as putting ourselves in another person's shoes and seeing if we can feel what they are feeling. As a relationship coach, someone who specializes in active listening, I consider myself an empathic person. Even as a little boy, I felt the feelings of others suffering, and my heart would break. Yet when conflict hits my own marriage, I am sometimes one of the least empathic people I know. In fact, this step wasn't even in the LUFU process until recently because I poo-pooed empathy as if it were already a part of who I am and what I do. *

Truth be told, in my highest-stakes relationship—my marriage—this is one of the hardest steps for me (notice which is hardest for you, that is where your work is). When my partner is struggling with something complex, one of the things she wants from me is empathy. For example, if she feels sad about something big in her life, she wants me to understand her perspective, relate to it, and feel her sadness. But I rarely want to sit and feel her sadness. Instead, I look right past it to seek solutions to take her sadness away. But that's not what she wants. So my work is to do my very best to put myself in her shoes and feel the sadness. I could then say, "That is sad," or "Wow, hearing you say that, I feel sad too."

Person I'm in conflict with:
What they did:
The feeling I have when I think of this person:
0-10 scale:
Timeframe:
My part in our unresolved conflict:
I imagine the impact on them is/was
If I speak up, what am I afraid they will do (behavior, action, inaction)?
If that happened, what will I have to feel in myself?

Diagram 11.1 Conflict Box
with Empathy

If you have a hard time feeling your feelings, this will be the hardest step for you, too. If you can't feel your own feelings, how

---

* As is often the case, my wife helped me wake up here and slowly become a more empathetic person.

could you understand much less feel someone else's?* The simple move with empathy is to finish this sentence in your conflict box. If you recall, we skipped row 7 and filled out rows 8 and 9. Now, we come back to 7. (See Diagram 11.1.)

Or, to keep it simple, fill out this sentence:

My part in our conflict is/was _____ [*behavior/action/inaction*], and I imagine the impact on them is/was

_____.

By the way, you don't need to wait until step 5 in LUFU to empathize. In fact, showing empathy could be the very first thing you do. Sometimes, you can skip all previous steps and lead with empathy like this:

♦ "Oh my gosh, I see how upset you are. Tell me more."
♦ "Whoa, I see how angry you are. I must have really fucked up. I know this triggers some old stuff for you."
♦ "Aw, I see that you're hurting. Something bad happened. What's going on?"

Empathetic statements like these can take a person from an 8 on the trigger scale to a 3, very fast. Do your best to really imagine the impact your actions have on other people.

Step 6. Validation

After we've put ourselves in the other person's shoes, we can see the world a little bit more from their vantage point. This allows us to

---

* A small percentage of readers might have an actual diagnosis such as Asperger's, autism, or narcissism that will make empathizing very difficult. I encourage you to find resources on the subject for further assistance. But most of us do have the capacity to empathize and it can be developed over time.

make sense of their world and validate it. Validation is another vital skill that took me years to get because I wanted to be right or to hurry up and get to my turn to speak. Validation allows the other person to feel even more seen and understood. We validate their experience because it helps them feel less crazy, less alone, and more cared about. Typically, validation dissolves any remaining defensiveness on their part.

Very important note: Validating their experience does not mean their experience is right and yours is wrong. It has nothing to do with that. It just means their experience is 100 percent valid in how they see the world. If you get caught there, you are missing the point completely and you'll keep going in a loop in conflict with the other person. Validation is done with three powerful words:

"That. Makes. Sense."

When you say those three words, you'll be surprised at how quickly a person begins to relax. However, there's one catch: It has to truly make sense to you. I can't validate a woman's experience and feelings around being objectified unless I truly get that objectification and misogyny really exist. I can't validate your political beliefs unless I understand where they come from.

Given the person you're in dialogue with, understanding who they are, their history, their baggage, their pain, and their values, does it make sense they feel a certain way? For example, when my wife and I get into a conflict, sometimes I raise my voice. Although I don't think I raise my voice, I know that defending myself on this one will go nowhere fast. And I know myself well enough that when things get heated, I get bristly, sharp, and I do change my voice tone, even though I think it's barely noticeable. But however subtle I think my tone is, it affects her. So, I can validate her and say, "Yeah, I can see that you got scared or upset. That makes sense because I'm on edge. I'm stressed about work and did have a tone." Here are some other examples:

* "Honey, it makes sense you're angry because I didn't text you back and I know you hate lag time in our communications."
* "I hear you and can relate. I hate it when folks don't respond to me in a timely manner too. I don't blame you for being angry at me. Your anger makes sense."

When people join our experience as best they can, it feels good. We feel safer and seen and understood, which are two of our core relational needs. This helps us reconnect.

Step 7. Ownership

As an emerging leader in your relationships, you already know how important it is to own your part. Backseat drivers blame, but raising your hand and owning whatever you did that upset them by saying something like "Yes, I did do that" can calm the other person down to the point of dissolving the conflict. Notice in the validation example with my wife, how I let her know that her being upset made sense because I did something that upset her. I did in fact have a tone. If you keep pointing out what they did or didn't do and you keep avoiding ownership, any great listening technique will fall short.

You are welcome to own your part at any time during LUFU, *as long as you don't hijack the conversation and go into all the justifications around why you did what you did.* There should be no explaining yourself, making excuses, or clever rationalizations. Just own your thing and keep listening. Usually this is done in one to three sentences: "I just want to own that I didn't return your text. That's so true. I blew it, and I know you got annoyed because you needed to hear from me to keep your plans. What else?"

Remember, you're still listening. If you feel like saying, "Well, you did that to me yesterday!" now is not the time. You're fielding *their* complaint and *their* upset, not yours. It isn't your turn yet. Be the adult and listen to them completely.

Step 8. Completion Through Shared Reality

Finally, you're at the point where you're about to switch and they can take a turn listening to you. To move on to your turn or to celebrate the fact that you got to zero, check in to see where they are. Be sure that you understand them to the point of them feeling understood. And remember, you are not the person to decide—they are. So ask two confirmation questions to close:

- ◆ "Is there anything else? Is there anything I missed? Is there anything else you want me to get about you and your experience? What else? Anything else before we transition to my experience?"
- ◆ "Do you feel understood for now?"

What if they say no? If they say no, one of two things is going on: (1) they really don't feel understood by you and you need to keep at LUFU until they do, or (2) there is a lot of water under the bridge. Maybe, as you start to listen better, they bring up older resentments from the past. If this happens, agree to complete the current issue and make a new time for the stuff that's coming to the surface.*

Most of the time, people are not unreasonable at this stage. They will feel your effort and appreciate it. Basically, you want to be on the same page and understand each other. At this point, they should be more present and their disconnection number should be closer to zero. And, yes, your turn to speak is coming up.

Although you might not yet be at zero, you'll notice that if you truly listen to someone, it brings you into more presence and lowers

---

* If you've avoided conflict for years, you might have a long list of unresolved conflicts that needs to be dealt with. Make a list and start chipping away so you can experience what getting to zero really feels like.

your number. Regardless, you want a turn to be listened to, right? That's where we're headed in the next chapter.

THE COMMITMENT TO LISTEN BETTER

Congrats! You now know how to LUFU your partner, family member, or a friend!

You might want to set the context for the people in your life and let them know you're learning how to be a better listener. It can feel less jarring for them if you give your friends a heads-up. As stated above, you'll want to practice LUFU in your everyday life while not in conflict as a way to strengthen your skill. You are an engaged listener who takes command of your listening process with the sole intent of understanding the other person's world. If you fall back into your passive listening role or an old pattern of defending yourself, notice that, and own it: "Hey, I'm doing that thing again where I defend myself instead of listening to you."

Like lifting weights, better listening is a new muscle that needs regular attention. The more you practice, the more this becomes the way you listen to other people for the rest of your life, and it comes out of you being genuinely who you are. If you don't practice, you're conveying to yourself and the other person, "I'd rather use my roadblocks of blame, apologies, distraction/avoidance, compartmentalization, time, FRACKing, hoping, and praying that things will somehow magically get better." (More on these soon.)

The rule of thumb is you don't understand the other person until they feel understood. If you are really stuck, you may need an outsider to help you understand each other. Now, you're probably ready for your turn to do the talking. You want to feel understood, too, right? In the next chapter, I'll teach you how to speak in a way that will give you the greatest chance of feeling understood.

ACTION STEPS

1. Validate someone (using the three words "That makes sense") in the next twenty-four hours just for fun and see what happens.
2. Which step in the LUFU process is your weak spot? (Mine is empathy.) What exactly are you going to do about it and by when? Write up a "practice plan" and share it with your accountability partner.
3. LUFU a stranger. Next time you're in line, on a plane, bus, or subway, give a stranger the gift of LUFU and watch what happens.
4. Ready for the full process? Pick one relationship in your life to start practicing LUFU with. Don't expect LUFU in return unless the other person is reading this book, too. For now, just commit to being a great listener and keep practicing on them. Give them a heads-up that this is your goal and that you want to practice with them. Ask for feedback along the way. Tell them to be honest (Need more examples? See the resource guide at the end of the book.)

How to Speak During
and After Conflict

> If you run from a challenge, the challenge is not on the outside.
> The challenge is your perception of the outside. So you
> carry that with you. You'll just run into the challenge in
> another form.
>
> —Dr. John Demartini

Now that you've learned how to listen better, let's cover how to speak better during conflict, which can feel just as hard, or even harder, depending on your personality and experiences. The sooner you learn to speak effectively during conflict, the sooner you get to zero because you're about to share your side of the story.

Let's start by learning how to better communicate. Good communication has two parts, effective listening and effective speaking. Part of speaking well in stressful conversations is understanding, as a speaker, what works and doesn't work. This chapter is broken up into two parts: thirteen reminders before you speak, and eight steps to do as you're speaking.

First, your ability to communicate and feel understood will develop much better if you've applied the tools already discussed. That means you're aware of your relational history, your inner conflict, and your scared animal and you've practiced listening. In addition, to be a skillful communicator, you need to understand some basics of human behavior and what other people value and care about. That way, you can include them, relate to them, and consider them as you speak. It's okay to be messy, selfish, and miss the mark. The goal is not perfection. The better you get at speaking, the easier it becomes to clean up whatever mistakes you make.

THIRTEEN REMINDERS BEFORE YOU OPEN YOUR MOUTH

Reminder 1: Speaking from the Back Seat Garners Limited Results

It goes without saying that in the heat of the moment if you're above a 5 on the trigger scale, you're in the back seat and are more likely to do and say stupid shit. Not only that, when you claim to know the truth and you're in the backseat part of your brain, your memory is unreliable and incomplete. This has been proven in research.[1]

Reminder 2: Minimize Conflict by Setting Context

Context frames your relationship and frames each conversation. Without context, you allow yourselves to be run by your reactions and emotions. If you want to get to zero with someone, you need to set the stage for what you want to talk about and what outcome you want. For example, by starting with "Hey, I'd like to spend the next thirty minutes trying to work through our conflict so we can both feel better. Are you up for that?" you have focused the conversation and helped the person understand your motives.

Context frames each conversation and is essential for conflictual conversations. For example, let's say you and a friend had a big disagreement two days ago that was not resolved. You agree to meet for coffee. Your friend is conflict avoidant and, knowing them, they won't bring up the conflict. Before you leave the office, you look at your phone and see you have one hour exactly before you need to be back at work. Factoring in driving time and parking, you realistically have forty-five minutes. Even though you're nervous, you want to bring up the conflict from the other day because it's affecting your mood and sleep.

As you sit down in the coffee shop, you remember to start with some micro context. You say, "Hey, friend, I have about forty-five minutes with a hard stop at twelve forty-five and I want to address what happened between us the other day."

They tentatively say, "Uh, okay."

Being considerate you ask them, "Is there anything you want or need during our time together?" This gives them an opportunity to check if they might need or want something. By setting context, you just advocated for what you want to happen so you don't leave your time together feeling upset or resentful. Setting context allows you to get more of what you want and provides a framework for the content to go more smoothly.

Reminder 3: Attune to the Other Person

When you tune in to a radio station, you have to turn the dial until you get a clear signal. Similarly, when you're with another person, sometimes you have to turn the dial up or down on your voice, your presence, how close or far apart you are sitting, the amount of eye contact, and so forth. This process is called attunement. Attuned communication is the best communication because it's where both parties are really with each other.

When you attune, you're trying to locate the other person, how they are thinking and feeling, and how they are responding to you. You're trying to sync up with them. Are they present? Are they with you? Are they interested? Do you have their full attention, or is it better to try again later? Are *you* ready and available? What is *your* vibe? If you don't tune in before speaking, you might create more conflict.

Playing catch is a classic game of attunement. By throwing a ball back and forth, we begin to feel a rhythm. Good conversations are like playing catch, back and forth with no one hogging the ball. When we make a bad toss or drop the ball, we have a disconnection. No big deal; we pick it back up and try again.

Sex is another playground in which to explore attunement. Can we really be tuned in to each other's signals, words, and bodies? Can we sync up, or are we constantly missing each other, which results in more disconnection and frustration, leading to shame and hurt feelings?

Attunement is an instinct in the context of relationships. We are supposed to notice when others get upset or need help. However, if nobody ever adequately tuned in to you as a child, your ability to tune in to others may be compromised. As a kid, maybe you got used to the family norm of tuning out because you learned that "negative" emotions caused problems, so you dealt with them on your own. Or maybe you grew up in a family where everyone talked over each other and no one was really listening. Reflect on your own life and recall whether the adults were tuned in to you, your needs, and your boundaries. If you can't see the power of in-the-moment attuned communication, you may not have ever received it and therefore might not understand the value of seeing or being seen.

However, with practice and through learning to be more present you can awaken this innate capacity and become good at attunement, which also means being aware of a few other things—such as monologues, nonverbal communication, eye contact—as you move into, and away from, a conversation.*

Reminder 4: Avoid Monologues

After we tune in to the other person, we want to be considerate about *how* we communicate. As a kid, whenever I was in trouble, my parents would lecture me and tell me to look them in the eye. Sometimes my

---

* If you cannot attune or you are with someone who cannot attune, you might consider getting an Asperger's/autism assessment or a neurological assessment. There might be an underlying biological condition that undermines this capacity.

dad would poke me in the chest and stare down at me with the most intimidating glare while he lectured me. As you can imagine, this was pretty scary, yet I found a strategy to get through it. I got pretty good at looking at his nose to give the appearance that I was looking him in the eye and listening. But I was really somewhere else, mentally and emotionally checked out. I was hunkered down in the back seat of my own mind.

When someone is triggered, their brain cannot process a lot of words. Remember, when they're in their scared animal moving toward the back seat, their front brain goes offline, which affects their ability to make rational sense, remember details, and speak or listen well.

If you are in the back seat, you will be unattuned with the other person and you might think that explaining yourself is the way to go. Pretty soon, your story starts to sound like a monologue. And monologues hold other people captive. Most people cannot process, let alone remember, a big speech or lecture you give.

Instead, speak slowly, concisely, and in a way that the other person can digest. Speak for one to two minutes max. Anything over five minutes often results in you losing your audience. They will likely check out, shut down, or dissociate.

Reminder 5: Be Aware of Your Nonverbals

Many studies suggest that 70–93 percent of communication is nonverbal. Under stress, your nonverbal communication has a huge impact on the other person—from your tone of voice (yes, this is considered a nonverbal) to eye rolling, glaring, folding your arms, or looking at your phone during an important conversation. Just like in LUFU, pay attention to what you're communicating nonverbally through the entire connection, disconnection, and reconnection process. Your scared animal and other people's scared animals are sensitive to nonverbals. Notice the nonverbal behavior below that triggers your scared animal:

- Eye rolling
- Looking away
- Slamming doors
- Tone of voice
- Dismissive hand gestures
- Folded arms
- Furrowed brow
- Dirty looks
- Turning their back
- Leaving the conversation without saying anything
- An unreturned text message
- The other person moving too close to you
- The other person moving away from you
- Silence

Nonverbals can move us away from zero as we disconnect to protect ourselves. Tone of voice and facial expressions can escalate or deescalate a fight fast. Work to soften your belly, your shoulders, and your tone of voice.

Reminder 6: Create and Maintain Eye Contact

During conflict, many struggle to look at each other. Eye contact feels too intimidating, too vulnerable, or too upsetting. But according to Dr. Stan Tatkin, a leading expert on how couples read each other's faces, when a couple in a fight can make eye contact, they deescalate the conflict sooner and are less likely to misunderstand, misread, or veer into inaccurate memories of the past.[2] In other words, if you are not looking the other person in the eye, you're more likely to pull up negative memories of this person rather than focus on who they are in real time right in front of you.

For me, eye contact, though hard to do in the moment, actually helps me calm down more quickly when I see my wife's eyes. Tatkin recommends that you look directly at each other and that you never fight while driving or lying in bed staring at the ceiling. When we are next to each other but not looking at each other, we are more likely to go into a threat response because we can't read each other's facial cues, which triggers the amygdala more often. Bottom line: Make eye contact and notice how it softens the emotional charge. It's hard to stay angry at someone if you look directly in their eyes. However, note the opposite can be true for parents and teens. Too much intense eye contact with a teen can increase, not decrease, their anxiety. Be aware of who you're talking to.

Reminder 7: Move Closer, Not Farther

This one depends on how you both are wired and whether this is a business relationship or an intimate one. If you are occupying the same physical space, moving away from someone can feel threatening to them. Moving toward them can also feel threatening, yet it signals your desire for reconnection, more than moving away. In addition, sitting next to someone might feel less threatening than sitting across from them. My experience shows me that moving toward the person you are in conflict with, exuding your best nonthreatening vibe and with a soft gaze and tone of voice and any other behavior that communicates you're not a threat, can gesture that you care and want to resolve your issues.

Now, if you seek and pursue more than you avoid, push yourself instead to give the other person more space. Instead of blowing up the other person's phone with texts or demanding they speak with you, set a timer for one hour and try to relax with no distractions. Do a NESTR meditation and get comfortable being with your inner experience.

Reminder 8: Consider Physical Touch

Although physical touch can freak out some people during conflict, it helps other people calm down. Know what works for you and them. A gentle hand on the shoulder or leg can lead to instant relief. Try a few different gentle touches to see what works. This is counterintuitive when you feel threatened; however, embodied touch can be an immediate step toward resolving a conflict.

If appropriate for your relationship, a standing hug with five deep breaths can reset the nervous system without words. (Notice if this moves your number up or down.) Allow your bellies to touch and see if you can sync up the breath. You'd be surprised at how quickly this can soothe the scared animal. Think about how you calm a scared dog that doesn't know you. Eventually, after you've given the dog enough space, you might move closer, soften your tone of voice, and reach out to soothe the dog by petting it.

Reminder 9: Distinguish Between Personhood and Behavior

Some of us are very sensitive to anything that comes across as criticism. It's a common human tendency, and it's worse when we're under stress. Knowing this, remember to be sensitive in how you speak. When people are under stress, most conflate behavior (what we do) with personhood (who we are), but there's a big difference between the two that we should not forget.

In adult relationships, conflict tends to bring out our all-or-nothing, black-and-white thinking. Under stress, the scared animal needs simple choices, and if things are either/or, then it's easier on the scared animal. "You're wrong and I'm right" can easily translate into "You're wrong as a person and therefore bad." Please identify the behavior rather than judging the person. Here are a few examples:

- "You're an asshole" versus "You're acting like an asshole."
- "You're rude" versus "You're acting rude."

Even better is to say something like: "I don't like that behavior. It feels rude."

Here's a simple reminder from the sharing impact tool (discussed on page 188) to practice:

When you _____ [*behavior*], I feel _____ [*own the feeling*], and it has me _____ [*share impact*].

For example:

- "When you behave in that way, like raising your voice, I feel scared [feeling] and it has me want to move backward and retreat [impact]."
- "I love you (and who you are) and when you behave this way, I feel upset."

During conflict, do your best to stick to speaking about behavior. This is you being a sensitive and thoughtful person. It is a responsible way of speaking and it goes a long way.

Reminder 10: Remember Their Values and What Matters to Them

When we are scared, we get very I-centric. Me, myself, and I. We can increase our chances of reconnection when we remember what the other person cares about. Knowing their values and being sensitive to them facilitate a smoother resolution process. Review the validation section of the SHORE process (discussed below) and Chapter 16, which discusses how to work through value differences.

Reminder 11: Be Responsible and Respectful

How you communicate matters. The more responsible and respectful you can be, the better the process will go. Disrespect leads to disconnection. If you really want to get to zero, speak responsibly and respectfully. Use I statements and take ownership of what you did or didn't do. Too triggered? Back up by setting a boundary for yourself or hitting the pause button with a return time so you can go cool down and climb back into the front seat.

Reminder 12: Remember the Cost of Not Speaking

Some folks would rather keep their truth inside because they believe it could make things worse if they let it out. We've all had an experience where an honest conversation turned into a nightmare. As we've discussed many times throughout this book, stuffing your self-expression is a recipe for resentments and unfulfilling relationships, where you squelch your truth just to keep the relationship going. I never recommend this as a consistent habit or approach to real, raw, great relationships.

Reminder 13: Speak Up as Soon as Possible

Sometimes you and the other person are not willing to meet back up. It feels too difficult and painful; but push yourself to make an attempt sooner rather than later. Some of us spend too much time calculating the right timing. I like to speak after I've listened. A good rule of thumb with timing is to speak *as soon as possible*. If you've waited days or weeks, it's too long.

I hope these thirteen reminders help you prepare for your next conflict. You may want to refer back to the chapter on how to be with your scared animal, too. Now that you've gone inward and have learned something about yourself, it's time to finally speak to the person in your conflict box! I know that was a lot of prep work before having a chance to speak, but I'm sure it will help you move through conflicts more efficiently as you keep these ideas and practices in mind.

THE SHORE PROCESS

I call the speaking process SHORE, which stands for speak (S) honestly (H) with ownership (O) to repair (R) empathetically (E). Think of your two boats far out at sea and in conflict. The conflict has created a storm with big waves. By heading to the SHORE, you help the waves of discord die down. The SHORE process helps us regroup, reconnect, and get to zero before heading back out together into the vast ocean. Like LUFU, there are eight steps, and maintaining presence throughout is critical:

Presence
1. Context
2. Own
3. Empathize
4. Validate
5. Share impact
6. Request
7. Lessons
8. Collaborate

Presence

We already covered how to be present through a conflict in the section on LUFU in the previous chapter. You'll notice skills in listening and speaking overlap. The more present you can be when speaking, the more tuned in you are to your listener, and the more your message will be received by them.

Step 1. Context: Stand for Three

Why do you want to reconnect? Be transparent by sharing with the other person your context and intention: "I know you might still be upset after what happened. That makes sense. I want to reconnect because our relationship is important to me."

As a reminder, Standing for Three is where you hold yourself, the other person, and the relationship all with equal regard and consideration. Repairing conflict is not just good for me, it's good for you, too, and ultimately, it's good for us. Holding this view prior to speaking reminds you to act in a pro-relationship kind of way. You are speaking up because you believe it's good for both of you and your connection.

Step 2. Ownership: Start with "My Part Is . . ."

This foundational tool of taking personal responsibility helps move conflicts into reconnection more quickly. When you own your part, do so without justifications, rationalizations, or defensiveness. If you want to help things move along even more, be as vulnerable as possible.

Step 3. Empathize: "I Imagine the Impact on You Is . . ."

As you own your part, stay extremely curious about the impact your behavior has had on the other person. When you acted that way, what did they go through? What thoughts, feelings, and sensations are they dealing with? Try to put yourself in their shoes and see them in their pain around what you did or didn't do. Use the model sentence from Chapter 11:

> My part in our conflict is/was _____ [*behavior/action/inaction*], and I imagine the impact on you is/was _____.

For example:

- "I raised my voice and I see that scared you."
- "I didn't return your text and I can imagine how frustrating that was for you."
- "As I look at your face right now, I see and feel the pain I caused you."

Need more help with empathy? Review Chapter 11 and the steps in LUFU.

Step 4. Validate Their Bigger Picture: "That Makes Sense"
We covered validation in the LUFU process. But it's important here to add a few subtleties because you're now speaking, not listening. In LUFU, you validated *how they feel*. In SHORE, you validate *what they are going through* so you have a better chance of being heard. Empathizing and validating soften the other person and put them in a more receptive state to hear you out. Instead of defending, they might actually participate and listen to you.

For example, if you and I are in a relationship, and you consistently avoid the hard conversations that would allow us to reconnect, I must remember why conflict and talking it out is hard for you. So, using my listening skills, I put myself in your shoes and imagine what it's like to be you. If our relationship has lasted many years, I likely know what causes you to retreat to the back seat. I might remember the household you grew up in and how difficult your life was back then. If I don't know, I ask with a statement like this: "Hey, I don't really understand why you're reacting this way and I'd like to understand you more."

Then I might say, "I see how hard this is for you. I can appreciate how rough it must have been growing up with no one to listen to you. It makes sense why you go away, because you don't think this is going to help. And . . ."

If you were someone who hasn't learned to empathize and address the other person's values first, the conversation would instead sound like this: "Hey, can we talk? It feels like you're ignoring me. I'm so tired of you withdrawing and not working this out with me just because of your money issues. It stresses me out. And you need to start showing up for me." (Notice how many times the word *me* is used.)

As you can imagine, this self-centered blaming approach will go south fast. To stand up *for us* is to put yourself in the other person's shoes even in the way that you speak to them. If you cannot or will not do this, you'll be using the next few steps as a way to think only of yourself and they will likely defend themselves. We must work to genuinely include understanding if we want the other person to get the impact of their behavior on us. We want their behavior to make sense to us. The second half of the validation statement "That makes sense" is the next tool.

Step 5. Share the Impact of Their Behavior on You

After you've validated their bigger picture, you get to share the impact their behavior has on you. I call this tool *sharing impact*. With sharing impact, you always consider *them* first, which can help preemptively mitigate their defensiveness.

Sharing impact is what some consider an "I feel" statement. Start with a fact or observation about their behavior, action, or inaction. Then talk about how it affected you using feeling, emotional, or descriptive words:

"When you _____ [*name a factual behavior, action, inaction*], I feel/felt/experience(d) _____ [*your feelings about yourself*]."

Here are a few examples of sharing impact while considering the other person's bigger picture first:

- "I know how much you like things orderly and clean. It helps you relax [empathize first], *and when you raise your voice and ask me why I haven't cleaned yet, I feel like I'm in trouble* [sharing impact]."
- "Friend, I know you work sixty hours plus a week and you're juggling your family, which is so demanding [empathize], *and when you don't return my texts for a full day, I feel anxious and dropped* [impact]."

Sharing impact can be scary, especially if we haven't done a great job advocating for ourselves in the past. If you do this well, even masterfully, don't expect roses when you address them. No matter how skillful you are, you cannot rob them of their reaction. Just be sensitive. Once you've shared impact, you get to make a request for behavior change.

Step 6. Make a Reasonable Request for Behavior Change

At the end of a conflict, sometimes we can include a request that the other person do something in the future. Ideally, we first own what we can do differently in the future. Then we ask them to do something different, as well: "I'd like to be more considerate of your feelings moving forward, and it would be cool if you would do the same for me."

Examples of changes you can ask for:

◆ Ask them to tell you when they will be late instead of just showing up late.
◆ Ask them to let you know if they're going to spend more than $100 on something so you can discuss it first.
◆ Ask them to keep the kitchen tidy and participate in cleanup.

Requests are invitations to change behavior that ultimately consider and benefit the other person and the relationship. If both of you are flexible enough to make a behavior change, the relationship can get stronger. But your ask has to be reasonable. Here is another example of airing a reasonable request for behavior change:

"My request is that you pick up your socks and put them in the laundry basket. That would help me feel more considered around how clean I like things."

See how there are no demands or threats here? Those don't work. Ideally, you both agree ahead of time that making requests is okay in your relationship (refer to Chapter 15). Both people need to see the value in the change and agree to how it will help the relationship. When you make a request, you want to follow it up with consideration and make sure it will be good for them too. Be realistic and understand that people's habits are hard to change. Can they be a work in progress around that thing you want them to change? More on how to make a request for behavior change in Chapter 17.

Step 7. What Did I/We Learn?: "What I'm Learning About Me, You, and Us"

Remember, when you become a student of conflict, you become a student of you, them, and the two of you together. You Stand for Three. If you're not learning through the process of conflict, you're missing the boat entirely. As a conflict starts to cool down, be looking for lessons learned.

Journal about your insights and share them with the other person when they are ready to hear and move on to the next step. Here are two examples of lessons learned:

> "This conflict has been hard. It's really teaching me that I do a poor job of standing up for myself. I'm also learning that you do a better job at standing up for yourself. I wonder if we can utilize that strength of yours somehow?"

> "I just learned something valuable. When you don't text me back on time, I feel like I'm back in my family when my dad sometimes never came home. I felt so scared and alone then, and I sometimes project that situation onto this one."

Step 8. Collaborate Toward Future Agreements and Strategies

Whether you are in listening or speaking mode, as you move closer to zero, it's time to dig in and collaborate on how to move forward in the best possible way. Now that you are on the other side of the conflict, you can look back at it. Hindsight can give you new insights about each other, and your relationship will be stronger as a result. This is a great place to create agreements, update old ones, or create some kind of conflict plan moving forward. This particular issue may come back again or a new issue will most definitely emerge. What is your plan moving forward? Be proactive boatmates. Another storm will come in due time. How can you both better handle things when the waves grow monstrous and you're at odds? Sit down and make your plan (refer to Chapter 15 on agreements).

With the SHORE process, used in combination with LUFU, both parties play a part in the Getting to Zero process.

These listening and speaking tools and techniques should help with the reconnection process. A good reconnection process means you're at zero, or very close to it, you feel secure again, your scared animal has let down its guard, and your heart is online and willing to be vulnerable and in connection again. Check in with your number on the trigger scale. Ask yourselves the four relational needs questions again:

+ Do *they* feel safe? Seen? Soothed? Supported and challenged?
+ Do *you* feel safe? Seen? Soothed? Supported and challenged?
+ Are *we* at zero?

Notice whether the relationship has been strengthened or not. If done well, this level of repair rebuilds trust. Stay focused on doing your part and cleaning up the mess in the best way possible.

SIGNS YOU'RE AT ZERO

Your nervous system will tell you if the issue is resolved. It will feel like your shoulders are no longer raised up to your ears, your heart rate decreases, you can breathe more deeply, and best of all you will be able to sleep better. In relationship to this person, you won't feel that low-grade stress anymore. Your scared animal will be offline and in the back seat. Your creativity will be accessible again. You may feel more interested in life and more connected to yourself.

Now, it may be that you get to zero with this person but still feel the immense stress of your job, finances, or life. That's a separate issue that I'm not addressing in this book. I want you to get to zero in your high-stakes relationships so you can more easily, and with support, tackle the other challenges in your life as a team.

Neither of you can fake a zero (but it's amazing how often we try!). And remember—everybody's baseline is different. My zero might be different from yours. Honor the other person's sensitivity. Honor your own. Sometimes you can clear a big charge with the other person, but one of you still has residual issues. If you don't get to feeling safe together after a disconnection, please go to Chapter 17 and we'll do some troubleshooting.

If you can't clear the charge between you two on your own, pay good money to hire someone with solid skills, like a relationship coach (see the resource guide in the back of the book for more info). There is absolutely zero reason to hang on to small or big hurts. If you're really stuck and staying there, a skilled relationship guide can help get it done for you and teach you a proven process that works every time.

ACTION STEPS

1. Practice setting context. Next time you have a call with a friend, family member, or coworker, experiment with setting context and a time frame for the conversation. See if it helps you consider them better and get more of what you want.
2. Be aware of your nonverbals. Write down the top three non-verbals that trigger you the most. Educate the person in your

conflict box about this without making them wrong. Own how sensitive you are to those cues.

3. Identify your weakest spot in the SHORE process. Write down what you're going to do to improve and by when.

4. Try the SHORE process in your next conflict and report back. Journal about it, then share key takeaways with your practice partner who's reading this book with you.

PART 3 | DO'S AND DON'TS OF CONFLICT—HOW TO STAY AT ZERO

The Five Most Common Fights
and How to Face Them

Sooner or later relationship brings us to our knees, forcing
us to confront the raw and rugged mess of our mental and
emotional life.

—John Welwood

M ANY YEARS AGO, I WENT TO ROCK CLIMB THE CIRQUE OF
the Towers Traverse in Wyoming with my good friend and
climbing partner, Max. The hike in was an eight-mile backpack with
all our camping and climbing gear on our backs. Our packs easily
weighed eighty or ninety pounds. Backpacking way out in the back-
country presents many stressors: mosquitoes, water filtration, heat, the
aches and pains of carrying a huge pack—and, of course, your com-
panion. Max is a slow hiker. I am fast. When I finally got to camp, I
found a good campsite and waited and waited. The longer I waited
for him, the more irritated I became.

When he finally got there, he was beat. I was rested. We started
to argue over where to set up camp. Although some small part of
me wanted to collaborate, I had already picked our campsite, en-
visioning it fully set up during my wait time. He didn't like it. We

proceeded to have what felt like a silly fight over where to camp in this endlessly beautiful area. I mean, the 360-degree views were stunning. But we were disconnected and retreated to our tents like two grumpy old men.

The next morning, we were going to be holding each other's life in our hands on the end of a thin rope, hundreds of feet off the ground. While the climb itself was easy for me, what made everything hard was that Max and I never resolved our conflict. Being two shut-down, emotionally unavailable guys, we just sort of stuffed it. Two days later, we hiked out after successfully reaching the summit and didn't say a word about our conflict, ever.

Looking back now with more self-awareness, I can see the layers. I had a resentment toward him and likely he toward me. We had un-spoken judgments and never worked through any of them. Overall, the trip sucked. I missed out on the magnificence all around me be-cause I kept stewing and stewing over what was unsaid. I blamed him for this for a few years until I learned about owning my part. I didn't see that I had the power to change anything. I had set up camp in the valley of victimhood where I stayed until many years later.

My disconnection with Max is something we've all experienced—we slog through it knowing we won't see this person again for a while, or we think we'll "get over it." Although the five most common types of fights often happen in a partnership or long-term relationship, they also happen in families, in close friendships, and in work relation-ships. If the relationship is high-stakes and you've known each other a long time, chances are you'll encounter all of these common fights.

So, what do people typically fight about?

1. Surface fights and disagreements (the little stuff)
2. Childhood projections
3. Security fights
4. Value differences
5. Resentments

In a long-term partnership, when you move out of the rush of the infatuation stage, you begin to notice that your partner irritates you—the way they chew their food, slurp their smoothie, or leave their socks on the floor. Your value differences emerge, and you begin to see parts of them that you don't like. Naturally, you may begin to distance yourself, or you do your sneaky unconscious habit of trying to change them by reminding them it's laundry day. Little issues become bigger issues, and you start to experience disconnection, dissociation, irritation, shutting down, loss of interest, and many more symptoms that don't feel good.

In a family, because you've all lived together for so long, what can break you apart is not the differences themselves but each family member's inability to work through conflict. Most families don't know how to work through a resentment, let alone a simple conflict. Some parents struggle to truly accept their kid's values if those are completely different from their own. Adult siblings fight over family money as their parents age. And most of us have been a part of a holiday dinner where politics, gossip, or somebody's addiction takes center stage.

At work, an unanswered email can turn into a bigger fight weeks later. A curt Slack message without context can create a conflict where there didn't need to be one. In a business partnership or at the workplace, differences in values can lead to significant breakdowns in a leadership team. And when one person gives in to another person's strong opinion when they didn't really want to, a resentment is born that will fester until addressed.

If you understand the five common conflicts, you can better understand each particular challenge and how to work through it. In an intimate partnership, conflicts typically emerge between the six-month and two-year mark. In a family, they are ever present, depending on how the family addresses conflict. At work, most people avoid them, but the conflicts are still running underground.

Let's break down what these types of fights are all about.

1. SURFACE FIGHTS AND DISAGREEMENTS

What they are: These conflicts are the everyday stuff—fighting about who said what last night, the unreturned email, a misconstrued text, how late you were to a meeting or appointment, how the dishwasher was loaded, or whose turn it was to pick up the kids—and countless other fights that seem small or superficial in nature.

How to recognize a surface fight: Surface fights usually feel like a big deal initially, but after things calm down, and you're both in the front seat, the fight seems petty, like a waste of time. When the level of activation doesn't match the crime, it's a surface fight with a deeper tributary underneath. If you say things like, "You're overreacting," or "This isn't that big of a deal," you're in a surface fight.

Getting to Zero: To get to zero with a surface fight, you need to first be open to the strong likelihood that there's more to the story. Try to identify what you're really fighting about, then you can make progress. You might get lost fighting about the content, when in reality you're fighting about *how* the content was discussed. For example, it might be that you raised your voice, or the other person turned and looked at their phone while you were talking to them. Let's say your friend innocently gave you some unsolicited advice about something important to you. You might feel a tiny bit defensive and your tone of voice shows that. This turns into a surface fight that most people brush off. But if it happens a few times, it might bring to the surface an unresolved conflict you've had with this person for many months that never got dealt with. Most of us are sensitive to tone of voice, and what might seem like no big deal can be the tip of the iceberg.

Sometimes it's just about the tone, but other times it's a giant resentment that has never been dealt with. Whatever the case, you can say something like, "Hey, it seems like you're upset about something bigger and I'd like to explore that." Or you can take personal responsibility and say, "I keep noticing that I'm overreacting to this tiny thing. That tells me it's probably not about you. I think there's something from my past going on here that has nothing to do with you." Remember to keep a sense of humor about this common dynamic. "I can't believe we were stuck fighting about the _____ [*surface issue*] for so long, when really it was about how you are feeling criticized by me again [*deeper issue*]."

Word of caution: Most couples get stuck focusing on superficial issues and are not aware that there may be a bigger resentment below the surface or that their security as a couple is at stake. Most people can brush off surface fights and disagreements and return to normal. However, if a surface fight festers and repeats, there's always more to the story. The family dramas that happen during the holidays often start with surface conflicts yet involve bigger value differences or resentments below the surface. In addition, there's often something much deeper that no one knows how to deal with, so people gossip, backstab, and avoid.

Rule of thumb: If you continue to fight about the "little things" over and over, there's likely an unaddressed resentment underneath it.

---

2. CHILDHOOD PROJECTIONS

What they are: Ever feel like you're married to some version of your parents? Do you have issues with authority? Have you ever "fallen in love" with a mentor, musician, or hero? These are versions of childhood projections. Psychology teaches a lot about projections. It's common to hear someone who's done personal growth work say something like this: "Hey, I think you're projecting your dad/mom onto me."

A projection is when we project (like a movie projector) a past negative or positive experience onto someone in the present. Anytime you are in high-stakes relationships, projections are part of the game. For example, if you grew up in a family where one of your parents was critical, you may find yourself in a close relationship where you always feel like the other person is criticizing you. Let's say your dad was hypercritical and nothing you did was good enough. As an adult, when a boss or partner gives you feedback, you might feel like you're in your childhood home again, getting shamed for "not doing it right."

There are actually scientific reasons for projection that have to do with implicit and procedural memory, but we won't delve into that level of detail in this book. Basically, the old memory (feeling criticized by Dad) and the new interaction with your boss (receiving constructive feedback to improve performance) feel the same to you. Of course, this clouds your ability to see your boss for who she really is and receive the grain of truth in her feedback (gender doesn't always matter with projections). If you miss that there might be a projection going on, you'll keep thinking the other person needs to change. In this case, you'll keep hoping your boss doesn't give you critical feedback.

Childhood projections, and projections in general, are completely unavoidable when you partner with someone or when there is a power difference in the relationship, such as between employee and boss. In a partnership, it's common to project a past image or experience of your parents (or other influential figures) onto your partner. At work, most of us have had a boss we looked up to or despised. If we worked there for a long period of time, we might have projected past experiences with our parents onto this boss, which creates a sticky dynamic.

Take Sylvie. She grew up in a family where her dad left the family when Sylvie was ten. Naturally, this was devastating, and children her age tend to create meaning out of such events, such as "It's my fault that my dad left. It's because of me." Over time, Sylvie adapted and developed a new strategy to get her dad back. She began to excel at everything, mainly school. She thought that if she could be perfect, her dad would return and give her the love she always wanted.

Of course, this never happened and when she entered into an adult relationship, she always tried hard to please the man she was with, worrying that if she didn't "get it right," her boyfriend would leave her. Her "abandonment fears," as she called them, would create so much anxiety in her intimate relationships that she would drive her partners away. She reported they would feel nagged, intruded upon, and turned off by her clinginess. Sylvie was projecting her past abandonment fears onto her current partners, worrying that if she wasn't perfect, they'd leave. This also heightened her trust issues and made it very hard for her to trust her boyfriends. Then the men would break up with her, confirming her worst fears.

How to recognize when you're projecting onto someone: It's easiest to see our projections in long-term partnerships. Ty projects parts of his relationship with his mom onto his wife to this day. And his wife projects parts of her experience with her dad onto him. It's normal and unavoidable. Our partner brings up old familiar feelings from our childhood that we want to push away. Although often uncomfortable, learning how to work with our childhood projections is incredibly healing. For example, sometimes when Ty's wife is stressed, preoccupied, or simply tired, Ty projects a negative experience with his mom onto her.

Growing up, when his mom was struggling in some way, Ty would feel disconnected from her and thought it was his fault. This disconnection created a lot of anxiety in him as a boy. As an adult man, it might appear silly that he would react the same way when his wife is underresourced, but this is the terrain Ty works with to this day. Although this type of projection has happened plenty of times in his relationship and he's improved how he responds, his scared animal still reacts because the situation feels familiar. Part of this is his relational blueprint talking, so he understands in real time that his wife isn't mad at him, nor is she leaving the relationship. Ty is becoming a relational leader and knows this is his childhood attachment pattern talking. Knowing this has allowed him a little more wiggle room to regulate himself and reconnect with his wife.

Getting to Zero: The first step is for you not to take everything so literally when the other person is too distant or too close. Although it might feel like death at times, it's not death. Relax. If Ty's wife is feeling underresourced and it goes on longer than he's comfortable with, Ty speaks up and says something. The conversation goes best when he is able to lead with vulnerability versus complaint.

Complaint: "Hey, you seem distant and I don't like it. You should come back around and we should work this out."
Vulnerability: "Hey, honey, I know you've been going through a lot and are stressed and tired right now. I'm projecting you're also mad at me. I feel hurt and a bit alone over here."

Notice the difference between the two options. Though neither are perfect, Ty and his wife have coached each other on the type of responses that work best for them. You can do the same.

In at least one of your high-stakes relationships where you think projections might be going on, identify the two key projections you have put on the other person and ask them if they'd be willing to share theirs. *How* you do this matters:

- Rather than say, "You are so mean," you can say, "I sometimes project onto you that you are criticizing me."
- Rather than say, "You're mad at me," you can say, "I'm projecting that you are mad at me."

Another great way to work with this is to lead with "I'm making up a story that . . ." This can be even more disarming to a person because you're owning what you are doing—making up a story. That feels much less threatening than blanket statements such as "you are," "you always," or "you never." To make this practice even stronger, lead with a considerate statement about the other person, then share your projection, like this: "I know your plate is full and you're super stressed about finances; I'm making up a story that you're upset with me and that you don't want to connect with me."

3. SECURITY FIGHTS

What they are: Security fights in parent–child relationships and adult partnerships can be very stressful. Security issues bring up the deepest layer of our relational blueprint, where the very old attachment need and the core fear of abandonment live. Here, a partner in a relationship might wonder, "Are you really with me, both feet in, and not going anywhere?" If any of your four relational needs—feeling safe, feeling seen, feeling soothed, and feeling supported and challenged—is unstable in any way, it will impact your sense of security, and every surface conflict will be more intense because of the unresolved security issue. Endless stress and countless hours are wasted fighting about other issues when, in actuality, security is the issue.

How to recognize a security fight: One of the hallmark features of a security fight in an intimate partnership is that one or both people feel that the other person isn't "all in." One or both people feel like somewhere — just around the corner — their partner is going to bail. Often sex and money fights fall into the security category because there is so much at stake. For example, you might be financially dependent on someone and therefore do not want to leave the relationship because your sense of security is at risk. And, if you don't feel secure in your intimate partnership, you might not want to open up to the other person sexually. Security fights keep coming up until you both commit 100 percent. Imagine if you had a business partner who was one foot in and one foot out. You'd probably feel on edge and not want to keep moving forward with the business until you felt their full commitment and willingness to take risks equally. Or imagine if this same business partner had no interest in working through conflict and brushed it all under the rug. Over time, you wouldn't feel safe.

Insecurity in the parent–child relationship occurs when the child perceives the parent is inconsistently available for comfort, soothing, or connection or when disconnections are not repaired. The parent is preoccupied with their own schedule, demands, addictions, stress, image, work, or anything else that takes them away from offering their child the four relational needs. It goes without saying that when a power dynamic is unequal, such as in the parent–child relationship, it's not up to the child to provide security for the parent. For example, as a child, you may have felt it was your job to take care of an alcoholic or depressed parent.

Or maybe your parents were mean, belittling, or sham-ing. If your caregiver behaved in a way that ignited your scared animal too often, too intensely, or they outright ignored your need for reassurance and reconnection during times of stress, you likely had an insecure relationship dynamic. This is when children create negative stories about themselves, such as "I'm not wanted" or "relationships are not trustworthy," and therefore will be more likely to have insecure adult relationships.

In adult romantic relationships, security becomes the de-terminate of long-term relationship success or failure. If you are not in a secure adult partnership, giving and receiving the four relational needs, then your fights will come back to security, even if it seems like your fights are about what was said at dinner last night. For example, a couple can get stuck in conflict be-cause they do not address the deeper threats to the partnership. One partner gets stuck in avoiding, running away, blaming, and feeling terrible. The other partner keeps talking, nagging, and trying to work through the issues, but it's all done from an anx-ious, fearful place that often drives the other person farther away.

Early on in my relationship with my wife (then girlfriend), we fought a lot. In fact, a close friend once took me to dinner and said, "Bro, you guys fight all the time. Do you really think this is the right person for you?" Imagine two therapists/psychol-ogy nerds going in circles about who's projecting what onto the other person. We worked hard to find solutions to our conflicts. We always got to zero, but sometimes it would take *days* of pro-cessing and talking. Although it seemed like most of our fights were about surface subjects, projections, and values with the oc-casional resentment sprinkled in, I would later learn that one of the reasons we were so inefficient in our conflict resolution was because I didn't have both feet in. As much as I loved her, I was ambivalent about partnership. I didn't want to feel suffocated or trapped, yet I wanted a relationship. So I kept distancing and pulling away when things got too close. Naturally, my wife felt insecure and I felt annoyed at her insecurity, not quite getting that my lack of having both feet in was creating the insecurity. This dynamic completely changed when, after two intense breakups over the course of three years, I finally put two feet in and asked her to marry me.

Getting to Zero: Security is a great goal to achieve for a parent, a couple, and even business partners. Like any of the other types of conflicts, to get to zero you both must be a student of relationships, first and foremost. If you recall from Chapter 4, this means you both grow and develop yourselves. Then you navigate this challenging conflict as a team and collaborate to repair and reconnect. But both of you have to be 100 percent committed to the relationship. You decide that you're not going away and that no matter what you're going to make reconnection happen. If your partner is unwilling to be a student, then it will be next to impossible to learn and achieve security in a partnership.

So, what happens if you have a difference in commitment level and the other person is courageous enough to be transparent that they are not all in? The good news is they are being honest, which helps you decide what you want to do. But no great couple, team, or band happens when all the players are not 100 percent in.

The good news here is that if you have a willing partner, you can easily create security over time, even if you had a difficult childhood. Once you earn the right to call yourselves a secure couple or secure business partners, you will still experience surface fights, projections, resentments, and value differences, but your foundation will be solid when there are no threats about someone leaving. Your nervous systems may continue to feel threatened at times, but because you are now taking a stand for security, you both feel the strength of having a rock-solid foundation. This feeling is what most committed couples are after.

4. VALUE DIFFERENCES

What they are: Value differences can be deal breakers. A value is something you care about, such as monogamy, parenting philosophy, wealth, health, work style, and religion. (It's not a deeply held belief.) Initially, a new friendship or work relationship can seem great, but over time and under stress value differences—along with your true colors—will push through to the surface. You can't hide what you really believe. It often turns out you value different ways of living and loving, different ways of dealing with money, children, conflict, family, work, spiritual beliefs, and so on. When you first met, it might have seemed like you valued the same things, but over time, you've polarized. None of these differences are problems inherently; however, they become challenging for people to navigate, especially if you have no tools or methods to work through them. Understanding value differences requires that you know your values; you identified some of them in Chapter 8.

Examples of Big Deal-Breaker Value Differences
- Spiritual or religious beliefs
- Positions on culture, race, ethnicity, heritage, tradition
- Growth mindset versus fixed mindset
- Spending money versus saving it
- Drugs/alcohol versus sober living
- Politics and ideologies
  - Guns or no guns
  - Pro-life or pro-choice
  - Democrat or Republican

- Marriage or no long-term commitment
- Monogamy or open relationship
- Live in a city or in a small town, near ocean or mountains
- Kids or no kids
  - How to raise the kids
  - Parenting philosophy
  - Public or private school

How to recognize a conflict over values: From the list of deal-breaker value differences, see if you can identify at least two conflicts you've had that revolve around any of those subjects. Circle them. If you've ever had a conflict over politics on Facebook or at your in-laws' or at Thanksgiving dinner, you know how charged these conflicts can be. Value differences appear to be belief differences. "I believe in God; you don't." Although this is a difference in beliefs, it's also a difference in values because of how we live on the basis of our beliefs. "I value a religious way of life, while you don't." We often cling to our values because it's where we are least likely to change, especially if we are not on a growth path.

For example, parents can have big value differences over how to raise their kids and which schools the children will attend. Fights over value differences can create huge rifts for a couple. Married partners often have value differences around money. For example, one person has financial resources and is very organized and responsible, and the other person has a lot of debt and is disorganized. This value difference often becomes a big source of tension and unresolved conflict.

If someone you care about continues to say they are "too busy" to meet with you to work through a conflict, they are essentially saying through their actions, "You and whatever happened between us aren't that important to me." They aren't valuing the relationship. People are communicating through their values all day long by the actions they take and by the way they live their life.

Getting to Zero: When value differences emerge, they can be deal breakers. But people can learn to negotiate the differences in a mature way; their diversity is the very characteristic of their relationship that helps them accomplish more together and form a strong team. Sameness is not what we're after here. To get to zero with value differences, you both need to set context and agree to face the differences. Pretending like they are not there only creates more tension and conflict. Remember conflict creep?

Using the skills outlined in Chapter 11, listen to each other intently. Be sure you both feel understood. Ask each other how open you are to change. Remember that most people don't change their values unless they see that doing so will help them get what they want. For example, Margaret believed in living in the now and, in her words, "enjoying her life," and her husband valued saving for retirement. They fought about this all the time until, using the tools in Chapter 16 (for how to resolve value differences), they finally were able to accept their differences and come up with a win-win together. They negotiated and moved forward with these value differences in place. Are both of you willing to make room for and accept the other person's values? Or are you too different to move forward with the goals you want to accomplish separately and together?

Next, you need to do two things: (1) see how their values are beneficial to you in your life and actions, and (2) sell them on your desires through *their* values. For example, Margaret had to see how saving would help them enjoy their life more, and her husband had to see how Margaret's spending would help both of their futures as well.

Think, "How do their values help me?" This is a simple yet profound question that reframes the other person's behavior and choices into a potential benefit for you. For example, "How does my husband watching sports all day with no job help me?" My guess is that his choices are helping you get even more rooted in your values. His choices might be helping you make choices that you deem as better for you and for your kids. If you continue to judge him and feel superior to him, he will only shut down and distance more.

I mention this because you might be stuck trying to change someone in your life. Trying to change someone who doesn't want to change rarely works. When it does work, it's because you've done a masterful job communicating to them on how doing what you want them to do helps them, not you. In Chapter 16, we'll dive back into value differences and take all of this one step further.

5. RESENTMENTS

What they are: The Oxford English Dictionary defines a resentment as follows: "Bitter indignation at having been treated unfairly." Notice the blame that comes with this lame definition. "Treated unfairly," but according to whom? Doesn't this definition imply that, according to me, I deem something as unfair? Yes, unfair is about *our* values. In other words, if you don't conform to my values or to an explicit or implicit agreement we had, I will suffer bitter indignation and resent you. Again, blame! I prefer a more personal-responsibility-based definition:

A resentment is another form of conflict when I try to change you (get you to live by my values) or when you try to change me (get me to live by your values).*

---

* Not once in three years in grad school did I learn anything about resentments. Eek. Eventually, I found Dr. John Demartini, and he opened my eyes to how much resentments can ruin relationships. He also taught me how to clear them, which I share in this book.

If I don't conform when you want me to change, you'll resent me. If I do conform when you want me to change, I'll resent you. For example, if you and I are married and you agreed to move to the city because I pressured you, but you're really a country person, you'll resent me. Because you chose to betray yourself to move to the city. This is classic Strategic Self versus True Self conflict.

Resentments typically emerge because we agree to something reluctantly. We hold back our true self-expression for fear of losing the relationship or driving the other person away. Resentments are also born when you expect the other person to be who you want them to be or who you thought they were, and you struggle to embrace them as they really are (classic in families and marriages).

I once tried to help a couple that was in gridlock over the husband's occasional pot use. The wife wanted him to quit, and he wanted to be free to smoke whenever he wished (which wasn't that often, but it still upset her). For a while, he tried to quit for her, which required that he betray his true self-expression, so not surprisingly he began to resent her. When he finally stood his ground and let her know that he was an adult and he would smoke when he wanted, she resented him. Can you see how she was trying to change his values to be more like hers? He couldn't see that by quitting smoking pot it could help their relationship and help him. And she couldn't see how his occasional use could be helpful to her or them. So they both remained locked in their positions.

They were in gridlock because neither one of them was Standing for Three, neither could see how their current way of being could be workable and possibly even serve their relationship. It became either/or, win or lose. A win-win would have been if she accepted some occasional pot use so long as it didn't hurt their relationship or connection, and he chose to smoke less, knowing it upset her and also hurt their connection. Both would have felt more considered and accepted for their values. If you want to be rigid in your beliefs and values, be single and don't partner.

Resentments might start small but can keep people stuck for years without solutions. People typically bury resentment because they minimize how important the issue is, feel skeptical about it getting resolved, or are too scared or too uncomfortable to go there. For many people, resentments come out as repetitive surface fights and disagreements, when in reality they are most often value differences.

Resentments are born when:

1. You try to get me to live by your values.
2. I try to get you to live by my values.

How to recognize a resentment: You know you have a resentment when you have an unmet expectation. For example, if you value being on time, and your friend is chronically late, and you keep getting irritated, you have a resentment because you want them to do life like you do. Here's another example: if you're mad because you keep wanting your parents to ask you questions about yourself and they always talk about themselves, you have a resentment. Or, if you have an employee who keeps falling down at their job, you likely have a resentment.

Getting to Zero: How do we get through resentments? Here's a simple yet profound exercise to help you see how expectations and resentments go hand-in-hand. I call this the *Quick Resentment Process*.

1. Take 100 percent responsibility. Own your resentment as such: "I resent that . . ."
2. Replace the word *resent* with *expected* and notice what happens: "I expected that . . ." Interesting, right?
3. Write this down: "The expectation was mine and I was ___ percent transparent with X person about my expectation of them." (Own it.)

Here's an example:

1. "I resent that you were late, again."
2. "I expect you to be on time and never be late."
3. "I put this expectation on you. I was zero percent transparent, meaning I never told you that I have this expectation of you."

What if you were 100 percent transparent with your expectations? I'm a big fan of making expectations clear and transparent so you can negotiate a better outcome for both of you. Expectations and requests can be fine in high-stakes relationships, but you'll want to understand how to speak them. We'll cover expectations in Chapter 17.

Try the resentment exercise with at least one current resentment so you can see how you are projecting your expectations (and values) onto someone else. If you want to take the next step toward resolution, it's important to see how having this expectation is helping you wake up and do something different in this dynamic. Near the end of the book, we will take another step. We'll also revisit what to do if someone won't come to the table and work out conflict with you—because surely you're going to have a resentment built up with that kind of person.

COMING BACK TO THE CONTEXT

Identifying what type of conflict you are facing in your relationships allows you to then address the exact problem. To get to zero, it is essential to learn *what* you are fighting about. Get on the same page about the *context*—then you can work through the *content*. People waste countless hours fighting when they don't even know what they are fighting about. One helpful question is for one of you to stop the conversation with a statement like this: "Hey, can we zoom out for a minute? I'm not even clear what we're fighting about anymore. That will help me orient better and listen to you better. Is it X or Y?" At times, you might need an outside facilitator to help you pinpoint the exact problem. A relationship coach or facilitator can see from a higher view and remain objective to help you through this. Their first job is to help you get clear on what the underlying issue is.

Get on the same page about the context—then you can work through the content.

No matter the type of fight, resolving conflict is about getting an education, which is only accessible to those with their student hats on. Conflict is a massive opportunity to learn about yourself and other people. It's an opportunity to learn new skills and tools that will help you get stronger as a person. Plus, you'll be better equipped, and you and the other person will behave more like a team when new challenges come down the road. And, yes, they never stop coming.

It's our similarities *and* our differences that make us strong, not just our similarities. But you have to work with the differences. That requires going into conflict. Standing for Three has to be in place. If I don't, or can't, accept your values, we won't make it very far on our journey together. To accept your values, I have to work through conflict with you—because if I'm in opposition to your values, it means that I'm not accepting you. If I'm not accepting you, I'm against you and can't really work with you.

ACTION STEPS

1. In your conflict box from Chapter 2, determine which type of fight you are having (surface, projection, security, values, resentment). Now write an action step that you are going to take to resolve this conflict. For example, if it's a resentment conflict, are you going to address it? If so, by when?

2. Find one resentment in your life and run it through the Quick Resentment Process so you can choose differently. Notice the expectation.

3. If you want more on value differences, skip to Chapter 16 for in-depth information on how to deal with them.

4. Share any of this with a friend who supports you taking owner-ship of the fights you are in and what you're doing about them.

The Ten Roadblocks to Reconnection and What to Do Instead

I cannot recommend love if you want to feel good.
If you want to feel alive, the most alive you're ever felt,
this is the game.

— Annie Lalla

M Y DAD IS A BADASS. I'VE LEARNED SO MANY THINGS FROM the guy. I learned every sport I know from him, along with the value of hard work. I also learned to bottle up my feelings and not talk about them. Ever. Though he never said, "Hey, son, I have a good idea to get you through life: stuff your feelings. It's awesome!" He just lived that way, so I followed suit. After all, he was my model of how to be a man in the world. This behavior was reinforced in just about every group I was a part of, from the classroom, to sports teams, to my circle of friends.

It's essential to acknowledge that we all learn how to do conflict in our childhood by watching the big people, day in and day out, year after year. How they treated each other and how they treated us taught us how to navigate challenges with other people. But now it's up to you to take responsibility and upgrade how you do it. Otherwise, your history becomes your destiny.

Before we dig into how to repair and reconnect after a conflict or disconnection, reflect on how repair and reconnection have happened in your life. When conflict happened as a child, did anyone comfort you? Did your parents own their part in what happened? Or were you the one to slowly reach out and get the connection back? Who initiated the apology? Did apologies even work? Did time just sort of take care of everything? Or did you distract yourself from the pain of disconnection through sports, food, video games, books, or friends? What were you taught, through day-to-day modeling, about this reconnection process? As a parent, I understand the profound concept that *you create what you are*. If you're reading this book, chances are the Conflict Repair Cycle just didn't happen that much, or at all.

Most adults use ten common conflict coping strategies. I call these the *Ten Roadblocks to Reconnection*, and it's essential we cover these first to dispel any myths about them being effective.

1. Blame
2. Apologies
3. Distraction/avoidance
4. Time
5. Compartmentalization
6. FRACKing
7. Hope and pray
8. Defensiveness
9. Stonewalling
10. Gaslighting

These ten tired approaches arrive once you've disconnected by way of the Four Disconnectors (posture, collapse, seek, avoid). They are all symptoms of an unwillingness or inabilty to work through con-

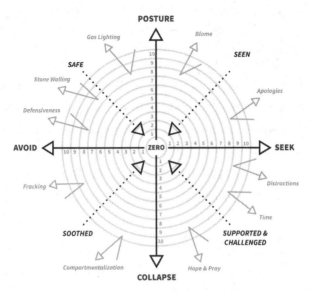

Diagram 14.1 Ten Roadblocks to Reconnection

flict. Like misfired arrows, they keep bouncing off the target of zero. (See Diagram 14.1.) Hence the term *roadblock*.

In conflict, sometimes it feels like you're way off trail, down some hidden dirt road, when in actuality you're taking the path of least resistance, which is more like a freeway. And as you may have experienced, these common roads lead to dead ends the vast majority of the time.

When we disconnect, if we are not practiced in conflict or the repair and reconnection process, we will resort to these ten feeble attempts to get back to zero. Unfortunately, these keep us stuck right where we are, ashamed and disconnected. As we unpack each roadblock, notice which one you typically get stuck in. Before I studied psychology, I got my master's degree in these in the school of hard knocks.

1. BLAME

The temptation to blame people is always there, especially when you are in the victim seat. I watch my kids do this all the time. For example, when they were younger, my son would point his finger at his sister and say, "She did it." And then my daughter would point her finger at him and say, "He did it." Any parent knows how frustrating this can be. When we disconnect via the Four Disconnectors, we employ blame as an additional feature of posture (blame them) or collapse (blame yourself). To blame is to assign responsibility "over there." When we do this, we put the solutions to our conflict "over there" also. For things to improve, "they" have to change, which keeps you powerless and off the hook. This is so rudimentary to learn, yet so difficult for many of us to change.

Self-blame is a collapse and another way we keep the conflict stuck. So long as I blame myself for our problems, *you* don't have to take any responsibility. It's all *my* fault. Then I get to create a bunch of bullshit stories about myself and stay in the valley of victimhood, where I hope and pray that someone pulls me out.

Clues that you're blaming: You're using language such as "You always," "You never," or "If only you would _____ [*insert behavior you want them to change*], then our relationship would be better." Whenever we put the fulcrum for change in the other person's court and make them responsible for our solution, we're in blame. Basically, if you start your sentence with the word "You," you're likely in blame. On the other hand, a self-blamer might use an I statement to blame themselves: "I can't believe I did that. I'm such an idiot."

How to stop: It's unrealistic to think you can get to a place where you don't blame. For years I tried not to blame or judge. As a meditation instructor, I also tried to teach other people not to do it. My personal experience is that it's next to impossible. What's more interesting to me now is to get underneath the blame. I find it helpful to allow myself to blame the other person quietly in my mind. But then, as quickly as I can, I work to see the habit, stay curious about my blame, and dig deeper. I look at what's driving my blame. I can ask, "What am I really scared or upset about right now?" I can turn the whole conflict around and look at my side. I can take personal responsibility instead: "My part of our conflict is _____" (just like you learned in Chapter 4). Instead of noticing and speaking everything *they* did wrong, I can focus on myself and what I may have done or not done that contributed to the conflict.

2. APOLOGIES

There are two types of apologies: (1) rushed and (2) paced.

The Rushed Apology

Sadly, most of the time, "I'm sorry" is said way too soon and way too often. Used in this way, it only reinforces the problems we want to solve because it never gets at the underlying issue of two people not understanding each other. Nor does it tap into the wealth of growth opportunities available if we just looked a little deeper at the problem or miscommunication.

Did you know the average person apologizes eight times per day? Look closely the next time an impulsive apology comes flying out of your mouth, and you'll see that it's probably a posture covering up shame for how you've behaved.

If these types of apologies really worked, we'd be so efficient at clearing conflict that we wouldn't be afraid of it. Why be afraid of a problem that gets completely solved with two words? Yes, parents should teach their kids to say "I'm sorry." It's a good social grace for all children to learn. However, a rushed apology rarely works to settle a child's nervous system, and usually it's not enough to help an adult move from the back seat to the front seat. Stack on enough unaddressed disconnections and watered-down apologies over many years, and kids get used to not feeling seen or acknowledged in their hurt.

These kids turn into adults who remain caught in the same cycle of incompletion. They don't know how to repair and reconnect effectively because they were taught only to apologize. Rushed apologies are a sidestep that is insufficient to settle the activation of the scared animal and gain legitimate reconnection.*

Paced Apologies

A well-timed and well-paced apology can sometimes be just what the doctor ordered. If you are attached to the apology and it works for the other person and they've told you that, then feel free to use it.

A paced apology means that you know when to use it to get to zero. Sometimes it's right up front: "Whoa, I'm so sorry I just did that." For example, if I just said something inappropriate to my wife and I can see that she's reacting, I can say, "Ah shit, I'm sorry, I can see what I just said was lame. My bad there." Then you work to own up to things and work to understand the impact of your behavior on the other person.

At other times, the paced apology should not be given until the very end of a process such as LUFU. Once in a while, after you've done everything I recommend in this book and you sense the other person could benefit from your apology, then tell them you're sorry, but do so while looking them right in the eye with tremendous vulnerability. Otherwise, your apology is just two meaningless words.

> **Clues that you're shortcutting with apologies:** Greg and Tevra were newlyweds. Greg had a history of "fucking things up" (his words) with Tevra. He made mistakes like forgetting

---

* Sometimes and for some people, apologies do work; celebrate that! But if you want to get good at conflict, it can't be your only tool. Know that if you overuse apologies and don't do the other stuff I recommend in this book, your chances of getting to zero decrease rapidly and substantially.

her birthday, or, as she complained, "He signs up for these on-line marketing programs for his business and he never finishes them. He never follows through."* When they came to me, they were in a huge conflict that wasn't about the programs he was signing up for. He apologized about fifteen times in the first few minutes. He wasn't even aware that he was doing so much apologizing until I pointed it out. I told him to ask her if his rushed apologies were helping. She said no. I asked him to tell her why he was still using apologies. He didn't know. And he really didn't. It was an unconscious bad habit that he fell back on when he was scared. It was his default setting. He genuinely thought that the way to get back in control, back in the front seat, was to apologize.

Turns out Greg had been a doormat his whole life, a classic "nice guy." He rarely took the lead and was agreeable to just about anything. He chose a woman who was a type A personality, always wanting to be in charge and rarely taking no for an answer. When conflict happened, she would blame him and he would apologize. That was their pattern. But not one of his apologies had worked in their five years of being together because it never addressed the actual issue.

In working with them, we discovered that Tevra had not said anything about the apologies. Not once did she say something like, "I don't need an apology, I need ownership and understanding of the impact your behavior has on me." She didn't know how to tell Greg his way wasn't working, and she was caught in her way, which was to blame him for just about everything, which also wasn't working. They both learned that apologies worked for Greg, but not for her. I instructed them to get in touch with the vulnerable feelings behind their respective walls.

---

* Notice the exaggeration. But this is how people talk in conflict.

They began to reconnect and soon learned what worked to settle their scared animals.

How to stop: If you do the rushed apology, the very first step is to recognize your bad habit and how ineffective it is. Start by asking the person you most frequently apologize to, "Did that help?" Or, "Could I be doing more to help settle your nerves?" Then, pay close attention. After you apologize, do you feel reconnected and great? My guess is that you're not at zero yet. Start noticing whether you feel relaxed and settled when other people apologize to you. Or do you need more?

3. DISTRACTION/AVOIDANCE

Frequently, you will want to distract yourself from what is uncomfortable, which is why I'm asking you to increase your discomfort threshold. Distractions are "medication." We want to medicate away the uncomfortable feelings. Totally understandable. But distraction doesn't heal conflicts, nor does it help us reconnect. Any couple knows that a day or two after a fight, watching a good movie together can take the edge off and help them both focus on something more enjoyable. But did it help them resolve anything and get to zero? If distraction worked for reconnection, the very best thing to do would be to watch a movie and eat some ice cream while scrolling Instagram. At some point, you would look at each other again and realize, "Oh yeah, there's still that big shit pile between us. Hmm. Should we deal with that?"

Many people can go decades and even might die having "changed the channel" to something more enjoyable.

Clues that you're distracting: Recognize that you distract. List your top five distractions when you are in conflict or avoiding it. Here are a few examples:

- Reaching for the phone and texting someone, or opening any number of apps, such as Facebook, Instagram, Google News, games, Snapchat, or TikTok
- Watching TV, Netflix, or porn
- Eating food—particularly sugary foods, chips, or crunchy stuff
- Using drugs—alcohol, painkillers, weed, and so forth

How to stop: The first step is to recognize that distraction produces limited results. I used to take naps in order to avoid my feelings. But whenever I woke up from a nap, my problems and pain were still there. Whenever you "wake up" out of distraction, try setting your phone timer for five minutes and do the NESTR meditation. Explore what's going on inside and ask yourself, "What feeling am I running from right now?" Or, "What am I scared of?" See where these introspective questions take you. Once you learn how to be with your experience by increasing your discomfort threshold, you'll be far more agile in stressful conversations.

4. TIME

Back in my wilder days, after a night of serious binge drinking, I would wake up the next day with a raging headache, regretting that I'd had "that one last beer" at two a.m. But I knew that I'd feel better by evening because the hangover would wear off. And if it didn't, I could always crack another beer in the afternoon to take the edge off. Although very shortsighted, this is how most people treat conflict. Just wait it out and eventually you'll forget and feel better, right? Wrong—your unresolved conflicts stack up on top of each other and get shifted into long-term memory. You're priming yourself for more and more unresolved conflicts, the very thing you're hoping will go away and get better.

Time rarely heals relationship wounds.* If it did, we'd be living in a world full of happy, connected people because all we would have to do is wait for things to get better. When you don't address relationship conflicts as they come up, you compound unresolved conflict onto unresolved conflict. This creates added burden for you and your future relationships to deal with.

The good news (or maybe bad news for some of you) is that painful relationship experiences tend to repeat until we face them.

Clues that you're hoping time will take care of it: The time technique for resolving conflict builds off the distraction technique. Add up enough distractions and now you're employing the time approach. The reason you keep using time is that it sort of works. You've trained the people around you that you'll be better the next day, or in a few days, so you don't even need to talk about it. After all, "it's in the past." You probably learned this from your parents, and they learned it from theirs.

How to stop: As I said, the first step is to recognize you do this. Remember that hitting the snooze button on a conflict does nothing to change the conflict. Own up to the fact that sometimes you try to let time take care of your problems. Look a friend in the eye and let them know this is how you do things sometimes. Ask them if they are okay with you using time to try to resolve conflict the next time it comes up between the two of you. My hope is that your friend isn't down with that and would rather feel understood by you and rather get to zero with you. Surrounding ourselves with growth-oriented people who want our truth forces us to step up.

---

* Research in 2017 done at the University of Arizona confirms this assertion.

5. COMPARTMENTALIZATION

Depending on the context, consciously shoving issues under the rug or putting them on a shelf can be helpful to get through the immediacy of the situation. For example, on a sports team, it's pretty important to stuff your beef with a teammate until the game is over because not being able to control your anger during play could cost you your reputation and the game. However, after the game—if you want to be better team players—you can address the conflict on some level. Sometimes the coach might have to help you.

In other words, there is a time and a place for sucking it up and compartmentalizing emotions. For example, if a big crisis comes, such as a death in the family, job loss, or health crisis—two people who were at odds may put aside their individual differences and face the challenge together. But once the storm passes, how's the vibe? There are still issues to address. Each subsequent storm highlights your weak spots, and at a certain point those weak spots become a liability. We'll never become stronger if we don't learn to address the unresolved issues between us.

A seventy-year-old couple asked for my help. I quickly found out that for the man's entire life he had "buried his fears and concerns" (his words). He had been through hell in his business off and on for forty years. When I asked the woman how she supported him all those years, she said he never talked about any of it. So, she would just make him a nice meal, and that was that. As a result, their long-standing marriage lacked the emotional depth that they both longed for. Compartmentalization is like putting things in your garage or that messy junk drawer when you clean off your desk. It looks like it's been dealt with, when in reality, you just put it somewhere where you don't have to see it every day. And over time the mess gets bigger and harder to deal with.

Clues that you're compartmentalizing: Unlike distraction or time, we often do compartmentalization consciously. You might think to yourself, "I'd rather do work than deal with this right now." Or, "Let's go grab a beer so I can take my mind off work." When we put things on the shelf, we table it for later . . . or do we?

My parents' generation is notorious for sucking it up to get through hard times. I applaud my own parents for this because I think it's one of the only tools they had back then. I'm grateful for their sacrifices and their approach because, had they done things differently, I wouldn't be writing this book. But one of the challenges with compartmentalization is how deeply it affects our ability to empathize and relate to other people who are also going through challenging times. When you compartmentalize, you're essentially saying, "I don't want to deal with that." Again, my question for you is, "What are you so afraid of?" I mean, if you really examine the conflict and feel that discomfort all the way down, what is the worst thing that can happen? Do you really want to live in fear of whatever emotions and sensations that are going on internally?

How to stop: First, know that we all need to compartmentalize at times. That's okay. Just don't make it your go-to approach during conflict. If you live by compartmentalization, you'll miss out on the possibility of learning about yourself and growing stronger.

To stop using this technique, you have to *want* to stop. Get clear on that first. Feel free to take a break from the stressful situation. No problem. Then add in the all-important next step: return and deal. Start owning this by saying, "Friend, sometimes I bury things and I compartmentalize them. I don't want to deal with them." Admitting this makes you an authentic person and brings you back into choice. Want to turn up the heat?

Ask the other person if they are okay with you doing that in your relationship: "Hey, are you cool if I stuff my feelings around our conflicts?" See what they say. Telling the truth about yourself instead of burying it increases your discomfort threshold, increases intimacy, and invites more honest relationships. It's good to remember that you can't be fulfilled in life when you bury parts of your experience.

6. FRACKING

Another huge roadblock to getting to zero is what I call *FRACKing.** Under stress, most of us rely on ineffective speaking and listening skills: we talk too much, we blame, we wait for our turn to speak, not really listening. I can relate. Recall the conversation I had with my wife in Chapter 11. Here is another part of that same conversation:

> Her: I have a problem with Teresa. I'm so frustrated. [*she lists her complaints about Teresa*]
>
> Me: [*after trying to be a good listener*] Why are you frustrated? She always does this. Have you thought about challenging her or confronting her?
>
> Her: [*feeling defensive*] Um, not really.
>
> Me: [*feeling her defensiveness but proceeding anyway, like a dumbass*] Teresa is so difficult. I can talk to her for you if you want. I mean, let's cancel our plans with her. I don't want to hang with her anyway.
>
> Her: [*shutting down*] Never mind. I don't really want to talk about it anymore.

---

* I first heard a similar term from a guy at Threshold Passages, a rite-of-passage organization for men and boys. He called it FRAP. I modified it to an acronym that worked for how I wanted to teach people about listening. Fracking is also the controversial process of pulling oil and natural gas from deep beneath the earth. This is not the type of fracking I'm talking about.

> Me: [*feeling anxious*] What's wrong? I'm just trying to help.
>
> Her: [*walking away*]

Can you see the problem here? If not, you're not alone. When I'm stressed, in blame, or impatient, I still FRACK instead of listening. Let me unpack what I was doing wrong in the above example so it's clearer.

F is for fixing. Notice how I tried to fix it. This is typical masculine behavior.* Guys love to fix things—cars, appliances, gadgets, and problems. A masculine partner can feel very good about himself if he fixes things. In my view now, people don't need fixing because no one is broken. Feel free to try to fix the conflict, but not the other person.

R is for rescuing. Notice how I tried to bail her out and fix the problem for her, which sends a message that I don't think that she can handle her own problems. This can feel condescending for the other person. Remember the triangle of victimhood? People don't need rescuing from their relationship problems. They need to be understood first. Then, they need challenge and support to overcome the problem through their own wisdom and inner guidance.

A is for advice. A lot of men like to give advice. "You should do this." "Try this next time." Depending on the context, advice

---

* I'm going to use masculine instead of male in the book to be more inclusive. That said, masculine can still be off-putting for some readers. Feel free to substitute for men, or whatever the fixing partner's label is. I think this is one of those generalizations that feels true most of the time in my experience. From my experience men are socialized to fix problems, which is great in some parts of life and not helpful in others.

has a place, but during conflict if you give the other person advice and they already have a problem with you, it ain't going to end well. General rule: don't give anyone advice unless they ask for it.

C is for complaining or colluding. Complaining is like blaming. Colluding is taking sides and agreeing with her story about someone else. Instead of listening objectively, I came in taking her side (classic rescuer behavior). During conflict, most of us are in fact blaming the other person for something. Blaming and complaining usually push a person farther away from zero. Instead of working toward reconnection, you're helping them disconnect further—from you.

K is for killing. This means that we kill—or squash—someone's experience when we gaslight or deny their feelings. "You shouldn't feel frustrated," or "That didn't happen." When you kill someone's experience, you're denying what they thought, felt, or encountered. Remember, everyone's experience is 100 percent valid (which has nothing to do with right or wrong).

The bottom line here is that FRACKing will keep you disconnected and in conflict, so my mantra is "No FRACKing." Feel free to adopt what makes sense there.

7. HOPE AND PRAY

Another common and overused approach to conflict is to hope or pray that things get better. Maybe this is what people do when they hope time will take care of their problems? I'm not against hope, and I'm not against those who pray for spiritual or religious purposes. If you pray deeply and it helps you have the courage to learn how to work through conflict, great. But if your prayer is your way of not putting in genuine effort to work for a solution or take responsibility, then skip it because your conflict won't magically go away. If praying for conflict resolution worked, the world's religions would all get along and respectfully disagree, and there would be no wars. If you're going to pray, pray for the inner strength to learn how to apply the tools in this book.

Hope is like the time strategy. The idea is if you hope hard enough, in time things will magically get better. And, yes, sometimes we get lucky and things get better without us doing anything different. But that's the exception, not the rule. Far too many people sit on the sidelines and cling to hope as a solution to get through conflict.

Clues that you're stuck in hope and pray: The telltale sign that you're stuck in hope and pray is when you fail to learn anything. When the conflict is over, if you didn't learn anything, chances are you're in a hope and pray mindset. Imagine for a minute that you and a friend wanted to learn to ski. Now imagine your friend watched some YouTube videos on how to ski, read a book on the subject, and took eight private lessons with a ski instructor. Now imagine that you had access to those same resources, but you said, "No thanks, I've got this. I'm going to hope and pray that I learn to ski." Who will be the better skier in two months?

How to stop: Like all the roadblocks, owning your current style is the first step to removing it. "Friend, sometimes I just hope our conflicts would magically disappear." Or, "Sometimes I wish things would change, improve, and get better without actually doing anything differently myself." By taking personal responsibility over using hope and praying as a strategy to avoid the harder work of repair and reconnection, you help the other person trust you more because your words and actions line up.

8. DEFENSIVENESS

Whenever our scared animal is under attack, we rightfully defend. Yet, do we really need to keep defending ourselves in those surface fights? If your roommate or partner is upset that you forgot to pay a bill, and you defend yourself, it's likely going to go nowhere. The challenge with the human brain is that our memory is inaccurate. People waste years of their lives trying to defend something that may or may not have been said. I don't know about you, but when I'm in an argument with someone I really care about, it's painful to defend myself because I'm making the disconnection worse. Defensiveness serves to protect us from more vulnerable feelings such as hurt and shame.

There are two main types of defensiveness: (1) rigid and (2) excuses.

Rigid defensiveness looks like denial of your behaviors or actions: "I never said that." If someone is this defensive, the conversation won't go anywhere. In the excuses style of defensiveness, we admit we did in fact do something wrong, but then we immediately follow it up with justifications and rationalizations: "I did do that, but the reason is because . . ." Hmm. Here, you are taking personal responsibility (nice work) but then following it up with a justification or excuse as to why you did what you did. In my experience, either type of defensiveness immediately kills any potential of reconnection. It's like shutting a door in someone's face.

Clues that you're defensive: Anytime you make an excuse, explain yourself, or justify, you're in a defensive posture and working hard to prove your position. Most people don't respond well to this.

How to stop: As per usual, own it: "I'm being defensive." Better yet, before you even defend yourself, give the other person a heads-up about what's going on for you. "I'm about to defend myself. But instead of doing that, I'm going to keep listening." This helps you stay with the other person. It's not yet time to explain yourself. Listen first. Sure, at some point in the Conflict Repair Cycle, you'll want to feel heard, too. Eventually, if the people in your life are good listeners, you won't even need to defend yourself.

9. STONEWALLING

These last two roadblocks are much more extreme than the rest. Think of a literal stone wall. That's how it feels to be with someone who is stonewalling. They act like a solid wall, and chances are they are in fact behind an internal wall they've built, probably long before you came along. They may not even be aware of it. This type of person is shut down to any communication whatsoever. They refuse to respond. Instead of facing the conflict with you, a stonewaller tunes out, checks out, turns away, and continues to not deal with the issue at hand. Although this term wasn't around when I was dating, I would have most certainly been labeled a stonewaller because I wouldn't deal with any conflicts or upsetting moments. I walled them out.

Clues that you're stonewalling: You shut people out of your inner life. You feel something uncomfortable and might be aware that you don't want to "go there." You resist people who try to get to know you better by walling them off, especially during upsetting moments. You have a lot of rationalizations to support shutting others out, such as "People are too difficult," or "it's none of their business," or "I'm fine, I really am. You're the one who is upset."

How to stop: If you're willing to change your pattern, you can stop doing this to others. Start by taking responsibility for protecting yourself with this wall for such a long time because you really don't know what else to do. Then work with a coach or therapist to dismantle the wall, one stone at a time.

10. GASLIGHTING

Whereas the other nine roadblocks are pretty normal, gaslighting is an outlier and extreme. Gaslighting occurs when you use both lying and manipulation to get what you want relationally. You knowingly deny and fabricate reality. If you've ever been on the receiving end of gaslighting, you know it's extremely confusing because you begin to question your own sanity as the other person lies, denies reality, refuses to take any ownership, and skillfully turns every conflict back to somehow being your fault.

Clues that you're gaslighting: First, I really hope you don't gaslight anyone. You need to be a pretty sociopathic or narcissistic person if you use this in any way to get out of conflicts. That said, if during conflict you employ triangulation as a way to get people on your side, this can be a very subtle form of gaslighting. If you continue to not take personal responsibility for anything in the conflict, you're pulling out your flamethrower and burning down all possibilities that you might have a part in it. This is extremely dangerous in any high-stakes relationship, and soon enough you'll burn that bridge forever.

How to stop: For a normal person, watch your tendency to triangulate and get others on your side. For a true gaslighter person, you must become aware that you do this and want to change your behavior. If this is so, then seek professional help.

The good news (and bad news, of course) is that when we attempt to get to zero using any of these ten roadblocks, we continue to reach dead ends in our conflicts. We also feel bad feelings like shame, fear, anger, and disconnection. This is an opportunity to use the shame and the disconnection as intrinsic motivators to repair and reconnect. These ten roadblocks can be summed up in one word: Unwillingness. If you have an unwilling person it will show as any of the roadblocks and prevent you from getting to zero.

ACTION STEPS

1. Which of the ten roadblocks do you use the most? Own it. Journal about it.
2. Reflect on FRACKing and write down which letter you do the most. Journal about it.
3. Notice if any shame or guilt came up in this chapter. To help bust through any shame, share your answers above with at least one person.
4. Pick someone from the past with whom you've been in conflict (perhaps the person in your conflict box?). Own whichever roadblocks you did most with them. Then, ask them or wonder (if you are not speaking to them): "What was the impact on that person, given that I did this behavior with them?"

The Twelve Agreements
to Ease Conflict

If you do not address your childhood traumas, your romantic
relationships will.

— NEIL STRAUSS

BOTH PARTIES IN A CONFLICT OFTEN ARE UNDERRESOURCED
and stressed. One or both of you might claim it's too hard or
too much. If no one leads, you remain stuck and your issues go
nowhere. However, if you have an agreement that no matter how
bad it gets, you'll work as a team to figure it out, then there's always
a path forward.

Creating agreements is another tool to help avoid the common
pitfalls of conflict. If the context of your relationship is to grow and
work together as a powerful team, the agreements are the rules you
live by. Agreements help you rise above reactivity, return to what you
agreed on, and get to zero sooner rather than later. Ideally, and as
soon as possible, put some of these agreements in place in your high-
stakes relationships.

It's important to mention that not every relationship needs agreements. But the closer the relationship is and the higher the stakes,

the more essential agreements are. You might only need a few agreements with one to three people in your life.

For example, many couples choose to make a prenuptial agreement before they marry as a way to protect both parties' assets in the case of divorce. Divorced parents who co-parent often have clear agreements in writing about pickup and drop-off times, and other important boundaries. Co-parents do this to proactively minimize confusion and conflicts. Business partners often have lengthy legal agreements because without them in place a business partnership that becomes contentious can deteriorate fast.

I once facilitated two high-level entrepreneurs through a significant conflict because they forgot to add one important feature to their legal agreement. Because their agreements were not 100 percent clear, their conflict was full of emotional charge and challenge, and it put unnecessary stress on their relationship. But within two hours, using the tools in this book, they got through the conflict, got on the same page, clarified the language in their agreements, and became a stronger partnership as a result. The key to their conflict's resolution lay in their willingness to stay engaged and work through the conflict.

Depending on the relationship, the fact that you want to establish agreements might come out of left field. If you've been friends with someone for years and out of nowhere you decide to make new agreements for the relationship, don't expect your friend to jump onboard easily.

Relational leaders are willing to have the hard conversations that agreements sometimes require. A lot of people avoid agreements because they see a potential fight coming on that they don't want to deal with, worrying that they and the other person might not be on the same page. Don't let your fear of having this conversation be a good enough reason to avoid making agreements.

The process of talking about agreements itself can be a conflictual process. Agreements can't feel like rules, or else when they've been broken, people feel like they're in trouble. Think of agreements as guardrails that keep both of your scared animals in check. Under stress, guardrails actually help us feel safe just as knowing that we agreed to something ahead of time does. Under stress, the brain doesn't like ambiguity or things that feel unclear. Issues that are vague and open to interpretation and subjective bias all increase possibilities for threats and more conflict. When we both get emotional and reactive, with clear agreements in place we can relax back into the parameters that we agreed upon about conflict. So keep agreements short and simple. Read through the following agreements carefully, and think about which ones would be great for you and the other person. All of these agreements start with "I," but as you make agreements together, change the "I" to "we."

1. I AGREE TO MAKE CLEAR AGREEMENTS.

Making clear agreements prior to getting in a fight and even early on in your relationship allows for maximum connection and minimum pain/damage and disconnection. Here's an example of a clear agreement a couple made: "We agree to a weekly one-hour financial date to work through our money challenges. If we can't make progress after one month, we will hire outside help to support us in solving our money challenges as a team." Here's an example of an unclear agreement made by two high school friends who started a business together: "Let's call some people if we lose money." This ambiguous agreement is asking for conflict because it's so open to interpretation.

Think of agreements that will specifically assist you with conflict in your high-stakes relationships. For example, at work you might have an agreement that all team members will remain open to feedback and be coachable during team meetings. A couple in an open relationship, which can be rife with opportunities for hurt and misunderstanding, might require more specific agreements because there are more players involved: "If you want to sleep with someone else, we both agree that you'll tell me first so that I can veto it or we can discuss it." This type of agreement prevents a conflict from happening if all parties are on the same page about the agreement.

When making a clear agreement, make it so you both can understand it under stress. There's no interpreting. When an agreement no longer serves, change it together.

2. I AGREE TO GROW AND DEVELOP MYSELF.

As an emerging relational leader, put your student hat on and try stepping into a context in your relationships that is oriented toward growth and development. That way, when things get hard, you have one option—grow! Growth-oriented relationships can handle adversity, discomfort, differences, and conflict. Perhaps the only reason heavy metal band Metallica is still pumping out music decades after forming is because they are all open to growing and working through conflict.* Stanford researcher and author Carol Dweck has researched the growth mindset and her results are abundantly clear: people do better in life in just about every area if they adopt a growth mindset.[1]

Stop pretending you know how to listen well or talk effectively if you keep getting stuck in the same conflict patterns. You probably have something to learn that will help you and the other person get through the conflict. Every day I work with people who think they are great at listening and communicating. I ask them, "Why is it that you're having such a hard time with this person?" They often respond with blame and justify that they have a hard time only with this one difficult person. My reply is always the same: "Then this is where your speaking and listening skills matter most." Once they humble themselves and begin to take personal responsibility, they can start to

---

* Watch the amazing documentary *Some Kind of Monster* in which the band hires a psychotherapist to help them work through their challenges with each other!

learn and thus get different results. Everything in their relationships begins to change for the better. The reason this happens? They become students of conflict.

3. I AGREE TO LEARN HOW TO EMBRACE CONFLICT AS A NORMAL PART OF CLOSE RELATIONSHIPS.

In a close relationship, the goal isn't to not fight. That is a fantasy. You want to bring real stuff (your true self-expression) out in the open. By doing so, you may rock the boat and upset them. No problem. Your mindset must shift to thinking: *Conflict is a growth opportunity.* Conflict exposes the rift between our understanding of each other— which becomes an invitation to understand each other better. It also exposes the inner conflict, the rift between our True Self and our Strategic Self. When we say yes to conflict, we open the door to more truth-telling. On the other side of conflict is a deeper connection. You cannot and will not have a good, solid, lasting relationship without learning how to deal with the shit that comes up between you and the people you care most about. To me, this is choiceless. The crux of any exceptional relationship is always determined by how two people handle conflict.

4. I AGREE THAT THE MOST RESOURCED PERSON LEADS.

Decades of observations have shown me that whoever has the most emotional capacity to take ownership or to listen to the other person's point of view usually starts. I call this "the most resourced person." If you are the person who is most resourced in any given moment, you advocate for a conversation, a dialogue about what happened, and you seek reconnection. If you are feeling like the least resourced, just let the other person know. "I'm really in it over here. Can you lead this?" Or simply, "Can you start? I'm still struggling."

Rule of thumb: The most resourced person starts.

---

5. I AGREE TO EXAMINE WHAT DRIVES ME TO BLAME YOU.

Years ago, I went through a stage where I blamed my parents for my past hurts and my relationship difficulties. It was very hurtful to them, and it put unnecessary stress and strain on our relationship. I eventually had to work though my blame of them, heal some past hurts, and then our relationship improved. I became a relational leader in my relationship with my parents. Today we have a great relationship and I look forward to spending time with them.*

If you truly dig deep and get curious about what drives your blame, you'll start to see that you do very normal things, like projecting your parents onto your partner or projecting past hurts and traumas onto current people and situations. If you dare to grow, these become breadcrumbs on the path to becoming a stronger person, because if you learn how to work through some of your past charges and triggers, you stay in the front seat more often and learn to be more adept and agile during conflict. If you can't go beyond blame, you'll never reap the rewards on the other side of conflict.

6. I AGREE TO OWN MY PART.

We've already talked about one of the quickest ways to dissolve a conflict: own your part. Your ability to work though conflict is directly proportional to your ability to take personal responsibility within any conflict. Ownership keeps the power with you. You have

---

* Important to note that I worked through my stuff with my parents without changing them. They never went to therapy, they never owned anything, and they just remained true to who they are. Very inspiring. This helped me deal with my fantasies and expectations. More on this in Chapter 17.

the power to change your behaviors and actions, you have the power to listen and speak in a way that works for the other person, and you are reading and learning how to do conflict differently right now. Own that.

7. I AGREE TO BE VULNERABLE AS QUICKLY AS POSSIBLE.

Vulnerability is disarming. Try staying mad at someone who is crying. Try hurting someone when you are in your heart and feeling great. It's pretty hard, right? Although it might feel like the most counterintuitive thing to do, going into vulnerability will disarm a good partner or friend fast. Of course, many of us don't want to do this because we've had experiences when we were vulnerable and we got hurt. So, we remain on lockdown, blocking our hearts and tender feelings from the other person. Understandable, but if you want to work through things, staying behind your wall and lobbing grenades at the other person is going to keep you stuck.

Vulnerability doesn't have to look like tears; it can simply be more ownership. "Honey, I was a jerk." Or, "Friend, I see you hurting and I feel shame that I caused it." In my experience, the conflict will take a turn for the better when someone remembers to soften and move out of a fearful or defensive posture. Sooner or later one of you has to be vulnerable and feel something. "Honey, I feel hurt." "Friend, I feel scared." Then of course allow yourself to feel it, own it, share it. Be seen in your vulnerability, even though it can trigger your partner. Often it will soften them too.

8. I AGREE TO SPEAK WITH CARE AND RESPECT.

When we are our scared animal, we often speak from the back seat. Backseat drivers say and do stupid shit. So, make an agreement that no matter how intense it gets, you agree to demonstrate care and respect. If you truly care about the other person and you want to get to the other side of the challenge, you must communicate in a way that they can listen to and digest. Be a decent human being. No backstabbing, yelling, screaming, or speaking in a way that scares the other person. No sarcasm or making fun of each other either.* Stick to I statements.

It's important to remember a lot of our communication is non-verbal, so watch the eye rolling, arm crossing, sighing, and turning away from the other person. It's important to mention that no matter how skillful you are, the other person still might shut down or run away. Watch your fantasies that you can do it perfectly and not upset them. That's highly unlikely. Yet, you can mitigate some reactivity by behaving in a way that is safe for their scared animal. When you are not able to speak with care and respect (because sometimes you just can't), your job then is to clean up the mess that you helped create and work to repair and reconnect.

9. I AGREE TO STAY IN RELATIONSHIP.

Before working on myself, this would have been the hardest agreement for me to live up to. I have countless examples of cutting someone off and walking away or just not staying in the conflict. *Stay in relationship* means that you both stay with the conflict until you get to zero. This means you won't cut off the person or leave in complete silence with no return time. You can still take some time and space to gather yourself (hit the pause button) so you can think and speak clearly. But let the other person know when you will return. Always return to finish what you started until you both feel the issue is resolved.

---

* One of my teachers, Duey Freeman, taught me that sarcasm stops intimacy. I've digested that for years and it feels very true to me. Know the difference between sarcasm (words that can feel hurtful and bad leading to disconnection) and humor (words that can feel playful and funny leading to connection).

10. I AGREE NOT TO MAKE THREATS OF LEAVING.

In the heat of the moment, words come out of our mouths that we later regret. One of the worst things you can do in your long-term relationship is to make threats of leaving. In a marriage, mentioning the word *separation* or *divorce* in the heat of the moment is deeply damaging and can further embed fear and mistrust in your partnership. Threats tell the other person to stay vigilant and on guard because you might not be here tomorrow. That exacerbates insecurity in the relationship and invites more conflict. So, no more threats.

11. I AGREE NOT TO BRING UP BIG CONFLICTS OVER TEXT OR EMAIL.

A personal rule of mine for many years has been never to fight or argue over text or email. Face-to-face is always best. There are scientific reasons for this, but the bottom line is that a huge amount of information, such as voice tone and body language, gets left out when texting and emailing. Without these additional visible and auditory cues, people tend to read into things to fill in the gaps and go into negative memories.

How often have you received a text and misunderstood what the person was saying because you couldn't tell if they were upset or not? This agreement is very important if you want to navigate differences more efficiently. Here's some language you can use next time things get stirred up over email or text: "Hey, I appreciate what you're saying, *and* can we take this to an in-person conversation, please? Our relationship is too important for me to do this when I can't see your face or be with you." Sometimes we're forced to be apart, such as during COVID-19; however, even then we could do a Zoom or FaceTime call. "Hey, thanks for letting me know how you feel. I don't want to respond until we are on Zoom where I can see you. Can you talk tonight?" This is a great boundary and self-respect practice.

12. I AGREE TO LEARN HOW TO REPAIR
AND RECONNECT EFFECTIVELY.

When one of us distances or shuts down and times goes by, I understand it's my responsibility to repair whatever breach has occurred by owning my part, listening deeply, getting the other person's world, all in service of reconnecting. I understand that conflict is inevitable; therefore, I will learn how to clean up any mess we both participate in and get to a good place we both agree on. This is a good agreement to have for the rest of your life.

BROKEN AGREEMENTS

Despite our best efforts, most of us make and break agreements, intentionally and unintentionally. Think of how many agreements you broke as a kid—or as a parent. If they are broken once in a while, consider it an opportunity to repair and reconnect and use the tools outlined in this book to get there. However, consistent broken agreements means there's an underlying issue that is unaddressed. Often, the person breaking agreements is unconscious of these "sabotage-like" behaviors. When they take a closer look, they usually find one or more of the five types of conflicts occurring.

Natalia and Sammie were in a long-term partnership. Natalia continued to have energetic flirtatious exchanges with other women on Facebook. After Natalia and Sammie went in circles about the broken agreements and trust, they asked me to help. I helped both women see that Natalia had a huge resentment toward her wife because she did not want children. Now, in her late forties, with no children, Natalia was still angry at Sammie for not collaborating with her on starting a family. Rather than leave the relationship, though, Natalia chose to stay with Sammie but abandon her dream of having kids. She chose to stop fighting about it and "let it go." Bottom line?

Natalia didn't "let it go." She kept breaking agreements because she was hurt and angry and resenting Sammie.

Once these two courageous women got honest and looked underneath the surface-level fight, which was about breaking an agreement they had on flirting, they were able to get to the real resentment, work through it, and create a new agreement about dealing with resentments as soon as they arise. Natalia could finally do the work to truly let go of having children, and she did.

As you can see, agreements can play a vital role in your high-stakes relationships. You'll find that the parameters of your relationships are clearer and trustworthy as a result. More importantly, agreements help you deal with the regular conflicts that come over time.

ACTION STEPS

1. Think of which high-stakes relationship you want to add some agreements to. Pick three agreements from this chapter that stand out and commit to inviting the other person into this conversation. Allow yourself to be sculpted by the conversation and see if you can get a shared reality and at least one agreement.

2. Optional: If you've used agreements before, reflect on the agreements you had in place and what was hard about them, or why they worked or didn't work.

3. Share any of the above with a close friend and try not to hide. Remember, you want closer, more fulfilling relationships, right? If so, commit to sharing what you're learning about agreements.

How to Resolve Value Differences

You can have everything in life you want,
if you will just help other people get what they want.

—Zig Ziglar

MANY YEARS AGO, I WAS AN OUTDOOR EDUCATOR FOR THE Outward Bound School. As a lead instructor, I would take teens and young adults into the remote wilderness of Maine for fourteen- to twenty-four-day backpacking and canoeing trips. Each trip, I shared leadership with an assistant instructor so in case something happened to one of us, the other could take over. Sharing leadership was complicated when I had value and personality differences with someone.

One of the hardest trips was a twenty-day course I led with Danielle in late September. An unusual nor'easter hit us on day one, and a steady downpour pounded us for three straight days. Everything was soaked except for our sleeping bags. The creek we were supposed to canoe down was too shallow at some points, so we had to get out and walk our canoes for miles. But then, within twenty-four hours, this tiny creek rose six feet into a monster river. We would later hear that there was flooding all over Maine. The students were so wet and cold

that one of them became hypothermic and we almost had to evac-
uate him. As you can imagine, this rugged experience immediately
bonded the group. But not Danielle and me.

Danielle and I were like oil and water. My way of leading the
course and Danielle's were completely different. We were misaligned
about how to teach canoeing, how to pack a pack, how to cook food,
and how and when to teach the kids the necessary skills they needed
to be successful. During the trip, our relationship deteriorated. Not
because of the rain, flooding, and cold temperatures but because I
couldn't deal with my internal stress in relationship to Danielle. We
had a values clash and couldn't find common ground. In addition, I
didn't have the open-mindedness or skill that would have earned us a
collaborative experience.

My approach to remedy this? I did what I always did back then: I
tried to control the situation by trying to change her and getting her
to conform to my way of doing things. At a certain point, she relented.
I won, but it came at a price. Each day we had a few small conflicts
that would always end up with me getting my way. Not one conflict
did we successfully work through. Not one repair. By the end of the
twenty-day trip, we were barely speaking. Imagine twenty days in the
wilderness with someone you don't get along with! And guess what
we were teaching the kids in our course? How to be a team. Shit
sandwich anyone?

As discussed, one of the most common things people fight about
is our values because it feels like we are fighting for who we are. Some
people who have conflicts over values never get to zero because these
types of fights can be some of the toughest to resolve. We tend to
guard, hold close, and defend the values we cherish most. And when
other people threaten those values, we posture, collapse, seek, or
avoid, which creates more conflict. The reason value differences are
so hard is because, in conflict, the person's core sense of self can feel
attacked, disrespected, or not accepted.

We all know what it feels like when we don't feel accepted for who we are (core human split, remember?). It sucks. Value-difference conflicts poke at the core of our personhood, and over time these insults to our person force us to rebel or adapt into what, or who, others want us to be (Strategic Self). Then, we often make the classic relationship mistake that I made with Danielle—we genuinely believe that if the other person does things our way or is more like us, the conflicts will magically disappear and our relationship and our life will be better. Danielle did her best to avoid our conflicts and tried to appease me by keeping quiet (which pissed me off more). In trying to be who I wanted her to be, she had to abandon her values, and in doing so, she resented me. It turns out I resented her, too, because I was co-leading a course with someone who stopped standing up for herself. I didn't have this awareness at the time, I just knew I was irritated the entire trip and I blamed her for making me feel that way.

Standing for, and fighting for, your true values is essential for you to be fulfilled in your own life, and it is equally important in your high-stakes relationships. In these relationships, you also need to be flexible and learn how to work with other people's values that are different from yours, because everyone's values matter. This is why we Stand for Three. But back then, I stood firm in my values with Danielle, and I left no room for hers.

So, what are we supposed to do when it feels like we have to compromise our core values or beliefs? How do we get to zero if we are fundamentally two different people? How do we reach a resolution when we don't seem to share the same values? Getting to zero around your value differences requires a lot of maturity. Soon, like a skilled diplomat, you will be able to accept someone who is different from you, find alignment, celebrate your differences, and perhaps accomplish even more together. Or maybe you realize that your values are so misaligned that you must move on from that particular relationship. Either way, the question is always the same: "How can I be true to myself and my values, respect their values, and learn to collaborate with them so we both get what we want in the relationship?"

You and the person in your conflict box from Chapter 2 came into the world with different relational blueprints. Over time, each blueprint adopts values. When those values clash with another's, instead of gliding through the water like a team, your boats are constantly bumping up against one another. Not only are you experiencing outer conflicts and misalignment, but you also feel the tension and confusion of the inner conflicts and lose sight of where you really stand as boatmates.

Maybe you want to go north and they want to go west. Maybe you want to talk about your challenges with conflict, and they don't. Doh! One or both of you feel judged, criticized, neglected, or even attacked. How crazy is it to be out in the middle of the ocean, sharing resources, boats tied together, with no alignment on why you are there or where you are going? Yikes! It's always shocking to me that people get as far as they do without communicating about and working through their core value differences. For Danielle and me, it was only twenty painful days. In most of my relationships, it was months or years.

Paradoxically, it's the diversity of values that creates huge advantages if you learn how to collaborate with those differences.* If you don't, your relationship may polarize even more and the differences may become deal breakers. Think of winning teams. If everyone on a team was the same, you'd have conformity and a recipe for losing. Winners learn to accept differences, play to strengths, and find the path to collaboration even with difficult teammates.

Think of your favorite band, sports team, or the best long-term group experience you've had. Success was accomplished through the diversity of each person, not because of everyone's conformity. Then, think about the last time you asked someone to be like you.

---

* I didn't learn how to collaborate in a high-stakes relationship until I got married.

It might have been this week, especially if you're a parent. How did that work out?

It's important to respect people's values, even if you disagree with them. Why? Because they have the right to their values and because respecting differences helps you learn to love and accept other human beings as they are. Respecting their values doesn't mean you have to stay in a relationship with them. In fact, the opposite might happen—respecting their values while not trying to change them sets you free to leave.

To freshen your memory, here are the most common value differences as discussed in Chapter 13:

- Spiritual or religious beliefs
- Positions on culture, race, ethnicity, heritage, tradition
- Growth mindset versus fixed mindset
- Spending money versus saving it
- Drugs/alcohol versus sober living
- Politics and ideologies
  - Guns or no guns
  - Pro-life or pro-choice
  - Democrat or Republican

- Marriage or no long-term commitment
- Monogamy or open relationship
- Live in a city or in a small town, near ocean or mountains
- Kids or no kids
  - How to raise the kids
  - Parenting philosophy
  - Public or private school

So how do you get to alignment and resolve conflicts over value differences? Here are six steps to help you navigate these differences together.

SIX STEPS TO ALIGN YOUR VALUES

1. Know Yourself and Your Values

Conflict helps you find out where you stand because, under stress, your truth comes spilling out. Your relational blueprint and true self-expression make their way to the surface. If you avoid or deny them, you'll keep trying to be who they want you to be and stay in the same old patterns—and your conflicts will not resolve. Allow conflict to help you get clear on who you are and where you stand. This is why we welcome conflict, because it helps us locate and know ourselves. Use the compass exercise in Chapter 8 to identify your values and where they differ from the values of the person you're in conflict with.

2. Consider Their Values

When you look at your conflict box, ask yourself whether you know that person's highest values. Just take a guess based on their daily actions. The assumption here is that you've known this person for quite a while and that it's a high-stakes relationship. If that's true, you should know what makes them tick.

Draw their compass next to yours. Once you have a good enough rough draft of their compass, you should be able to see the problem clearly of where your values don't line up. They value money; you don't. Or they value having children; you don't. Or they value letting the dog sleep on the bed; you don't. You value talking about your problems and working through them; they value solitude and time away from you. You value health; they don't. You value being on time; they don't.

Next, if you know what drives or motivates them as their overall mindset or attitude, add that to the diagram as the "how" on the spine of their compass. Just guess if you don't know. If it's easier to draw the diagram like the one below, do that.

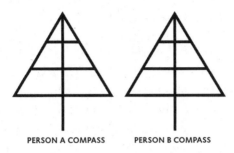

PERSON A COMPASS   **PERSON B COMPASS**

Diagram 16.1 Considering Their Values on Their Compass

3. Accept Your Value Differences as Fact

Although we all can change our values over time, that won't guarantee we'll ever have the same values as the person we're in conflict with. For example, co-parents might both value having a growth mindset but still be very misaligned around how they parent their children. No two people are the same and no two people have the same compass. Even if we have a lot of shared values, the nuances inside the values are different. The sooner you can accept that high-stakes relationships involve differences, the better.

4. Find Your Shared Values and Write Them Down

Next, draw two blank compass diagrams that overlap, each one representing the hierarchy of values for each person. The new triangle that emerges in the overlap is where you have common ground.* This overlap is where your values align, as shown in Diagram 16.2. In that shared compass, write down your shared values.

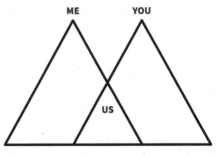

Diagram 16.2 Shared Compass

---

* It's like a Venn diagram but with pyramids!

258 – GETTING TO ZERO

This helps you see where you are different and where you are similar. You can evaluate your similarities and determine whether there's enough alignment to continue the relationship or not.[*] Having more shared values doesn't necessarily translate into a better relationship. That said, little to no alignment suggests a relationship on shaky ground with very little "glue" to bond you together. Low-stakes relationships can live without much common ground or alignment. High-stakes relationships cannot.

If you're in a high-stakes relationship with this person, there has to be some alignment, or you wouldn't be in relationship with them. Finding that alignment in your overlapping values is essential because it's one of the factors that holds you together during tough times. Shared values anchor you to a common vision, purpose, and direction.

For example, when two people go into business together, there must be strong alignment of values from the start because when the storms come, which they will, the shared compass helps hold their boats together. Same in a marriage, same on a team.

5. Find Alignment Together

This next step in the exercise is one you should do with the person you're trying to find alignment with. However, if you want to start answering these questions alone, know your answers are limited without the other person's input.

Draw the shared compass (Diagram 16.2) on a new sheet of paper and make it much bigger so there is room to answer the questions below. These questions are designed to help you determine how aligned you are:

---

[*] Do this exercise when you're connected to yourself. Why? If you are currently disconnected and stressed, the scared animal will be the one drawing this diagram, and the scared animal always paints a picture that has more differences than similarities, more negatives than positives.

1. WHY are we in this relationship?
2. WHAT are we creating? WHAT do we stand for?
3. WHERE are we going?
4. HOW are we going to get there?

These questions are geared to help you find alignment on the context, or purpose, of your relationship. Really dig in and engage with these questions. Doing a simple exercise like this, where you answer four questions together, can in itself create conflict and intense challenge for both of you. But that's no reason not to engage in this process. Remember, collaboration is inherently harder than doing things alone, so don't expect this to be easy. Partnerships and teams that don't have the courage to ask these types of questions are delegating responsibility for their future to the scared animal.

You'll notice that if you have a lot of alignment, you'll enjoy talking about these questions and creating your shared answer. Misalignment, on the other hand, might reveal beliefs or negative stories you haven't wanted to examine where things are challenging. Do this together. If your friend or partner passively participates in this exercise by simply agreeing with your answers, they are not doing the work and you're letting them off the hook. This will come back later to bite you both.

The bigger the differences, the more you'll have to negotiate alignment using the upcoming step 6. If you have trouble finding overlap and answering the questions above, you have two main options: (1) work for alignment by engaging in potentially hard, but liberating, conversations, or (2) work for alignment, but if the other person won't come to the negotiating table, *then* move on. It's impossible to work something out and align with someone who won't meet with you and practice this exercise. Don't waste your time.

Keep in mind that when conflict occurs in a high-stakes relationship, be sure to determine what the fight is about (Chapter 13). You can use these four questions to see whether it is a value differences conflict. If you find that you are indeed aligned, chances are the conflict is about something else.

6. See How Your Differences Serve the "Three"

Once you answer the four questions, you can examine your value differences together. If it's good for them and not for you, it won't be good *for us*. If it's good for you, but not for them, it won't be good *for us*. It has to be good for all three. You have to see how their values help *us*. They have to see how your values help *us*.

Connect the dots between your values and see how your differences are actually of service and benefit to each other and the shared compass. Imagine looping your boats together with more rope or twine to make the bond even stronger. Your differences have to be seen as valuable to each person's values and to the shared values of the relationship. Whatever you do, you have to see how a value, whether yours or theirs, serves both of you. If you can't see how it's good for you two, you won't be onboard or aligned.

Rhonda complained for years that Dave was not "doing the work" on their relationship. She tried everything to get him to go to therapy, read books, and listen to helpful podcasts. But Dave was Dave. He was a heady engineer and really liked his work. He was paid well and worked for a good firm that gave him a lot of freedoms. He had a relational blueprint that suggested that relationships weren't all that helpful because as a kid he was left on his own a lot. Dave grew up with parents who blamed and compartmentalized their problems and conflicts. Dave learned to work better alone.

Rhonda grew up in a family of alcoholics where the caregiving was inconsistent. When her mom was drinking, Rhonda felt anxious and alone. When her mom was sober, she was mostly there for Rhonda, and Rhonda got her four relational needs met. As a result of this attachment pattern with her mom, she was much more relationally focused than Dave. Naturally, when Dave was under stress, he would isolate (moving away). When Rhonda was under stress, she wanted connection with Dave (moving toward).

This couple had some alignment with two shared values in their relationship compass—kids and travel. But they had never answered the four questions of why, what, where, and how. Their relationship was okay as long as they were traveling with the kids, but they had no real direction, and as the kids grew, so did their frozenness around the four questions. For ten years, instead of either one of them engaging in conflict, Rhonda was doing her best to change Dave. She perceived that if Dave could feel his feelings more and talk openly about them, he would be even happier and she would get more affection and connection.

Although her forecast may have been true, her approach wasn't working. Dave felt continually criticized and judged and would shut down and retreat to the garage where he did his hobby of woodworking. Dave felt relief in the garage all by himself. Rhonda felt anxious and insecure when she was alone. Neither of them knew this as a classic attachment dynamic and a very normal struggle in long-term relationships.

By the time they reached out to me, Rhonda was ready to throw in the towel. First, I helped them understand that their attachment pattern (one person seeking, the other avoiding) was normal. Then I had both of them see how each other's values were going to help each of them get more of what they wanted. After that, I helped them learn to communicate *through* the other person's values. (See Diagram 16.3.)

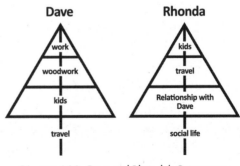

Diagram 16.3 Dave and Rhonda's Compasses

Rhonda wasn't convinced it would work but decided to give it a try. Within an hour, I helped Dave see that Rhonda's values of connection and intimacy with him and her social life could actually help him get a raise, be more focused at work, and expand his time in the garage. I helped Rhonda see that by letting Dave focus on work first and foremost, she would get more connection. How? Because then he wouldn't feel like he had to avoid her anymore. By feeling less of her anxiety and pressure, he has room to learn to communicate better with her. He finally saw that his avoidance in learning how to communicate better with his wife was actually creating more conflict, which bled into his time for himself. In other words, by learning some basic tools, he would actually get more time to do his woodworking. Then, because Dave would be less irritable, he'd be more approachable and available when Rhonda wanted connection. They were psyched.

Here's an exercise I asked Dave and Rhonda to do.*

1. Write down twenty ways the other person's number one value helps you live by your top value.
2. Write down twenty ways their number two value helps you with your top value.
3. Write down twenty ways their number three value helps you with your top value.
4. Bonus step: Write down twenty drawbacks of the other person having your exact same values.

In doing this simple exercise, you're "weaving" your boats together so they are stronger for when the storms come. You're also breaking down the fantasy that you "should" be with someone who holds the same values as you because "that would be easier." Remember, no matter who you join boats with, and no matter how similar your values are, there will be challenges.

---

* A modified exercise from Dr. John Demartini.

The next thing I had both Rhonda and Dave learn was how to communicate through the other person's values. For example, instead of Rhonda saying, "I want to feel more connected to you, Dave, because I need that to feel good," I had Rhonda rephrase as: "Dave, I want to help you focus more on work and get more time in your woodshop. I have a feeling that if we are in a better place and connected, it will help you feel stronger at work and more at ease in the woodshop. I also guess you'll become a better manager at work because you'll be able to handle a larger range of conflict. This could help your team get more done and, hell, you might even earn more money."

Instead of Dave telling Rhonda he needed space, I had Dave learn how to get his alone time by speaking through her values: "Hey, Rhonda, if I go on a walk with you and listen and share a little bit, will you support me in getting some focused time in my woodshop later today?"

Depending on your relational blueprint, you might need to speak through their values less. For example, someone who is overly focused on the other person all the time might need to share the impact of what the other person's behavior does to them. If you tend to not advocate for yourself, this is you. Time to share impact and use the speaking tools from Chapter 12.

DEFENDING YOUR VALUES

Know this: People defend their values because they don't feel understood or accepted with the values they have. Once they feel understood, they relax and are more receptive to your value differences. Too many relationships fail because inexperienced and inflexible people see their different values as incompatible or too different, concluding, "This will never work." In a case like this, the common approach is to stand for yourself and hope or expect the other person to stand for what you stand for. A partnership or a friendship isn't about holding steadfast to our own values, defending them tooth and nail, while neglecting the space between us called *our relationship*.

On the backpacking trip in Maine, had Danielle stood up for herself and fought for her values, it would have been better for her, but ultimately we would have still had a stalemate in aligning our values unless I was willing and flexible enough to include her values and soften out of my self-centered approach. If we both had Stood for Three and worked through our conflicts to find common ground, our relationship could have flourished, and the students might have witnessed a dynamic duo.

Negotiating any difference is about applying the listening tools first (LUFU—listening until the other person feels understood) and then the tools from Chapter 12 on speaking (SHORE—speaking honestly with ownership to repair empathetically). If you get stuck, always remember to speak in a way the other person can understand. The simple reminder is to speak *through* their values.

Collaboration makes you vulnerable. Sharing makes you vulnerable. Negotiating makes you vulnerable. Sharing resources makes you vulnerable. Loosening the grip around your values makes you vulnerable. It's much easier to do your own thing. Relationships are much more complex than going solo and require much more relational capacity. They demand that you become a bigger person. It is the combination of shared values and differences that makes relationships stronger, not one or the other. My differences with my wife are a total pain in my ass sometimes, but it's the very act of working through these differences that helps me, and her, grow to be better people, better partners, and better boatmates.

We all come with different life compasses, sometimes vastly different. The differences themselves are not the problem. It's our lack of understanding and inability to communicate with each other within these differences that create problems. When you don't get this, you'll loop in an endless cycle of asking your partner to be someone they're not, and they'll end up feeling judged, criticized, and unloved for who they really are. Which is another version of what happened to you growing up, right? Do you really want to ask your partner to be more their Strategic Self and fit into your box, or would it be more powerful to learn to embrace them as they are while cheering on their True Self? Isn't that what *you* ultimately want—relationships where you feel accepted as you are?

ACTION STEPS

1. Reflect on a value-difference fight. Knowing what you know now, write down what you could have done differently.
2. Do the six steps to value alignment outlined in this chapter. Ideally, do it with the person you have a value difference with. If they are not available, do it alone first. Then find a friend who will do the exercise with you. You have to learn how to do this. Practice in a lower-stakes relationship and see how it feels to see and connect around your different values.
3. Do what I had Dave and Rhonda do: bridge your value differences with twenty benefits and twenty drawbacks to each other, and practice speaking through the other person's values as you Stand for Three. Do this exercise with a partner.
4. Share actions 1–3 with your accountability partner (remember, this is a relationship book).

CHAPTER

17

If You Can't Get to Zero

The overwhelming need of the child to avoid pain and conflict
is responsible for the personality trait or coping style that later
predisposes the adult to disease.

—GABOR MATÉ

PULL UP A MENTAL IMAGE OF THE PERSON YOU LISTED IN YOUR
conflict box. See their name and check in to see how you feel in
relationship to their name. See their face. If you are not at zero with
this person, we have more work to do, right? The idea is that you
learn to choose to have friendships and relationships with people who
are a YES to working through conflict using the tools in this book (a
very important shared value). A great relationship or partnership is
one where both people upgrade and make choices that benefit both
people, not just one. If you want serious results in your relationships,
Standing for Three will become a guiding principle.

You are moving into the position of being a relational leader.
You understand how to move from being a victim to being an author. You also get that tomorrow, or next week, or next month, you
will fall down into the valley of victimhood again. But the difference now is that you know how to get back up. You know how to

repair conflict. You know how to get to zero. You are on the journey of empowerment, here, for yourself, your pain, your problems, your conflicts, and you're motivated to work through them. And, yes, you can still be a relational leader even when the other person doesn't show up.

WHAT IF THE OTHER PERSON WON'T WORK THROUGH THE CONFLICT WITH YOU?

If the other person won't meet you halfway to sort out a conflict, what then? This can be incredibly frustrating. Human beings can be tough nuts to crack. I don't know about you, but for me, the single biggest lever prompting me to change is pain. Pain is likely what brought you to this book. Your pain is guiding you to find a different outcome. But a resistant person who isn't interested in this book or collaborating with you to work through a conflict might not be in enough pain yet. As I told you previously, I was a resistant partner with every girl-friend I had prior to my wife. I had no outward interest in changing. It wasn't until my pain was great enough that I was ready to change.

Trying to Change Them to Get to Zero

Before we throw in the towel and write someone off who won't meet us halfway, let's try one last Hail Mary. It's worth trying a Hail Mary so you can be absolutely certain that the other person is not going to come to the table and work through conflict with you. If you are already certain the other person will not collaborate, feel free to skim this section and move to the section of this chapter titled "When the Person Won't Change."

Trying to change the other person is the most common tactic I see people use when they are trying to get to zero and work through difficult conversations. This "outside-in" approach is understandable. We all do it. How many times have you said the following to someone you are in conflict with: "This would be so much easier if you would only . . . "?

In general, asking someone to change their *values* or *who they are* is rarely a great idea, especially if they don't want to Stand for Three. It usually backfires. If they do change as a result of your consistent requests, the change won't stick because they are changing for you and not for themselves.

So, when is it okay to ask someone to change a *behavior?* It's always okay to ask, but be careful of your expectation that they will or that it even makes sense for them. Recall the SHORE speaking process from Chapter 12: speaking honestly with ownership to repair empathetically. Step 6 is making a request for behavior change. Your intent has to be that you see the proposed change as better for both of you, so you advocate for it. You invite the other person to learn and grow because you perceive that being better for the relationship, better for both of you, not just better for you or for them as individuals.

Before you throw a Hail Mary and ask for change—no matter which approach you try—here are a few important considerations:

Model change. Be the change. If you want someone to be into growth and development because you think it's awesome, just live that in an inspiring way, and they may follow or feel called to join you.

Work with your judgments. Are you coming from a place of superiority? Or are you coming from a place of neutrality with a desire to reach a win-win?

Understand requests. Most of the time a request for change leaves the other person feeling judged or criticized.

Check your resentments. Are you at the point where you resent them? If so, your request for change will be infused with that energy and vibe and thus is less likely to be met with open arms.

Keep an open heart. Come from an open heart and be willing to let go of the idea that the other person needs to be different.

Consider possibilities. Think through the real possibility that you might end up leaving the relationship and be alone or single. Really sit with this. Are you willing to lose everything to go after what you want?

Think about intent. Your intent has to be good for you, for them, and *for us*, and you need to be able to explain your intentions in a way that the other person can see the value in changing. If they can't see the value, and you can't communicate it well, it won't work.

In mutual relationships like friendships or partnerships, the power dynamics between people are equal, thus requests for behavior change are more complex. For example, if you and a friend have a conflict, it might be harder to navigate who's leading the conversation and what the boundaries, agreements, or expectations are. In a hierarchical work situation, on the other hand, it's much easier to ask someone you manage to change their behavior because your request is operating inside of a context that expects it. Either way, asking people to change can be difficult and often leads to more conflict.

Jessie and Patrick were together two years before Patrick asked Jessie to join him in his vegan lifestyle. He judged what she ate and thought his way of doing food was better. Jessie really liked Patrick and didn't have her own back, so she went along with it. For almost a year, she ate as he wanted her to. But any surface fight they had inevitably circled back to the food issue (underneath, this was a fight over values).

He really thought that if he changed her way of doing food, he would feel like he had a great partner and their relationship would be even more awesome. She really thought that if she did what he asked her to do, she would feel more connected and accepted and finally get the relationship she always wanted. But over time, their sex life diminished as her heart closed to him. Something wasn't working.

Initially, when she started the Getting to Zero process, she thought she and he just were not good at conflict, but she soon realized there was much more to the story—she was betraying herself to get love.

As Jessie learned about her inner conflict, conflict creep, values, and resentments, she started to stand up for herself. Naturally, this created more conflict and Patrick pinpointed her as the reason they were having so many challenges. He still really believed that if she conformed to his values, they would be so much better off. In his eyes, things had been going pretty well. He didn't realize the hidden resentment her going along with his lifestyle created.

Despite my best efforts to teach Jessie how to communicate with Patrick through his values, Patrick tightened his grip on his vegan lifestyle, which only served to drive the wedge deeper between them. As Jessie stood up for herself over and over, which did create conflict (remember choice C?), she began to resolve her inner conflict and the belief that she had to be someone she was not in order to feel loved and accepted. With my help, she eventually dumped Patrick.

This example is a bit extreme, but it happens all the time. Although Patrick had every right to ask Jessie to change, his approach was bound to backfire. Remember, we do get to ask the other person to change something, especially if it's a realistic, reasonable, and doable behavior change that might be better for the relationship.

Let's explore how to inspire people to change, notice the limitations of this approach, and also be willing to let some relationships go if the other person doesn't want to come along for the ride.

EXPECTATIONS

First, examine your expectations of the other person. What exactly are you expecting of them? Be honest and write it down like this:

I expect _____ [person's name] to _____ [behavior/action].

If you handed this person a slip of paper with this statement written on it, how would they react? Would they welcome it or get defensive? Earlier in the book, I covered how to clear a resentment by owning your expectation because much of the time expectations create resentments. Putting expectations on other people you care about is dicey ground. However, the fact is, we do have expectations of ourselves and other people. I expect my kids to do chores. I expect my wife to work on her emotional blocks, triggers, and issues. I expect my close friends to return my texts and voicemails. I expect my team to work hard and meet deadlines. And, of course, I have a long list of expectations for myself. Expectations are a part of human relationships.

But, if you're going down the road of having expectations, both parties must be open and clear about them. Make your expectations explicit. A few basic expectations are okay only when there is clear context and agreements around them. It is not okay to expect people to have a compass like yours and to live according to your values. Nor is it okay to ask people to change who they are or how they are fundamentally wired.

REASONABLE REQUESTS

As covered in the SHORE process in Chapter 12, you get to ask someone to change a little bit. Sure, they might shut down. But they might not. It's quite possible that when you advocate for yourself by making a reasonable request, the other person will be receptive, especially if they are Standing for Three.

A request for behavior change is most effective when you and the other person have a shared reality (agreement) that this behavior fits in the culture of your relationship. A request can be a great way to help that person be a better team player without requiring them to change to become who you want them to be. That's why we call our requests *reasonable*. Your request has to be reasonable in that it is doable and realistic.

Being in a partnership implies that you are open to reasonable requests because you're agreeing to the context that it's no longer all about you and whatever you want to do. It's a partnership, a friendship, or a collaborative work relationship. Remember how you tied your boats together? That was a choice; you did that. You chose to Stand for Three, not to travel alone, which implies you're willing to bend a bit, be flexible, grow, and adapt to how you travel together. But it's not enough to just assume this. High-stakes relationships really do have to explicitly create a context in which reasonable requests for behavior change are welcomed and agreed upon ahead of time.

Here's a short list of do's and don'ts when asking someone for a behavioral change. Remember, your request needs to honor the four relational needs—allow the other person to be safe, seen, soothed, and supported and challenged—and accommodate the difference between personhood and behavior.

DO'S: REASONABLE AND REALISTIC REQUESTS FOR BEHAVIOR CHANGE

MOST PEOPLE CAN ACCOMMODATE THESE TYPES OF REASONABLE requests for behavior changes:

- Helping out around the house (laundry, picking up, pulling their weight, etc.)
- Sharing the financial burden to get a business off the ground
- Getting outside help (coach, therapist, books) with relationship challenges
- Texting back within a reasonable time frame
- Staying in relationship to work through the conflict
- Showing up for practice and being a team player
- Putting the phone down when discussing important matters
- Maintaining eye contact during intimate, challenging, and serious conversations
- Using drugs/alcohol less around you

- Honoring your boundaries
- Respecting your "no"
- Being willing to create shared agreements, especially around conflict
- Meeting your four relational needs as you will meet theirs

DON'TS: LARGE REQUESTS FOR PERSONHOOD CHANGE

THE OTHER PERSON MIGHT VIEW THESE TYPES OF REQUESTS AS UN-reasonable, and unreasonable requests invite bigger conflicts:

- Living like you do or valuing what you value
- Getting in shape, losing weight, or gaining weight
- Contributing financially when it's unrealistic or impossible
- Being interested in growth and development
- Having children with you if it's not in their values
- Buying a house together
- Merging bank accounts
- Stopping their addiction
- Believing what you believe

There's no way around the fact that in the examples of unreasonable requests, you are asking someone to change something about themselves. Doable requests are most often behavior changes. Requests that are not doable are when you ask someone to change who they are. *Make all requests be about behavior, not personhood.* (Remember the section on personhood versus behavior in Chapter 12?) This is why a growth mindset is so vital to high-stakes relationships. A growth mindset means you're a student, and students are open to learning and changing, especially if it's better for the relationship (*for us*).

When you're not in the heat of the moment, make a list of reasonable requests. Any request has to be reasonable and doable; otherwise, it will fall flat and potentially backfire. Many years ago, when my wife and I had young children, I requested that my parents keep the TVs in their house turned off and not talk about violent or traumatic news around my kids. For years now, they have been amazing and respected my request, perhaps because they felt it was reasonable.

NONNEGOTIABLE NEEDS

When your requests fall short either because of how you approach asking for behavior change or because the other person just won't change, it's time to get clear on how much this requested change matters to you. If it's a very big deal, for example, if you're asking for monogamy because you cannot tolerate an open relationship, then your request is about something that isn't negotiable. I call anything that is not negotiable a *nonnegotiable need* because you "need" it in order to continue the friendship, partnership, or relationship.

In the context of conflict, we tend to have a hard time admitting we *need* something in order to feel safe again. Because our culture pathologizes needy people, we don't want to admit we need anything, even if we do. Just as a growing child needs a few things in order to feel safe, so do you. Remember, we are social mammals and for our nervous system to come out of a threat response, we *need* some things. Our scared animal operates in relationship.

The four relational needs to be safe, seen, soothed, and supported and challenged drive your safety, sense of security, and freedom to be yourself, express yourself, and explore your world. The four relational needs might be seen as optional in high-stakes relationships, but I think they are required if you want secure, strong, indestructible high-stakes relationships.

When you want to get to zero, ask yourself this question to determine your nonnegotiable need:

"What do I *need* in order to repair and reconnect during or after a conflict?"

Try plugging in the following relational needs and see if any are one of your nonnegotiables:

Safe: I need to feel physically and emotionally safe.

Seen: I need to experience the feeling of being accepted over time. I get that you will judge me and not accept me at times, but overall, you'll do the work to continue to accept me as I am.

Soothed: I need to feel soothed after an upset. I need you to repair with me so we can both feel good again

Supported and challenged to be myself: I need you to both support and challenge me to grow into who I am so I can continue to express myself and be me.

Are any of these statements true? Modify these needs so you can get behind them and stand up for yourself.

PUTTING INTO PRACTICE

As you're learning, start any communication in a high-stakes relationship by Standing for Three and considering the other person first. For instance, my wife might make this reasonable request of me: "Jayson, I know you're busy and want to get back to your project quickly, and you know I prefer a clean kitchen to cook in. Are you willing to take care of these dishes and put them in the dishwasher or wash them?" Later, she might add, "Are you willing to come up with a permanent solution that works for both of us? I think this will help me, you, and our relationship."

Really ask yourself: "Is my request reasonable, given who this person is?" Keep teasing out the differences between your expectations, requests, and nonnegotiable needs. My friend Roman requested that his business partner Smith attend relationship coaching with him to help them work through their value conflict in planning the company's direction. Smith understood they were stuck, and getting help made sense to him, so they went. It was a reasonable request.

When I coach couples, I encourage both people to keep their nonnegotiable needs very simple. Rather than a laundry list of expectations and "needs" that is overwhelming for most of us, I help them own the four relational needs because they are so foundational to strong relationships. And, yes, *how* you communicate your needs matters. Most needs can be boiled down to these four: feeling safe, seen, soothed, and supported and challenged. My wife and I have these needs in our marriage and if one of us was not able to meet them, we wouldn't be with each other. When I coach parents, I tell them they must be offering these needs to their children every day.

As always, know your friend's compass, their values. What do they care most about? If they don't see the value in how your request or need is going to help them get what they want, they won't do it.

WHEN THE PERSON WON'T CHANGE

Okay, so let's say the Hail Mary didn't work—you've made a reasonable request or stated your nonnegotiable need, and the other person is not willing to accommodate you. Then it's time to turn up the heat, move on, or work to resolve the conflict by yourself. Sometimes we choose to let someone go in our life; other times, they walk away from us.

Ending Relationships

Sometimes, we are not able to get to zero with someone, no matter how hard we try. Maybe a person has not learned the tools in this book, or maybe they have no interest in meeting us halfway. People come and go in our lives, and it's important to remember that it's okay to end relationships when you can't get to zero, no matter what the reason. However, if you do choose to end a relationship, be aware of this one thing that most psychologists, therapists, and coaches realize: whatever unfinished business or resentments you have with this person will likely follow you into the next relationship. All the more reason to work through things on your own, as explained later.

So, it might come to pass that you need to take a break from the relationship or end it. And sometimes, ending a relationship can feel harsh depending on how we do it.

Temporary breaks or "no contact" time periods can be so helpful. For example, sometimes when people break up, a period of no contact can really help them heal and move forward. It's all in *how* it's done. If you are going to take this route, show the other person respect by giving them context and a time frame:

> Hey, I know you want to stay in touch, but that's too painful for me right now. I'll probably be open to it down the road, but for now I need no contact. I ask that you respect this request and don't call or send me emails or texts. If you do reach out, I won't respond. I'm going to temporarily unfriend you on Facebook and other social channels as well. Not out of disrespect, but out of self-respect. Please understand that this is what I need to do right now. I'll send you an email three months from now. I wish you all the best. Thank you.

Sound harsh? Or caring? Notice your reactions to the boundary made in the statement. This is one of the most respectful and loving things you can say to another person because it's so clear and direct, providing the context around your nonnegotiable need stated as a reasonable request and setting a time frame. If you're used to taking care of people and not standing up for yourself, not valuing yourself, you'll think this type of boundary is harsh or mean. But look closer. Another possibility is that you are not yet ready to stand in your True Self and own what you need in your current conflict with another person.

For growth-oriented people, ending relationships and transitioning out of relationships are a part of life. Just watch children move from grade to grade, school to school. Kids show us all the time how to let go as you grow. If you are growing, you will outgrow friends and partners. If you are not growing, other people will outgrow you. It has nothing to do with you being better than them, or them being better than you. Whether relationships continue or end is governed by people's changing values and if we seek to align our core values and learn how to work through conflict. Sometimes our values are so different we drift apart, and that's okay, as relationships come and go.

How to Work Through the Conflict by Yourself

What if you're on the receiving end of a cutoff, sometimes known as an "estrangement," and still unhappy or hurt about it? Or the person in your conflict box is dead, gone, or won't come to the table? A relational cutoff is one of the most painful moves a person can make. Typically, we cut off a relationship when we feel like there's no other option.* Although it might not make sense to us, when someone cuts us out of their life on the basis of our values, if we really get to know the person, most of the time the move to end the relationship is understandable and makes sense given who they are, what they are going through, and what values they hold.

These situations can leave us feeling hopeless and powerless. I can appreciate how difficult it is when a person walks away, or dies, when there remains a huge unresolved conflict that was not dealt with. Although extremely difficult, these situations can also be opportunities.

---

* For further reading on relational cutoffs, I'd recommend Karl Pillemer's book *Fault Lines*, where he explores how excruciatingly stressful and painful cutoffs are and how to reconcile.

Many years ago, a close friend unleashed his rage on me and then abruptly cut me out of his life. I didn't know what to do. I just froze. Months went by with him not returning my calls, texts, or emails. I finally decided to let go of trying to reconnect, and for a couple of years I compartmentalized the whole situation. It was like I went through psychiatrist Elisabeth Kübler-Ross's famous stages of grief, passing through denial, anger, bargaining, depression, and acceptance.* Not only that, I enacted most of the Ten Roadblocks to Reconnection (as described in Chapter 14) to no avail. Nothing worked. When he randomly popped into my mind, I could feel my heart rate pick up.† I still was hurt, judging him, and wished the whole situation was different.

To get to acceptance (which is different from resignation; acceptance is explained more fully in the next section), I practiced a cognitive exercise I learned from Dr. John Demartini. I call John's method "The 180" because you force yourself to turn 180 degrees and look at a painful experience from another vantage point. Remember flipping the victim triangle into the author's triangle in the move from victim to author? Similarly, here we do a one-eighty and look at more possibilities with our student hat on. This is the same exercise I used in order to finally accept my parents as they are. I chose to see how my parents' way of doing things helped me become the person I am today. I would never have met my wife, nor would I be writing this book, had it not been for my parents' doing things exactly as they did them. I'm truly grateful. The 180 helps you "turn around" a painful situation or experience into an opportunity for healing, triumph, and empowerment.

---

* Some are critics of Kübler-Ross's stages, but I like them. They fit for my experience of relationship cutoffs, when another person won't work through a conflict between us.

† You know the feeling, right? Amazing how our scared animal can still feel activated and triggered in the present just by thinking of something that happened years or decades ago. That's a sign you're not at zero, folks.

With my friend, I started to see the benefits of his choice of cutting me out of his life and of me losing my friend. Then I examined the drawbacks to my fantasy of never losing him and maintaining our friendship. Trust me, I didn't like the exercise but nevertheless wrote out about fifty benefits and drawbacks. It took me a few weeks because it's hard to see things from another perspective sometimes. But as I made the list, things started opening up for me. I reached a place of genuine acceptance of the situation. Not resignation, but true acceptance. As my heart began to heal and lighten, I was able to see the ways in which I was a jerk to him at times and had behaved in ways that challenged his values and his way of living life. I could begin to empathize with his position and point of view. Not long after this, I called him up and owned my part in our relationship conflict. I let him know I didn't need anything from him and didn't need him to be any different. I just wanted to own my part of our dynamic. He thanked me, we had a great conversation, and we both moved on. I could have never done this unless I saw the benefits of the cutoff. Since that time, I've guided countless people through a similar process.

If you find yourself in blame and the other person will not come to the table or has cut you out of their life, you're left on your own to work this out alone. I know that can be traumatic, especially if it's family. But you can either sit in the valley of victimhood resigned to the fact that nothing can be done, or you can take ownership and claw your way to the top of the mountain as the author of your life. Can it be done? Most of the time, yes. Sure, in my experience, it's quicker to work through conflict with another willing person. But that's not always how life goes. We won't always have a collaborative Getting to Zero buddy. So it's important to learn the basic steps to work through your conflict with someone in their absence. Otherwise, you might stay stuck for years, hoping for a different outcome.

ACCEPTANCE

Once we accept that the other person won't ever come to the table and won't change, the only thing we can do is take resolution and healing into our own hands. Your healing, then, is completely and entirely up to you. This can be a difficult process, but it's a very empowering move. If we take the view that no one can pull us out of the valley of victimhood but ourselves, then there is only one choice—take full responsibility for our situation. We must climb, claw, or hike our way out of this conflict without this person helping us. But how?

What's Done Is Done

First, you must recognize the truth that whatever conflict happened, happened. It's done and it cannot be undone. It's complete. So, it's not a great use of your time or energy to ruminate on what should have happened. I call that *fantasy*, magical thinking that we could travel back in time and do something different. Such fantasies create more suffering for ourselves.

After accepting the fact that this person will not change, I take the view that there must be an upside. In fact, I take the view that every painful experience in life has an upside. Of course, the vast majority of the time I initially focus and get stuck on the downside. But what if there is always some kind of upside? What if there is something good or helpful that rises out of the carnage of a failed relationship? What if you're actually better off in life without them? What if the pain they caused you helped you get strong enough to leave an unhealthy relationship? What if them hurting you was the event that finally got you to take responsibility and hire a therapist or coach to get more help, to learn, to grow?

For example, all of my painful and hurtful relationship challenges growing up led me to my mission of helping the world do relationships better. I want to create a world where kids are raised in relationally sensitive and attuned ways by parents, teachers, and coaches who understand the concepts I'm writing about in this book. I want to arm the future generation with knowledge and tools to bully less, love more, and work through conflict successfully. There is no way in hell I would be doing what I'm doing now if it were not for all those failed relationships and the pain and challenges I faced in my childhood. Take a peek at your own childhood. Or just look at the very reason you're reading this book. You're likely reading this because of some relationship pain, right? So, is it fair to say that past relationship pain is helping you become a student of relationships? Isn't that a good thing in your life? Can you see how you might actually be empowering yourself as a result of past pain and a feeling of disempowerment?

We can't change the past, but we most definitely can change how we see the past. What matters is how you see it now, today. Focus on this question: "Given that's what happened in the past, what can I do to work through my pain, resentment, or trigger without any help from the other person?" Or, "Given that's what happened, how can I get to zero on my own today?"

Take the Steering Wheel

This attitude of empowerment helps me jump in the front seat, grab the steering wheel, put my student hat on, and take the healing and growth into my own hands. This approach is nothing I came up with. Countless victims of violence, oppression, and conflict have risen up throughout history to guide us in how to do this. When we lose our way, we can look to inspiring notable figures, such as Harriet Tubman, who escaped a hostile and violent environment as a slave, then went on to help hundreds of other slaves reach freedom through the Underground Railroad. And Malala Yousafzai, who fights for education for women and girls in Pakistan (where they were often banned from attending school) and who overcame being shot in the head by terrorists who wanted to stop her mission. And Misty Copeland, who rose above many challenges in her childhood to become the first African American principal dancer in the American Ballet Theatre's seventy-five-year history.

Even if you feel powerless to "fight" your situation, I recommend fighting to maintain your internal sense of dignity and respect, which won't involve the other person at this point. Get anchored in what you're fighting for. Maybe it's your own sanity, or your own voice. What is your bigger reason to work through this pain when the other person won't come to the table? Do you really want to continue to waste your breath trying to change them or wishing and hoping it was different?

What is your call to action here? What will you do to ensure your freedom from the prison of blame and the fantasy that they should be different? I'm offering you one powerful exercise taught to me by one of my mentors: The 180. Here are some additional questions to get you started.

Benefits of the conflict or the unresolved conflict—what are the lessons?

- What are five things this conflict has taught you?
- What are five capacities that you developed or are learning to develop?
- Name five strengths that came online as a result of this person and the conflict with them.
- Name five positive things you did with your time/energy/money as a result of the conflict.
- Name three people you sought support from while the other person was challenging you. How have those three people shaped your life for the better?

- Name three ways this conflict shaped your purpose or direction in life.
- What superpower(s) emerged as a result of this conflict?

Drawbacks to the fantasy of imagining your relationship would still be great if the conflict never happened:

- What would you have missed out on learning if this conflict or cutoff never happened?
- What capacities would you not have developed?
- What strength would you have missed out on increasing?
- Where would you have spent time/energy/money instead?
- Who would you have not met or deepened your relationship with if this event never happened?
- How would your career, vocation, or purpose have been impacted had the conflict or cutoff never happened?
- What superpower would you have been missed or not developed?

Your job is to make meaning out of the pain. Keep looking for what this relationship ending is trying to teach you or how it's helping you grow. Notice whether you feel defensive reading these types of questions. Notice whether you say things like "there are no benefits." When I struggle with myself, other people, or a life event, I run these types of questions. They help me get back on my feet and move forward because I don't like staying stuck in the valley of victimhood. These questions help me move up and out.

Hire Outside Help

I have facilitated countless couples, family members, and business owners moving through the Getting to Zero process. And I've been a part of many clearing conversations that other people facilitated.

In fact, a turning point in my relationship with my wife was when we had a few sessions with a skilled couples therapist. Meeting with an outsider who can take a more objective view of your conflict can really help move things forward. Ideally, you want to hire someone trained who can actually help you get to zero. But be aware of the water under the bridge. If you have semisuccessfully avoided your issues for years, don't expect any practitioner or facilitator to work magic. If you have a lot of unspoken and unresolved resentments and conflicts, it's going to take a while to get to zero. In addition, no therapist, coach, or facilitator can help an unwilling person. Willingness of all parties is required.

Wherever you are hurting in your relationship life becomes the path to freedom. Whenever you are stuck in a conflict, a breakthrough is on the other side, waiting for you. Your painful, hurt, trapped place is the exact location of your growth opportunity. In fact, the way to get over anything is right through the center of it.

ACTION STEPS

1. Are you actively trying to change someone? Perhaps the person in your conflict box? If so, own that's what you're doing. Be transparent. Find a new way to communicate by rereading Chapters 13 and 14, then move on to action step 2.
2. Reasonable requests (wants) versus needs: What is your request of the other person? Be sure it's reasonable. If it's a requirement, a nonnegotiable, a deal breaker, make it a need and own it as such. But don't bother stepping into a nonnegotiable need unless you're willing to lose the relationship completely if the other person cannot supply it.
3. Reflect on the four relational needs (safe, seen, soothed, and supported and challenged) in relationship to conflict. Do you

need any of these four? How does it feel to own that? Are you up for standing in these needs and offering them in a way that works for the other person?

4. Write down one big insight you gained from this chapter. Share it with a close friend and try not to hide. Do this within the next twenty-four hours.

Conclusion

It might not surprise you to hear (or be reminded) that of
all the factors in human life that predict the best positive
outcomes, supportive relationships are number one.
—Dr. Dan Siegel

B Y NOW, YOU'VE LEARNED THAT CONFLICT ISN'T THE PROBLEM.
You now know that you must return and reconnect, over and
over, as if your well-being depended on it because, well, it does. The
messiness and uncertainty of conflict will unearth your essence. They
certainly have mine. And though it's uncomfortable, this is good
news because it means we can integrate our Strategic Self into our
True Self. In addition, conflict invites us, encourages us, and pushes
us to be as we are (truthfully self-expressed), and find out if we can
also have great high-stakes relationships at the same time. If we value
good relationships, surrender to the fact that the Conflict Repair
Cycle is a part of life, and practice it for the rest of our lives with
presence, respect, and kindness, we will earn our way into powerful,
secure, and fulfilling high-stakes relationships.

When my wife and I had our first major conflict, I had already
opened up to her more than I ever had to anyone. But soon after, I
shut down. She didn't understand, nor did I. But my shutdown felt

very familiar, like a warm blanket I had been hiding under for years. I didn't like it, but it was familiar. I could feel the tug to stay under the covers and run away again. It seemed easier somehow. But as I thought about it, I didn't want to go backward. I wanted to shed the blanket and risk the uncertainty of having no shelter. I decided to "stay in relationship" with her and not run, even if I had no idea what was going on with me or what to do next.

Within a few hours, we met back up and began what was an entirely new process for me. That day, I chose to stay. I chose to work it out. I chose to return and reconnect, even though I was scared and had no clue what I was doing. That day, with wobbly legs, I chose a new pathway, and in doing so, I chose a new frontier, and a new me. And what did it get me? An amazing partnership where together we learned how to work through conflict and be true to ourselves at the same time. Our relationship eventually became a refuge, a launching pad, a home.

Throughout this book, you've been learning to become a relational leader. If you recall, there are four steps to this process:

1. Admit you're stuck and need help.
2. Take personal responsibility for the outcome you want.
3. Learn, grow, develop.
4. Embrace and engage in conflict.

If you've made it this far and you've done the action steps at the end of each chapter, you're on your way not only to being a relational leader but also to extremely fulfilling high-stakes relationships, where you get to be true to yourself and get what you want at the same time.

By reading this book, you have gone off trail and ventured into new territory. Although it might seem scary and unfamiliar, keep going, keep exploring. The breadcrumbs are here for you to follow. I've guided you to the edge of the ocean and now you must launch your boat and venture forth to the kind of relationships you might not have experienced before—better ones that are full of truth, depth, and meaning. Relationships that are good at the Conflict Repair Cycle. Your boat is full of gear now. Your scared animal is at your side, and you have the skills and ability to manage it. You know how to move from victim to author. You can Stand for Three. You choose to be honest, even if it rocks the boat.

You have my support (and challenge) in the pages of this book. You are an emerging relational leader. As you look to the horizon, know that a storm is brewing in the not too distant future. But fret not. You're just the person to meet it. I'm excited for what awaits you on the other side. You've got this.

FINAL ACTION STEP ————————————————

Check in. Feel this moment. Be right here now. Seriously, take a few deep breaths before you read the next sentence. Notice what it feels like to be more empowered around conflict. Take that in. Describe what you notice out loud in a word or perhaps a sentence: "I feel _____." As always, share this with a friend.

Acknowledgments

EVER SINCE THAT intense breakup in the Whole Foods parking lot, my life has taken a turn for the better. That day I chose to become a student of relationships meant that every day after that I'd be learning from people about how to improve my life, specifically my relationship life. For years, and to this day, I have been in student mode. I learn best by teaching other people what I'm learning, thus I'm a teacher also. I like to synthesize what I'm learning by creating consilient maps and models of how to do relationships better. I do that by standing on the shoulders of giants and learning from mentors. Below are the people I want to acknowledge, who helped me learn and who had a slice of impact that led to the creation of this book.

First and foremost, I want to thank my incredible wife, Ellen Boeder, for being such an amazing human, friend, lover, wife, and co-parent. This book, and all the tools, concepts, and practices, would not have been possible without our relationship and the countless hours we spent nerding out on attachment science, trauma, parenting, relationship psychology, and human behavior. I am also in awe of how you love our children with such reverence and ferocity. Your holding and care for them allow me to serve others at deeper levels, including by getting the time and space to write this book. Thank you for proofreading every page out loud with me and providing critical feedback early on about the tone, direction, and examples. I couldn't have done it without you. Hard to express how grateful I am for you. I love you.

I want to thank my son, Lucian, for his inspiring and ferocious zest for life. And, when you came into the world, you oriented me and made my purpose crystal clear.

I want to thank my daughter, Neva, for her elegant stillness, sensitivity, and big humor. Like water, you've helped me soften around the edges.

Next, I want to thank my parents for raising me just the way they did. You did a marvelous job and gave me an endless amount of support (and challenge) to find my way in life. You provided me with plenty of resources so that I could make the journey and find myself. When things got hard between us, you could have easily cut me off and stopped talking to me. Instead, you loved me, and stayed. From the bottom of my heart, thank you.

I want to thank my sister, Terese, for remembering my childhood when I couldn't, including that time our brother Greg and I were so mean with the slingshots inside the house. And to my brother, Greg, who might just be as happy as I am out in nature. I love you both.

Thanks to my first agent, Nena Madonia Oshman, for all the massive legwork you did coaching me, encouraging me, and initiating me into the book-writing process. I was so pissed at your first round of feedback, yet it was spot-on. Thanks for getting me connected to Lauren Marino and Hachette. Thanks for the handoff to Jan Miller. And to my current agent, Jan, I appreciate your tremendous experience in the space and how you believed in me right from the start.

Thank you to my editor, Lauren Marino. You welcomed me into Hachette with open arms and challenged me to get even more clear and learn how to structure my concepts more effectively. Your constructive feedback made this book much stronger. Thank you for that push. I'm a better writer because of it. Thanks to the entire Hachette team, including Michael Barrs and my publicist Lauren Rosenthal.

Thanks to my editors! Jen, for helping me get my proposal in good shape. Thank you to Andrea Vinely, who helped me edit the first draft of the manuscript. You are awesome, in particular about teaching me stuff about grammar that I never learned! And thanks to Betsy Thorpe for editing the second draft of the manuscript and all the back-and-forths during a critical time. You challenged me to restructure things and helped me to get even more plain in my language. Big props.

Casey Stanton, for doing the reach-out webinar with Harville Hendricks and Helen Hunt. Through that, I met a marketer, Rob, who introduced me to my agent Nena. That intro helped me get here. Thanks, man. Wild how that happened.

To my friends. I want to thank my close friends Keith Kurlander, Will Van Derveer, and Reuvain Bacal, for your commitment to track my shadow and for loving me the past eighteen or so years through the highest and darkest moments of my life. It's an honor to be a brother with you cats.

To my friend Lisa Dion, who helped me dissolve some of my biggest emotional charges with people who annoy the shit out of me and for being my pal on the spiritual journey of life.

To Rick Snyder, who gave me some great pointers along the way through the book-writing process and for your friendship on the growth path.

Thanks to Krista Van Derveer for introducing me to Lloyd Fickett and his work!

To Kelly Notarus. Your guidance, advice, humor, and experience were pivotal in helping me navigate the book-publishing process. You rock.

Thank you, Tami Simon, for your wisdom and time early on in this process.

I want to thank my core team at The Relationship School®: Rebecca, Ashley, Jennifer, Ana, Vicki, Brendan. These folks have stood by me with the ups and downs of my personality, my irritation, my neuroses. Y'all are awesome. And to Ana Novaro and Martin, for helping me with some of the diagrams and details of putting the book together. Thank you.

Thank you, Relationship School students and coaches, who continue to invest time, money, and energy in the most in-depth and comprehensive relationship training in the world that I created called the Deep Psychology of Intimate Relationships (DPIR) and the Relationship Coach Training Program (RCT). So many webinars, videos, Zoom calls, and debriefs. Whew. You're all helping me sharpen my teaching, and every one of you made a contribution to this book. Respect.

Thank you to all of my clients who have allowed me into the most intimate aspect of their lives. From you being willing to face and get help with the conflicts in your life, I was able to learn and refine more effective ways to help you and other people work through their differences. Your willingness to face your own challenges is helping those who read this book. Just by asking for help and being willing to learn, you're helping hundreds of thousands of people.

I also want to thank all my podcast guests and social media followers and fans for your dopamine-filled likes, shares, and comments. And to The Relationship School Facebook group: Y'all are amazing how engaged you are. Damn. All of you social media peeps gave me bits and pieces that helped me strengthen the Getting to Zero model and method.

To Naropa University, where I studied psychology. What a special place to finally go inward and deal with myself. To all my TCP classmates and unconventional and talented teachers there, thank you.

I want to thank Jane Bryant and Chuck Litman at the Boulder Mental Health Center for giving me the hands-on experience with mental illness that I was lacking in my graduate program. I learned firsthand about mania, depression, schizophrenia, and countless other mental illness challenges people face every day.

Thank you to my early Gestalt teachers, including Duane Mullner, Duey Freeman, Victoria Story. You three took my learning to the next level with the pillows and chairs and tears and laughs we had at GIR. And my other psychology teachers, specifically Bruce Tift, for challenging my fantasy that if I found the right person, I could be pain and conflict free. And for reminding me that I'll experience conflict, however disturbing, for the rest of my life.

Thanks also to Dave Ventimiglia, who was boss at a wilderness therapy program for troubled teens and who taught me more directly how to work with conflict inside of a family system. And to Patrick Logan at Second Nature, for helping me get better at working with disgruntled teenage boys.

I want to thank my main meditation teacher, Reggie Ray, for teaching me how to be with my experience, especially the most disturbing and painful parts of it. Thank you for gifting me with a skill I will have for the rest of my life—how to come home to my own body and heart and to always remember that deep inside my experience there's fundamentally no problem. Just by watching you, you also taught me how to teach to multiple levels of development. I have deep gratitude for what you showed me about myself and my fellow human travelers.

Thanks to my trauma mentors Julie Green, Pat Ogden, Kekuni Minton, and Peter Levine. I've learned loads from all of you about how to work with trauma effectively. Thank you.

Shout-out to my first Gestalt therapist, Dawn Larsen. Thanks for helping me crack the code to my heart and my emotional world. You had a major impact on me, especially with that experiment where I was under a blanket reaching for you. Those three years of therapy helped me uncork a lifetime of locked-up emotions, pain, and joy. Thank you.

Big thanks to David Cates, who helped me navigate my midlife crisis and trust my body at a deeper level. Shit. You held me when I couldn't. You taught me how to trust the current of life at a much deeper level.

In the past several years, I've taken a keen interest in science and the more nuanced layers of relationships, including interpersonal neurobiology, the brain, and our complex nervous systems.

Thanks, Dr. Dan Siegel, for your time and being such a trailblazer around attachment science and helping me see that our brain is relational and how we develop is a relational process.

Thanks, Stephen Porges, for your time and helping me understand my social engagement system, how I operate under threat, and how the vagus nerve works.

To Bonnie Badenoch, for helping me grok trauma and the brain at a deeper level. Your mentorship helped me begin to understand the brain and trauma.

To Gabor Maté, for your kindness, for replying to my emails, and for teaching me about our core need to survive and thrive. Your frames on attachment, relationships, and addiction have changed my life. By courageously challenging the limitations of Western medicine, you have modeled how to be a better leader. Thank you.

To Dr. John Demartini, for shattering what I thought was possible with psychology. John, you gave me a clear, science-based solution for resolving resentments, without the other person being involved. You're the first person to integrate science, quantum physics, and spirituality in a way I could understand, which made the Universe so much more magical and inspiring. I'm immensely grateful for the body of work you have put into the world and I am still learning from it every day.

To Stan Tatkin, for providing the science to validate my sensitivity in partnership and, more importantly, what to do about it. You also taught me that resolving conflict together is more efficient than resolving conflict alone. Oh, and for years, you taught my wife ways of being that have strengthened our marriage so much. Dude, thanks. You've helped our relationship a ton!

Finally, I want to appreciate the countless challenging interactions I've had my entire life. The unresolved conflicts, the traumas, and even the haters. The pain from each of those interactions helped fuel this book.

More Resources

I<small>F YOU WANT</small> to explore more tools and access downloadable PDFs, sample conversations, guided meditations, and if you want to find a practice partner, go to: http://gettingtozerobook.com. Here is a preview of the Getting to Zero website so you can continue to get to zero.

GETTING TO ZERO CHECKLIST

Because you'll forget some of the Getting to Zero process when you're in the back seat, I created a short checklist you can tape to your fridge to help you remember what to do first, second, third, and so forth.

> **Triggered?** Try this short process by downloading the one-pager here: Stop, Drop, Feel, Deal, & Get Real. In addition, **get very good at being with your experience**. Download the free NESTR meditation in which I guide you through a triggering moment (one for each of the Four Disconnectors). When you don't know how to "be with" your triggers, Getting to Zero is harder.

If no one helped you feel your emotions as a kid, it's time to learn how. Sometimes, when you're hurt by another person's behavior, it can trigger what feels like a younger part of you. **Download the Hurt Kid meditation** to explore this part of yourself.

Commit to becoming a better listener, especially under stress. Download the LUFU cheat sheet and sample conversation. If you really apply yourself, this skill alone will change your relationships for life.

Commit to being a better speaker. Download the SHORE cheat sheet and sample conversation. The SHORE process increases your chances of being understood.

Need hands-on help with Getting to Zero? Hire a Getting to Zero relationship coach, who is well versed in the material presented in this book and who knows how to get to zero. We have coaches all over the world.

Feeling alone and want more community? Join with others who might be reading this book in my Free practice community.

Like audio learning? If you didn't purchase the audiobook, do that, and subscribe to my podcast *The Relationship School,* which is available on all the major podcast platforms. We have hundreds of episodes on all things relational and countless episodes on conflict.

Bonus book club. Want to study and practice with other readers? See if the book club is still available and join our free Facebook group.

Social handles for daily bites of relationship support:
Instagram, TikTok, Clubhouse: @jaysongaddis
Twitter: @jaygaddis
Facebook: /jaysongaddisfanpage

Does your organization want to hire me as a speaker or facilitator of the Getting to Zero process? I can work with you, you and the other person, or your organization privately. Just apply.

All of these resources can be found at
http://gettingtozerobook.com.

References

CHAPTER 1: MY LIFE OF CONFLICT

1. George E. Vaillant, Charles C. McArthur, and Arlie Bock, "Grant Study of Adult Development, 1938–2000," Murray Research Archive Dataverse, Harvard University, 2010, https://doi.org/10.7910/DVN/48WRX9.

2. Robert J. Waldinger and Marc S. Schulz, "What's Love Got to Do with It?: Social Functioning, Perceived Health, and Daily Happiness in Married Octogenarians," *Psychology and Aging* 25, no. 2 (2010): 422–431.

3. Julianne Holt-Lunstad, Timothy B. Smith, Mark Baker, Tyler Harris, and David Stephenson, "Loneliness and Social Isolation as Risk Factors for Mortality: A Meta-Analytic Review," *Perspectives on Psychological Science* 10, no. 2 (2015): 227–237.

CHAPTER 3: HOW MOST PEOPLE DO CONFLICT

1. "Triangles," Bowen Center, https://www.thebowencenter.org/triangles?rq=triangles.

CHAPTER 4: HOW TO BECOME A RELATIONAL LEADER

1. Daniel J. Siegel, *The Developing Mind: Toward a Neurobiology of Interpersonal Experience*, 2nd ed. (New York: Guilford Press, 2012), 4.
2. Siegel, *The Developing Mind*, 24.
3. Siegel, *The Developing Mind*, 23.
4. Nelson Mandela, *Long Walk to Freedom: The Autobiography of Nelson Mandela* (Boston: Little, Brown, 1994).
5. Mandela, *Long Walk to Freedom*, 329.
6. Mandela, *Long Walk to Freedom*, 296.

CHAPTER 5: YOUR RELATIONAL BLUEPRINT

1. Daniel J. Siegel and Tina Payne Bryson, *The Power of Showing Up: How Parental Presence Shapes Who Our Kids Become and How Their Brains Get Wired* (New York: Ballantine Books, 2020).
2. Daniel J. Siegel, *Brainstorm: The Power and Purpose of the Teenage Brain* (New York: Tarcher/Penguin, 2015), 142, 145.
3. Siegel and Bryson, *The Power of Showing Up*, 5.
4. Siegel, *Brainstorm*, 142.
5. Ed Tronick and Claudia M. Gold, *The Power of Discord: Why the Ups and Downs of Relationships Are the Secret to Building Intimacy, Resilience, and Trust* (New York: Little, Brown Spark, 2020).
6. Rick Hanson, "3 Steps to Become More Resilient Before, During and After a Fight, with Dr. Rick Hanson—SC 67." *Relationship School Podcast*, August 31, 2016. https://relationshipschool.com/podcast/3-steps-to-become-more-resilient-before-during-after-a-fight-with-rick-hanson-sc-67/.
7. Dan Siegel, "The Verdict Is In: The Case for Attachment Theory," *Psychotherapy Networker*, March/April 2011, https://www.psychotherapynetworker.org/magazine/article/343/the-verdict-is-in.

CHAPTER 6: YOUR SCARED ANIMAL

1. Nadine Burke Harris, *The Deepest Well: Healing the Long-Term Effects of Childhood Adversity* (New York: First Mariner Books, 2018), 74.
2. Robert M. Sapolsky, *Behave: The Biology of Humans at Our Best and Worst* (New York: Penguin Press, 2017), 45.
3. Jayson Gaddis, "3 Steps to Become More Resilient Before, During and After a Fight, with Dr. Rick Hanson—SC 67," *Relationship School Podcast*, August 31, 2016. https://relationshipschool.com/podcast/3-steps-to-become-more-resilient-before-during-after-a-fight-with-rick-hanson-sc-67/.
4. Harris, *The Deepest Well*.
5. Gabor Maté, *When the Body Says No: The Cost of Hidden Stress* (Toronto: Alfred A. Knopf Canada, 2003), 183–184.
6. Jayson Gaddis, "Money, Powerful Questions, and 8 Dates to Have with Your Partner—TRS 229," *Relationship School Podcast*, March 11, 2019. https://relationshipschool.com/podcast/money-powerful-questions-8-dates-to-have-with-your-partner-julie-john-gottman-smart-couple-podcast-229/.
7. Greta Hysi, "Conflict Resolution Styles and Health Outcomes in Married Couples: A Systematic Literature Review," paper presented at the 3nd International Conference on Research and Education, "Challenges Toward the Future" (ICRAE2015), October 23–24, 2015, University of Shkodra "Luigj Gurakuqi," Shkodra, Albania.

CHAPTER 9: HOW TO BE WITH YOUR TRIGGERS DURING CONFLICT

1. Daniel J. Siegel and Tina Payne Bryson, *The Power of Showing Up: How Parental Presence Shapes Who Our Kids Become and How Their Brains Get Wired* (New York: Ballantine Books, 2020).

CHAPTER 11: HOW TO LISTEN DURING AND AFTER CONFLICT

1. Byron Katie, with Stephen Mitchell, *Loving What Is: Four Questions That Can Change Your Life* (New York: Harmony Books, 2002).

2. Jayson Gaddis, "Healing Trauma, with Peter Levine—TRS 328," *Relationship School Podcast*, February 2, 2021. https://relationshipschool.com/podcast/healing-trauma-with-peter-levine-peter-levine-328/.

CHAPTER 12: HOW TO SPEAK DURING AND AFTER CONFLICT

1. Daniel J. Siegel, *The Developing Mind: Toward a Neurobiology of Interpersonal Experience*, 2nd ed. (New York: Guilford Press, 2012), 71–90.

2. Stan Tatkin, *We Do: Saying Yes to a Relationship of Depth, True Connection, and Enduring Love* (Boulder, CO: Sounds True, 2018), 188.

CHAPTER 15: THE TWELVE AGREEMENTS TO EASE CONFLICT

1. Carol S. Dweck, *Mindset: The New Psychology of Success* (New York: Ballantine Books, 2008).